AUSTRALIA, THE EUROPEAN UNION AND THE NEW TRADE AGENDA

AUSTRALIA, THE EUROPEAN UNION AND THE NEW TRADE AGENDA

Edited by Annmarie Elijah, Donald Kenyon,
Karen Hussey and Pierre van der Eng

Australian
National
University

PRESS

ANU PRESS

the Australia and New Zealand
School of Government

Published by ANU Press
The Australian National University
Acton ACT 2601, Australia
Email: anupress@anu.edu.au
This title is also available online at press.anu.edu.au

National Library of Australia Cataloguing-in-Publication entry

Title: Australia, the European Union and the new trade agenda /
          Annmarie Elijah, Donald Kenyon, Karen
          Hussey, and Pierre van der Eng,
          editors.

ISBN: 9781760461133 (paperback) 9781760461140 (ebook)

Series: Australia and New Zealand School of Government (ANZSOG)

Subjects: International economic relations.
          Australia--Commercial treaties.
          Europe--Commercial treaties.
          Australia--Foreign economic relations--Europe.
          Europe--Foreign economic relations--Australia.

Other Creators/Contributors:
          Elijah, Annmarie, editor.
          Kenyon, Donald, 1936- editor.
          Hussey, Karen, editor.
          van der Eng, Pierre, editor.

Cover design and layout by ANU Press.

Contents

Section 3

Conclusions

Acknowledgements

The editors gratefully acknowledge that this project was funded from the research project 'Australia and the European Union: A study of a changing trade and business relationship', (LP0990000) supported by the Australian Research Council, as well as the European Australian Business Council, the European Commission, the Department of Foreign Affairs and Trade, the Department of Agriculture, Fisheries and Forestry and the Department of Industry and Innovation.

Abbreviations

AANZFTA	ASEAN–Australia–New Zealand Free Trade Agreement
ACCC	Australian Competition and Consumer Commission
ACEA	European Automobile Manufacturers' Association
ACP	African, Caribbean and Pacific Group of States
ANZCERTA	Australia–New Zealand Closer Economic Relations Trade Agreement
APEC	Asia Pacific Economic Cooperation
ASEAN	Association of Southeast Asian Nations
AUSFTA	Australia–United States Free Trade Agreement
BIS	Bank for International Settlement
BITs	bilateral investment treaties
CAB	conformity assessment bodies
CAP	common agricultural policy
CER	Closer Economic Relations, short for ANZCERTA
CETA	Comprehensive Economic and Trade Agreement
CSR	corporate social responsibility
CTC	change in tariff classification
CTM	Community Trade Mark
DDS	duty drawback system
EC	European Commission
ECIPE	European Centre for International Political Economy
EEC	European Economic Community
EECT	European Economic Community Treaty
EFTA	European Free Trade Association

EGA	Environmental Goods Agreement
EU	European Union
EU28	28 members of the European Union
EUSFTA	EU–Singapore Free Trade Agreement
FDI	foreign direct investment
FTA	free trade agreement
G8	Group of Eight
GATS	General Agreement on Trade in Services
GATT	General Agreement on Tariffs and Trade
GDP	gross domestic product
GI	geographical indications
GPA	Agreement on Government Procurement
HQB	high-quality beef
ICSID	International Centre for Settlement of Investment Disputes
ICT	information and communications technology
ILO	International Labor Organization
IMF	International Monetary Fund
IP	intellectual property
IPPA	Investment Protection and Promotion Agreement
IPPC	International Plant Protection Convention
ISDS	investor–state dispute settlement
IT	information technology
ITA	International Technology Agreement
JSCOT	Joint Standing Committee on Treaties
KORUS	Korea–US
LDCs	least developed countries
MEQR	measure having equivalent effect to a quantitative restriction
MFN	most favoured nation
MRA	mutual recognition agreement
NAFTA	North American Free Trade Agreement
NTB	non-tariff barrier

NTM	non-tariff measure
OECD	Organisation for Economic Co-operation and Development
OPEC	Organization for Petroleum Exporting Countries
PDO	protected designation of origin
PGI	protected geographical indication
PSE	producer support estimate
PTA	preferential trade agreement
R&D	research and development
RCEP	Regional Comprehensive Economic Partnership
RoO	rules of origin
RTA	regional trade agreement
SPS	sanitary and phytosanitary
STC	specific trade concern
TBT	technical barriers to trade
TFEU	Treaty on the Functioning of the European Union (Lisbon Treaty)
TiSA	Trade in Services Agreement
TPP	Trans-Pacific Partnership
TQ	tariff quota
TRIPS	Trade-Related Aspects of Intellectual Property Rights Agreement
TSE	total support estimate
TSG	traditional specialty guaranteed
TTIP	Transatlantic Trade and Investment Partnership Agreement
TTMRA	Trans-Tasman Mutual Recognition Arrangement
UK	United Kingdom of Great Britain and Northern Ireland
UNCTAD	United Nations Conference on Trade and Development
UNECE	United Nations Economic Commission for Europe
UR	Uruguay Round of Multilateral Trade Negotiations

USA   United States of America

WTO   World Trade Organization

Contributors

Roderick Abbott is a former EU Ambassador to the World Trade Organization (WTO). He served as deputy Director General in Directorate General for Trade at the Commission (1996–2002) and Deputy Director General at the WTO (2002–05). He is currently a member of the Steering Committee and Advisory Board, European Centre for International Political Economy (ECIPE) and a Visiting Fellow at the London School of Economics and European University Institute in Florence.

Carsten Daugbjerg is a Professor in the Crawford School of Public Policy at The Australian National University and the co-editor of the *Journal of Environmental Policy & Planning*. His field of research is comparative public policy, specialising in agricultural policy reform, trade negotiations in the WTO, public and private food standards in global trade, government interest group relations and environmental policy. His recent research addresses global food security policy and governance. He has published widely on these issues.

Annmarie Elijah is Associate Director of the Centre for European Studies at The Australian National University (ANU). She has worked as a policy officer in the Australian Department of the Prime Minister and Cabinet, and has taught politics at the University of Melbourne, Victoria University of Wellington and ANU. Her research interests include Australia–EU relations, comparative regionalism, trans-Tasman relations, Australian and New Zealand foreign policy and federalism.

Deborah Elms is Founder and Executive Director of the Asian Trade Centre. She is also a senior fellow in the Singapore Ministry of Trade and Industry's Trade Academy. Previously, she was head of the Temasek Foundation Centre for Trade & Negotiations and senior fellow of international political economy at the S. Rajaratnam School of International Studies at Nanyang Technological University, Singapore. Her research interests are negotiations and decision-making, and her current research involves the Trans-Pacific Partnership (TPP), Regional Comprehensive Economic Partnership (RCEP), ASEAN Economic Community negotiations and global value chains. Dr Elms received a PhD in political science from the University of Washington, an MA in international relations from the University of Southern California, and Bachelor's degrees from Boston University.

Bruce Gosper was appointed Australian High Commissioner to Singapore in September 2016. From 2013–16 he was Chief Executive Officer of the Australian Trade Commission (Austrade). Prior to that he was Deputy Secretary with the Department of Foreign Affairs and Trade. He was Ambassador and Permanent Representative to the World Trade Organization from 2005 until 2009. From 2000–05, Mr Gosper was First Assistant Secretary, Office of Trade Negotiations, in the Department of Foreign Affairs and Trade.

Paul Gretton is a Visiting Fellow in the Crawford School of Public Policy at The Australian National University. He was formerly Assistant Commissioner at the Australian Productivity Commission where he led the Trade and Economic Studies Branch. This branch is responsible for trade policy reviews, assessment of the impacts of national economic reforms and quantitative economic modelling. He managed the commissioned studies into preferential Rules of Origin, Bilateral and Regional Trade Agreements and has had responsibility for a number of studies into national economic reform in Australia.

Karen Hussey is Professor and Deputy Director at the Global Change Institute at the University of Queensland. Trained as a political scientist, Karen undertakes research in the field of public policy and governance, with a particular interest in public policy relating to sustainable development. Her recent research has focused on water and energy security, the role of the state in climate change mitigation and adaptation, the links between international trade and environmental regulation, and the peculiarities of public policy in federal and supranational systems.

Yoo-Duk Kang is Head of the Europe Team at the Korea Institute for International Economic Policy. He received an MA in International Trade and PhD in Economics from Institut d'Etudes Politiques de Paris (Sciences Po). His main research fields include international trade, economic integration and comparative area studies on Europe and East Asia.

Don Kenyon is Associate Professor and Visiting Fellow in the Centre for European Studies at The Australian National University. During 1993–96 he was Australian Ambassador to the General Agreement on Tariffs and Trade (GATT) and WTO in Geneva, and during 1997–2000 Ambassador to the European Union, Belgium and Luxemburg. He was a senior trade negotiator for the Australian Government with many years' experience in bilateral and multilateral trade negotiations and retired from the Australian Department of Foreign Affairs and Trade in October 2001.

Pascal Kerneis is Managing Director, European Services Forum, Brussels. He was lecturer in European law in the Law University of Rennes during 1985–87 and Legal Expert in the European Commission in Brussels (Belgium) during 1988–90. He worked for the European Banking Federation, Brussels, during 1990–99, dealing notably with international affairs, before his appointment as Managing Director of the European Services Forum in 1999.

Jacqueline Lo is Associate Dean (International) for the ANU College of Arts and Social Sciences and Executive Director of Centre for European Studies at The Australian National University. She is also the ANU Chair of Academic Board (2016–18). Her research focuses on issues of race, colonialism, diaspora and the interaction of cultures and communities across ethnic, national and regional borders.

Hosuk Lee-Makiyama is the director of European Centre for International Political Economy (ECIPE) and a leading author on trade diplomacy, EU–Far East relations and the digital economy. He is regularly consulted by governments and international organisations on a range of issues, from trade negotiations to economic reforms. He appears regularly in European, Chinese and US media, and is noted for his involvement in WTO and major free trade agreements. Prior to joining ECIPE, he was an independent counsel on regulatory affairs, competition and communication, Senior Advisor at the Swedish Ministry of Foreign Affairs, representative of Sweden and the EU member states towards the WTO and the UN, including the World Intellectual Property Organization and the UN Economic Commission for Europe. Lee-Makiyama is also a Fellow at the Department of International Relations at the London School of Economics (LSE), and currently shares his time between LSE and ECIPE.

Anne McNaughton is a Senior Lecturer in the ANU College of Law at The Australian National University. Anne researches and teaches European Union law. Her particular research focus is on the European Union as a legal system and the Europeanisation of private law within the EU Member States. She is currently Deputy Director of the Centre for European Studies at ANU.

Hazel Moir is an Adjunct Associate Professor in the Centre for European Studies at The Australian National University where her work focuses on the 'intellectual property' dimensions of possible trade agreements, including with the European Union. Her academic background is in economics (Cambridge) and demography (Brown). After brief stints in the private sector and in overseas aid, she spent 20 years in the Australian Public Service and followed this with a second PhD in public policy. Hazel has made a number of submissions to government enquiries into aspects of patents, copyright and trade policy. More recently she has written several papers on geographical indications.

Alan Swinbank is Emeritus Professor of Agricultural Economics at the University of Reading. His research has focused on the farm, food and biofuel policies of the EU, particularly its common agricultural policy, and the process of trade liberalisation. More recently, the UK's pending departure from the European Union ('Brexit') has come to the fore. Recent publications include *The Interactions Between the EU's External Action and the Common Agricultural Policy for the European Parliament* (2016).

Carl Tidemann is a research assistant in the Fenner School of Environment and Society at The Australian National University, where he completed a first-class honours thesis entitled 'Addressing carbon leakage in climate policy: A synthesis and assessment of the strengths and weaknesses of key policy responses'.

Pierre van der Eng is Associate Professor in the College of Business and Economics at The Australian National University. He is an economist and historian with interests in business history and international business, as well as economic history and development economics. His current research interests include aspects of business development and company organisation, particularly the management of political imperatives and liability of foreignness by continental European firms in Australia.

1

Introduction: Australia, the European Union and the New Trade Agenda

Annmarie Elijah, Donald Kenyon, Karen Hussey
and Pierre van der Eng

This book examines issues relating to the prospective trade agreement between Australia and the European Union (EU). It takes the position that robust, informed debate about this potential agreement is timely and useful. As the title of the book suggests, the aim is to situate the debate in a rapidly changing international context. The collection has its origins in an important conference held at The Australian National University (ANU) Centre for European Studies in November 2013. The conference proceedings took place in an atmosphere of reflection about whether a trade deal between Australia and the EU would ever come to pass, with participants arguing the case for its consideration. It is a mark of the changing relationship that at the time of writing the preliminary scoping for this agreement is underway.

The European Commission's recently released trade policy strategy, *Trade for All*, commits the Commission to requesting authorisation to negotiate free trade agreements (FTAs) with Australia and New Zealand (European Commission 2015a: 32). In November 2015, Prime Minister Malcolm Turnbull together with European Commission President Jean-Claude Juncker and European Council President Donald Tusk agreed to work towards the launch of 'comprehensive' trade negotiations, in a context of deepening the Australia–EU relationship (European Commission 2015b). These are steps in a process that will be slow to unfold; nevertheless, the debate about this agreement—and indeed the Australia–EU relationship at the centre of it—has moved on.

Historically, the path of the Australia–EU economic relationship has not run smoothly. The bilateral relationship is littered with examples of trade politics souring the broader terms. The difficulties have been well documented (see Benvenuti 2008; Kenyon & Lee 2006; Elijah 2004; Murray, Elijah & O'Brien 2002) and it is not the purpose of this book to reiterate them, but it is for these reasons that even a decade ago the notion of a trade agreement seemed remote. For Australian policy makers the difficulties appeared insurmountable. For European policy makers there would have been no obvious rationale for undertaking negotiations with Australia. What then has changed?

Australia and the EU: From adversaries to allies

The common agricultural policy (CAP) was a major problem in Australia–EU trade relations through to the end of the 1980s. Australia also maintained a somewhat closed and protected (especially on manufactures and services) economy up to the mid-1980s. CAP reforms and the creation of the EU single market in the 1990s, together with domestic economic reforms in Australia from the mid-1980s, have changed these fundamental issues (Kenyon 2012: 34–39). Reform of the CAP enshrined in the Uruguay Round Agreement on Agriculture, especially disciplining the future use of export subsidies, took much of the heat out of the decades-long dispute between Australia and the EU over agricultural trade policy (WTO 1994). Former Trade Minister Mark Vaile was able to declare in 2002 that 'there was more that united than divided Australia and the EU' on trade policy issues (Vaile 2002).

Australia and the EU emerged from the Uruguay Round in 1994 with a much greater level of agreement over future reform to the global trading system than at the beginning of the negotiations in 1986. The economic policy reforms in both Australia and the EU from the mid-1980s onwards have made them strong allies in the push for greater trade liberalisation on manufactures and services trade and in strengthening multilateral rules aimed at reinforcing the World Trade Organization (WTO) as the mainstay of an open global trading system.

These developments delivered a significant change for the better in the bilateral relationship after a long period of conflict. Australia and the EU became strong and active proponents of a new round of WTO trade negotiations from the beginning of the 21st century. The aim was to pursue the unfinished business of the Uruguay Round on the liberalisation of agricultural, manufactures and services trade—the so-called 'inbuilt agenda' for future negotiations foreshadowed at the end of the Uruguay Round—to further develop the new rules agreed during the Uruguay Round on services and non-tariff barriers (NTBs) more generally and to extend the General Agreement on Tariffs and Trade (GATT) rules into new areas. As this volume will show, the EU was particularly active in promoting the development of new WTO disciplines; for example, trade and the environment, labour standards, investment, competition policy and trade facilitation through the simplification of customs procedures. Young and Peterson refer to the EU as 'the most aggressive and persistent advocate of a broader international trade agenda' (2006: 796).

When the Doha negotiations were finally launched in 2001, Australia and the EU both pursued the new multilateral trade round as a top priority trade policy objective (Lamy 2002). The EU declared a moratorium (1999) on further bilateral trade negotiations in order to accord priority to the WTO negotiations. Yet, despite more than a decade of sustained effort, the Doha negotiations have not progressed to a successful conclusion. There are a number of reasons for this.[1] These include ongoing differences on the depth of cuts to domestic subsidy levels for agriculture in the developed world and the magnitude of further cuts to industrial tariffs among developing countries. Linking these key, unresolved issues in the negotiations has not assisted their resolution.

Fuelled in part by the limited success in advancing the multilateral trade agenda through the Doha negotiations, the EU signalled a new direction in trade policy with its *Global Europe* strategy (2006). The EU identified key markets in Asia (Association of Southeast Asian Nations (ASEAN), South Korea and Mercosur) as targets for 'new generation' trade

---

1　For an in-depth discussion of the failure of the Doha Round and its significance, see Muzaka and Bishop (2015).

agreements aimed at liberalising trade beyond what was possible in the WTO; particularly, overcoming 'behind-the-border' barriers impacting on services, standards, investment, public procurement and competition policy problems. Recognising the limitations of current WTO rules, the EU argued in 2006 in *Global Europe* that trade agreements can go 'further and faster in promoting openness and integration ... preparing the ground for the next level of multilateral liberalisation' (European Commission 2006: 5–8). Since 2006, the EU has concluded agreements with South Korea, Singapore, Vietnam and Canada, and is now negotiating with Japan. The status of the proposed agreement with the United States of America (USA), the Transatlantic Trade and Investment Partnership (TTIP), is unclear.

Australian trade policy from the beginning of the 21st century has followed a similar trajectory. Beginning in 2003, trade agreements with an increasing emphasis on NTBs as well as tariffs have been concluded with Singapore, Chile, Thailand, USA, ASEAN (together with New Zealand), Malaysia and, in 2014, Korea, Japan and China. Australia is now seeking to conclude trade negotiations with India. Notwithstanding these bilateral and regional agreements, the Australian Government continues to accord primacy to the WTO and the multilateral agenda (DFAT 2015).

The new trade agenda

The term 'new trade agenda'—sometimes referred to as the 'deep trade agenda'—is shorthand for the changed nature of international trade, 'in terms of both content and process' (Young & Peterson 2006: 795). The changes have recently gathered speed, as analysts have widely noted. The changed *content* of the new trade agenda is characterised by several factors. First, the trend towards global supply chains, where industries (e.g. motor vehicles) are increasingly global and where trade is in parts or components (or even intellectual property such as design) rather than in finished products.

Second, the new trade agenda explicitly recognises the rapid increase in the importance of services in world trade: professional services, financial services, services as part of the digital economy, education, tourism, transport and business services. Third, the new trade agenda is in the growing importance of foreign direct investment around the world as enterprises, especially from developed economies, increasingly seek to invest in manufacturing, mining and services activities in other countries to take advantage of resources, labour conditions and proximity to markets in order to maximise the productivity of their enterprises.

As a consequence, the new trade agenda is as much concerned with behind-the-border barriers as it is with straightforward at-border market access. Current policy makers, therefore, engage with how domestic standards and regulations impact on trade. They aim to address regulatory divergences between countries and regions relating to technical and environmental standards for manufactured goods and basic agricultural and food products; licensing, qualifications and certification procedures impacting on the supply of tradeable services; conditions applying to foreign direct investment, including rights of establishment, investment protection, repatriation of profits and dispute settlement; and competition policies, including the disciplining of monopoly and oligopoly power and public procurement policies.

The changed *process* of the new trade agenda is impacting on the way governments (and indeed other actors) are now seeking to achieve their objectives. In part because the importance of new trade agenda issues has advanced significantly since the launch of the Doha negotiations in 2001, trade liberalisation is no longer predominately being dealt with in a multilateral setting. Multilateral rules designed for a time in which a much less integrated global trading system could be kept open by reducing and eliminating visible barriers to trade—notably import tariffs and quotas—were effective in delivering progressive liberalisation of the world trading system from the late 1940s to the early 1980s. The focus then was on elimination. With the creation of the WTO at the end of the Uruguay Round of Multilateral Trade Negotiations (UR), the focus has shifted increasingly to regulatory cooperation. This is proving more of a challenge for the multilateral trading system.

According to the WTO, the eight rounds of trade negotiations that were completed during the 1980s and 1990s saw tariff rates on manufactured goods in developed countries fall steadily to less than 4 per cent (WTO 2014). The GATT progressively sought to deal with emerging issues since the 1980s; however, the system has not entirely succeeded in creating effective new rules to discipline new trade agenda and NTB problems. Even the signature reform reached in the Uruguay Round in the form of a new set of rules designed to liberalise trade in services—the General

Agreement on Trade in Services (GATS), aimed at mirroring the original GATT rules of 1947—has suffered from these shortcomings. To some extent this explains why it has not been possible to repeat the Uruguay Round success in the WTO. As it is, the multilateral process is essentially stalled. Bilateral, plurilateral and mega-regional deals have proliferated. At December 2015 the WTO has been notified of some 452 regional trade agreements (counting goods, services and accessions *together*) with 265 currently in force.[2] The incompleteness of efforts in the UR to bring new rules into effect, with the creation of the WTO, to discipline new trade agenda issues, is dealt with in more detail in the final chapter of this collection.

Thus, in the 1960s and '70s, an emergent Australian economy and a (then) European Economic Community of six and later nine member states endured a difficult bilateral relationship centred on straightforward 'at-border' market access issues. At present the 28 EU members states (EU28) and Australia find themselves partners in pursuing an agenda that includes revitalising credentials of the WTO; embedding GATT-plus commitments in other agreements in the meantime; and finding scope for trade liberalisation 'behind borders', with all of the complexity that entails. Further, the bilateral economic relationship between Australia and the EU is no longer adequately regulated by the WTO (Villalta Puig 2014: 300). It is in this context—a changed bilateral trade relationship; a vastly different international context—that an Australia–EU trade agreement becomes possible, and perhaps inevitable.[3]

The chapters that follow are in one sense deeply practical contributions to the forthcoming policy debate on the Australia–EU FTA. They are designed to contribute background information, provide case studies and directly inform the negotiations. The chapters highlight potential points of difficulty and possible gains from an Australia–EU FTA. They set out different perspectives on issues that will soon be front and centre in trade policy debates. Contributors from the Australian Productivity Commission, the European Services Forum and Austrade ensure that this book is policy relevant.

---

2   Counted separately, the figures are 619 notifications with 413 in force (see WTO 2015).
3   For a full account of the changing bilateral relationship, see Kenyon and van der Eng (2014).

The book seeks to make two further contributions. First, it constitutes a reappraisal of Australia–EU relations; particularly, but not only, the economic relationship. Here it complements a growing body of work that demonstrates that the Australia–EU relationship need not consist only of squabbles over agriculture (Kenyon & van der Eng 2014; Murray & Benvenuti 2014; Villalta Puig 2014). Whatever the past difficulties, the relationship described in this volume is multidimensional and maturing. The treaty-level Framework Agreement (concluded in 2015) between Australia and the EU is expected to underline the extensive cooperation underway across a range of policy areas.

Second, the chapters taken together present a snapshot of current issues in trade policy—the 'new trade agenda'—that is more complex and politically visible than ever. The issues that will arguably be confronted by Australia and the EU in forthcoming negotiations are those confronting policy makers around the globe. They are testing public tolerance of decisions once viewed as dull and technocratic, and are redefining the academic treatment of trade policy.

Structure of the book and key themes

This book is organised into three sections. Section 1 deals with lessons from abroad. The EU has recently sought trade agreements with several of Australia's major Asia-Pacific and Organisation for Economic Co-operation and Development (OECD) trading partners such as South Korea, India, Singapore, Canada, Japan and the USA. These new generation agreements are ambitious in scope and aim to go beyond border measures, such as tariffs. Proposed liberalisations extend to behind-the-border barriers, such as domestic regulation impacting on trade in both goods and services. What can we learn from recent trade deals the EU has concluded? This section examines the EU's trade deals with South Korea, Singapore and Canada. In doing so, it provides important background information about the likely shape of negotiations, the length of time that reaching agreements can take, and the obstacles to successful conclusion. What are the similarities with the Australian case, and what are the points of difference?

Section 2 consists of sectoral analysis. It addresses in detail two crucial aspects of a potential trade agreement between Australia and the EU. Trade in agriculture has historically been the principal source of tension in the bilateral relationship, a fact that dates from the United Kingdom's (UK) decision to join the European Community in 1973. Recent changes inside the EU and in Australia's export profile mean that this aspect of the relationship has altered fundamentally, such that scope for genuine gains exist for both sides in the negotiations; regulatory convergence across a range of NTBs is 'ripe for the picking'. Trade in services is now a key plank of the bilateral trade relationship and a much-lauded aspect of new generation FTAs. A successful Australia–EU FTA would contain ambitious measures relating to trade in services. The chapters in this section consider agriculture and services in detail.

Section 3 deals with the broad political and economic terms of an Australia–EU agreement. It brings together European and Australian perspectives on what could be gained from a potential agreement. It debates whether a trade agreement is the best format for pursuing cooperation and liberalisation, it details institutional questions about how trade agreements actually work, and it considers the risks to both sides of *not* undertaking the negotiations. A number of the contributions in this book present arguments in favour of Australia negotiating an FTA with the EU: the growing importance of bilateral services trade and scope for its expansion and mutual interests in agricultural trade, for example. Importantly, the Abbott and Lee-Makiyama chapter details the reasons why an EU–Australia agreement is also in the interests of the EU.

Several key themes emerge from the collection of chapters in this book. The list of five below is not exhaustive.

1. The current limitations of multilateralism and the search for alternatives

Without exception, the chapters that follow take as a starting point the apparent incapacity of the multilateral system to successfully conclude the Doha negotiations. Gretton describes prospects for finalising the Doha Round as 'bleak'; Gosper describes the multilateral possibilities as 'underwhelming'. Two issues feature repeatedly. First, governments seeking greater market access via tariff reductions and increased quotas need to secure this bilaterally given the lack of multilateral progress. The rationale for bilateral deals in this case is clear, especially given the all-but-finalised deals that remain in limbo pending the successful conclusion of Doha. Gosper's chapter notes that Australian negotiators could 'see the shape' of EU agricultural market access that Doha could make possible, still.

Swinbank and Daugbjerg's chapter deplores the failure of the international community to conclude the Doha Round, explaining the role of the WTO in locking in CAP reform in the past. In their view, the EU will not likely agree to further tariff reductions *except* in the context of a multilateral agreement, and in the meantime countries like Australia could potentially use a trade agreement to 'sidestep' continuing high EU tariffs on agriculture through increased tariff quota (TQ) access, much as has been secured in the Comprehensive Economic and Trade Agreement (CETA). Thus, the stalling of the recent WTO Round is seen as a motive for governments to embark on more diffuse trade strategies, including bilateral, plurilateral and mega-regional deals. The second issue, as Kang explains, relates to coverage. The limited ability of the WTO to deal with issues of concern to the EU such as investment, public procurement, competition policy and intellectual property rights has led directly to the strategy of institutionalising EU preferences in other trade agreements.

2. The changing nature of trade agreements

The chapters in this volume demonstrate that especially bilateral trade agreements increasingly broach new territory. The issues covered in the new generation agreements and the level of ambition that they articulate differ greatly from previous bilateral trade agreements. Particularly where developed countries have already substantially lowered their tariffs on manufactured goods, trade in services takes on new significance in negotiations and is considered crucial to the projected gains. Elms argues the centrality of services trade in the EU–Singapore deal and sees it as 'the primary offensive objective' of the EU. Elijah notes CETA was hailed as a major achievement by both sides, especially in relation to its treatment of services. Kerneis outlines the importance of services trade to both the EU and Australia and explains how negotiations about services trade liberalisation might unfold between the two. Hussey and Tidemann illustrate that while tariff reductions are unlikely to feature prominently in any potential Australia–EU FTA, the opportunities to remove technical barriers to agricultural trade are many, particularly where those barriers relate to environmental and human health objectives.

Investment provisions (recently elevated to the EU level by the Treaty of Lisbon, 2009) now feature across multiple trade agreements; for example, in the EU–Singapore agreement and in the CETA. The full implications of this development—for the EU and its trading partners— are still becoming clear. As Elms explains, the EU–Singapore agreement was delayed as a result. The investment provisions in CETA have become especially controversial and contributed to the so-called 'CETA-saga' of late 2016.

Largely because of the investment policy provisions of CETA—both 'direct investment', which following Lisbon is now an EU matter, and 'portfolio investment', which remains a member state responsibility— the European Commission decided to treat the ratification of the CETA treaty as a 'mixed agreement' requiring approval by all 38 national and regional governments in the EU rather than the simpler route of a 'qualified majority' vote by the 28 national governments in the Council. The government of the Belgian region of Wallonia threatened to veto the CETA immediately prior to its signature. Clarifications were sought from the EU (especially in relation to investor–state dispute settlement (ISDS) provisions), which finally enabled the CETA treaty to enter into force provisionally on 30 October 2016.

Trade agreements are more complex and broader in scope than ever. The complexities of entry into force, especially with the multiplicity of governments required to approve 'mixed agreements' has both political and practical implications.

3. Trade agreements are interconnected

Multiple chapters here attest to the interconnectedness between the different agreements that are now finalised or in prospect. It is clear that the sequence of negotiations matters greatly—in terms of potential trade diversion, but also in relation to the inclusion of liberalising measures, which are seen to represent the latest best possible outcome. The obvious example examined in this collection is the CETA. These negotiations were conducted with an eye to the proposed TTIP, as some of its 'wait and see' clauses demonstrate. Outcomes will ultimately depend on what the USA and the EU can agree. Meanwhile, Australian policy makers contemplate the CETA and its usefulness as a 'roadmap' for Australia. Abbott and Lee-Makiyama suggest that it is a deliberate strategy of the EU to pursue negotiations with a smaller, more flexible partner in a given region first, before engaging a larger trade partner (South Korea, then Japan; Canada, then the USA; and potentially New Zealand, then Australia).

Kang argues that South Korea may lose its competitive edge as the EU finalises more deals in East Asia, and underlines the need for Korean companies to make full use of the agreement's provisions. Elms traces the history of the EU–Singapore agreement to the failed EU–ASEAN negotiations, and notes the extent to which these negotiations were conducted by the EU with the aim of returning to an ASEAN-wide deal at a later date. Thus, the purpose of the EU–Singapore agreement is not simply trade liberalisation, but the building of a model that may form the basis of regional arrangements between the EU and ASEAN. Gosper outlines the place of the EU in Australian trade considerations. The fact that the EU is negotiating with Australia's trade partners 'adds to the logic' of trade negotiations with the EU.

It is clear in this volume that governments are pursuing defensive interests via trade agreements. It is less clear how the various agreements might ultimately relate to each other for the purpose of reinvigorating multilateralism, or even plurilateral initiatives. Bhagwati's concerns about the 'spaghetti bowl' and its impact on the multilateral trade system surface in multiple chapters (Bhagwati 2008). With their stated commitment to multilateralism, Australia and the EU share an interest in resolving this dilemma. The EU identifies the 'interoperability' of agreements as a priority in its recent trade strategy statement (European Commission 2015: 29).

4. Domestic settings and trade policy are inseparable

The domestic roots of trade policy have long been established. As Adams, Brown and Wickes (2013: 87) remind us, 'domestic policy settings form the basis of negotiating positions'. For the policy makers behind the new trade agenda, as the chapters show, domestic policy is not merely the source of negotiating positions, it is their prime target. The new trade agenda progressively inserts itself into national sovereignty issues in the determination of public policy decisions across a wide range of regulatory policies. Given the overall decline in the importance of tariffs, regulatory divergences have an increasing profile (Hussey & Kenyon 2011). These divergences arise more frequently from legitimate (e.g. historical) differences in public policy than protectionist motives. Nevertheless, the adverse impact of regulatory divergences—as intended or unintended NTBs—is incontestable. Dealing with the trade impacts of regulatory divergences is challenging (Mumford 2014). Further, it raises a raft of institutional questions that are far from resolved.

Kenyon and van der Eng conclude this volume by elaborating the possibilities for Australia–EU cooperation on the new trade agenda. It is argued that Australia and the EU are now set on a trade policy course with common objectives: to embed WTO-plus liberalisation in agreements with key trading partners in the context of frustrated multilateralism; and to ensure that current commitments can ultimately be 'stepping stones' in future, rather than 'stumbling blocks' to more effective multilateral trade liberalisation (European Commission 2006: 8). The concluding chapter examines how a new generation trade deal between Australia and the EU could advance these objectives.

5. The increased political salience of trade policy

Recent developments—notably the Brexit vote in favour of the UK leaving the EU in the referendum of June 2016, the near-scuppering of the CETA prior to its signature and the surprise victory of Donald Trump over Hillary Clinton in the US presidential election of 8 November 2016—have brought into sharp relief the political discontent that exists amongst those who have been left behind by the internationalisation of the global economy and technological change that have gathered pace through the second half of the 20th century.

In fact, these concerns have been growing since the end of the GATT Uruguay Round of trade negotiations in the mid-1990s. The Round broke new ground in moving beyond liberalising tariff barriers into the liberalisation of NTBs in areas such as agriculture, services, technical barriers to trade, investment and public procurement. Liberalising NTBs frequently results in adjustments to domestic regulations. With the decline in importance of tariffs as trade barriers the move into non-tariff barriers is a logical next step in the continuing liberalisation of global trade.

Opposition to aspects of the new trade agenda dogged the Doha Development agenda— intended as the successor to the Uruguay Round of the 1980s and 19990s from its inception in 2001. From the beginning of the Doha negotiations, the prospect of moving further down the path of liberalising particular NTBs was especially challenging to a number of developing countries, which were expanding their economies and enjoying increasing living standards for a growing proportion of their populations. At the same time, concerns about losing jobs to globalisation was growing in the developed world.

The political backlash now evident in the US and Europe is of particular concern for the trade policy agenda. Since the end of the Second World War, it has been the OECD countries that have driven global openness in trade as a key instrument in spreading economic growth and increasing living standards around the world. In key OECD countries it is now apparent that a rising tide does not automatically lift all boats—some have clearly been left behind. Jobs have been lost; pockets of poverty in even the richest of countries have persisted and expanded. Corrective action is needed to deal with these (not quite new) domestic political problems.

This collection brings together diverse perspectives, but none of the chapters here suggest turning back the clock on trade liberalisation. Much in terms of growth, better living standards and greater equality across countries in the world has been achieved. To fall back on increased protection, erecting new barriers against immigration and increased autarky in economic and security terms would only generate new conflicts. It is clear, however, that those who have lost out through the process of increasing global openness—in both developed and developing countries—need to have their interests more effectively taken into account. This is the task of individual governments. Domestic policy settings on job-enhancing programs and providing governments with increased financial resources will be needed. Noting the increased political complexity of trade negotiations, the focus of this book is on the role that trade policy might play in moving forward.

The point is now frequently made that Australia (with New Zealand) is one of the few OECD countries with which the EU does not have some kind of trade agreement. Australia and the EU appear to be entering a new phase in the bilateral relationship, and the push towards a potential trade agreement has been steadily gaining momentum. Chapters in this volume argue that a potential Australia–EU trade agreement has 'ample scope' for a substantive negotiating agenda and that the failure to act in this regard is untenable. Contributors to this collection have not assumed, however, that an agreement should be undertaken simply because there is not one in place. Trade agreements take time and resources. They are not self-evidently good, and the case must be demonstrated. With the prospect of an agreement under active consideration in both Brussels and Canberra, this volume begins to examine and explain the coming negotiations and inform public debate.

References

Adams, Mike, Nicolas Brown & Ron Wickes (2013), *Trading Nation: Advancing Australia's Interests in World Markets* (UNSW Press: Sydney).

Benvenuti, Andrea (2008), *Anglo-Australian Relations and the 'Turn to Europe', 1961–1972* (Royal Historical Society/Boydell Press: Woodbridge, UK).

Bhagwati, Jagdish (2008), *Termites in the Trading System: How Preferential Agreements Undermine Free Trade* (Oxford University Press: New York). doi.org/10.1093/acprof:oso/9780195331653.001.0001.

DFAT (Department of Foreign Affairs and Trade) (2015), 'World Trade Organization'. Available at dfat.gov.au/international-relations/international-organisations/wto/Pages/world-trade-organization.aspx.

Elijah, Annmarie (2004), 'Better the Devil You Know? Australia and the British Bids for European Community Membership', PhD dissertation, University of Melbourne.

European Commission (2006), *Global Europe: Competing in the World – A Contribution to the EU's Growth and Jobs Strategy*, COM(2006) 567 Final (Commission for the European Communities: Brussels).

European Commission (2015a), *Trade for All: Towards a more Responsible Trade and Investment* (DG Trade: Luxembourg), October.

European Commission (2015b), 'Statement of the President of the European Commission Jean-Claude Juncker, the President of the European Council Donald Tusk and the Prime Minister of Australia Malcolm Turnbull', Brussels, 15 November.

Hussey, Karen & Donald Kenyon (2011), 'Regulatory divergences: A barrier to trade and a potential source of trade disputes', In Australia's Trade with Europe: Potential unfulfilled, Special Issue *Australian Journal of International Affairs* 65(4): 381–93. doi.org/10.1080/103 57718.2011.586668.

Kenyon, Donald (2012), 'Australia and the European Union: A Relationship Driven by Trade', in *No EUtopia: The European Union Today*, AIIA Policy Commentary No. 12 (Australian Institute of International Relations: Deakin, ACT).

Kenyon, Don & David Lee (2006), *The Struggle for Trade Liberalization in Agriculture: Australia and the Cairns Group in the Uruguay Round*, Australia in the World: The Foreign Affairs and Trade Files No. 4 (Department of Foreign Affairs and Trade: Canberra).

Kenyon, Donald & Pierre van der Eng (2014), 'Defining the relationship between Australia and the European Union: Is the Framework Treaty enough?' *Australian Journal of International Affairs* 68(2): 225–42. doi.org/10.1080/10357718.2013.840558.

Lamy, Pascal (2002), 'Stepping stones or stumbling blocks? The EU's approach towards the problem of multilateralism vs regionalism in trade policy', *The World Economy* 25(10): 1399–413. doi.org/10.1111/1467-9701.00498.

Mumford, Peter (2014), 'Regulatory coherence: Blending trade and regulatory policy', *Policy Quarterly* 10(4): 3–9. Available at apo.org.au/resource/regulatory-coherence-blending-trade-and-regulatory-policy.

Murray, Philomena & Andrea Benvenuti (2014), 'EU-Australia relations at fifty: Reassessing a troubled relationship', *Australian Journal of Politics and History* 60(3): 431–48. doi.org/10.1111/ajph.12068.

Murray, Philomena, Annmarie Elijah & Carolyn O'Brien (2002), 'Common ground, worlds apart: The development of Australia's relationship with the European Union', *Australian Journal of International Affairs* 56(3): 395–416. doi.org/10.1080/1035771022000019723.

Muzaka, Valbona & Matthew L. Bishop (2015), 'Doha stalemate: The end of trade multilateralism?' *Review of International Studies* 41(2): 383–406. doi.org/10.1017/S0260210514000266.

Vaile, Mark (2002), *Australia and the Multilateral Trade Round: Defining the Common Ground*, National Europe Centre Paper No. 54 (The Australian National University: Canberra).

Villalta Puig, Gonzalo (2014), *Economic Relations between Australia and the European Union: Law and Policy*, Global Trade Law Series (Kluwer Law International: Alphen aan den Rijn, The Netherlands).

WTO (World Trade Organization) (1994), *The Results of the Uruguay Round of Multilateral Trade Negotiations: The Legal Texts* (GATT Secretariat 1994: Geneva), 39–68.

WTO (2014), 'Principles of the Trading System'. Available at www.wto.org/english/thewto_e/whatis_e/tif_e/fact2_e.htm.

WTO (2015), 'Regional Trade Agreements'. Available at www.wto.org/english/tratop_e/region_e/region_e.htm.

Young, Alasdair R. & John Peterson (2006), 'The EU and the new trade politics', *Journal of European Public Policy* 13(6): 795–814. doi.org/10.1080/13501760600837104.

Section 1

2

Korea–EU FTA: Breaking New Ground

Yoo-Duk Kang

Introduction

The European Union (EU) is an important economic partner for Korea in both trade and investment.[1] If the EU is considered a single economic area, it is 14 times larger than the Korean domestic market and it has always been an important export destination of Korean companies. In 2014, trade with the EU accounted for 10 per cent of Korea's total trade, making the EU the equal second-most important partner after China (21 per cent), alongside the United States of America (USA) (10 per cent). European companies have been very active in investing in Korea. According to European statistics, they represent more than 40 per cent of the cumulative total of foreign direct investment (FDI) since 1962 (Delegation of the EU to the Republic of Korea 2013). During 2008–12, European companies were the largest contributors to inward FDI into Korea with investment totalling US$22 billion.

Korean companies are also increasingly active in investing in Europe. Half of Korean cars sold in European markets are produced in the assembly lines in Slovakia and the Czech Republic, and Korean electronics companies made a number of important investments from research

---

1   For the purpose of this chapter, Korea refers to the Republic of Korea.

and development (R&D) centres to production facilities in Europe. In financial sectors, Korea's economy is more closely related to European financial markets. According to statistics from the Bank for International Settlement (BIS), European banks have very important exposures to the Korean economy. Almost half of Korea's external liabilities are with European banks, which means that both economies are increasingly interdependent. In this context, creating a more stable economic framework can be beneficial to both Korea and the EU and this was the background upon which Korea and the EU agreed to launch free trade agreement (FTA) negotiations in 2007. By 2015, the Korea–EU FTA was the only FTA that the EU has implemented with an Asian country.

This chapter reviews Korea's economic relations with the EU, focusing on the Korea–EU FTA implemented in July 2011. The FTA should be understood from mutual economic interests as well as Korea's overall trade policy. The Korea–EU FTA was the first FTA that Korea implemented with a large trading partner, and it is the EU's first 'new generation', or 'WTO-plus' FTA. This chapter firstly reviews the background of the Korea–EU FTA from both the Korean and EU perspectives. It describes the economic and political background of the FTA in the context of the overall trade policy of Korea and the EU. Secondly, it sheds light on the negotiation process of the FTA, focusing on arguments raised during the process. Thirdly, it examines the trade statistics over four years of the FTA. To compare changes in trade before the FTA and after its implementation, important factors are considered that affect trade from both sides. Finally, this chapter discusses future prospects for Korea's economic relations with the EU in the context of the Korea–EU FTA.

Background of the Korea–EU FTA

Korea's perspective

Negotiating an FTA with the EU was included in Korea's FTA roadmap announced in September 2003. This medium-term FTA plan reflected and expanded upon Korea's first FTA, the 2003 Korea–Chile FTA. Even though trade with Chile accounted for a small part of Korea's total trade, this first FTA provoked significant controversy and its ratification took more than one year. In order to obtain public support, the Korean government set up the FTA roadmap, which stated four principles of the Korean government's FTA policy: 1) multiple-track FTAs; 2) advanced and comprehensive FTAs; 3) transparent procedures in FTA preparation; and 4) diplomatic consideration in FTA policy (Ministry of Foreign Affairs and Trade, Korea, 2003, cited in Kang 2009: 16).

The roadmap also announced trade partners to be considered for FTAs on the basis of concrete economic criteria, such as economic feasibility and large and advanced economies. It organised prospective FTA partners into two groups: short term (negotiation within two years), and medium term (negotiation in more than three years). The EU was included in the list of medium-term prospective FTAs, along with the USA and China. One reason for this longer time frame was that the impact of FTAs with large trade partners would be much more significant than FTAs with small countries. Also, the EU exercised a *de facto* moratorium on new FTA negotiations during 1999–2006 in favour of the Doha Round of multilateral discussions in the context of the World Trade Organization (WTO) (Lamy 2002).

Table 1. Korea's FTA roadmap and list of FTA partners according to time schedule

Time frame	Countries in consideration	Remarks
Short term (within two years)	Japan, Singapore	• Start negotiations as soon as possible, including joint feasibility studies
	Association of Southeast Asian Nations (ASEAN), Mexico, European Free Trade Association (EFTA)	• Prepare negotiations or joint studies when appropriate conditions are met
Medium and long term (in three–five years)	USA, EU, China	• Progressive approach
	Israel, Peru, Panama, New Zealand, Australia	• Countries who have shown their intention to conclude FTAs with Korea
	Canada, India	• Prospective FTA partners

Note: Canada and India were reclassified as FTA partners of short term, when the roadmap was revised in May 2004.

Source: Ministry of Foreign Affairs and Trade, Korea, 2003.

In the meantime, trade and investment with European countries increased rapidly. In 2007, the EU became the second-largest trade partner for Korea after China. After its first FTA with Chile, Korea first initiated new FTA negotiations with the European Free Trade Association (EFTA). The FTA with the EFTA was generally considered as a preparatory step to one with the EU, because its member countries had maintained free trade status with the EU, adopting most of the EU's trade regulations. The Korea–EFTA FTA was concluded after only 10 months of negotiation.

EU's perspective

In the mid-2000s, EU business circles and external trade surroundings put increasing pressure on the EU to pursue bilateral FTAs. There were increasing concerns that industries of emerging countries such as India, Brazil and China would become more competitive than European industries. In this context, the arrival of the new trade commissioner, Peter Mendelssohn, brought a new point of view on bilateral FTAs. He argued that wisely constructed and ambitious bilateral agreements with carefully chosen partners could create new trade and improve the competitiveness of EU companies in key foreign markets experiencing high growth.

Incorporating new objectives in external trade policy, the European Commission announced a new trade policy in October 2006, later known as 'Global Europe' (European Commission 2006). The strategy emphasises the role of the EU's external trade policy, which contributes to the EU's competitiveness in foreign markets. Considering that it proved hard to make progress with investment, public procurement, competition and intellectual property rights issues in the WTO Doha Round, negotiating comprehensive FTAs with like-minded countries was regarded as the second-best option.

In order to select FTA partners, the European Commission proposed key economic criteria: 1) market potential (economic size and growth); 2) level of protection against EU exports (tariffs and non-tariff barriers, NTBs); and 3) potential partners' FTA negotiations with EU competitors (potential discriminatory impact on European firms). On the basis of these principles, the European Commission identified the Association of Southeast Asian Nations (ASEAN), Korea and the Mercosur bloc of countries in South America as priorities.

In addition to using economic criteria for selecting FTA partners, Global Europe is notable in several other respects. First, it aimed for ambitious and high-level FTAs. New competition-driven FTAs are aimed to be comprehensive and ambitious in coverage, aiming at the highest possible degree of trade liberalisation, including far-reaching liberalisation of services and investment. Second, ongoing or scheduled FTA negotiations with the EU's competitors (implicitly the USA) were taken into account. Third, the new FTAs would explicitly focus on tackling NTBs through regulatory convergence and contain strong trade facilitation provisions, intellectual property rights and competition. This means that the new FTA model that the European Commission sought to construct was seeking deep integration, including harmonisation of trade-affecting rules. These objectives of the EU's FTA policy corresponded to what Korea had been seeking for its FTA roadmap.

Negotiating the Korea–EU FTA

Negotiation process

Official Korea–EU FTA negotiations were launched in May 2007 after a series of preparatory meetings held the previous year. It took over two years, eight rounds of negotiations and many technical meetings to finalise the agreement in October 2009. By this time, Korea had already finished FTA negotiations with the USA and had signed the Korea–US (KORUS) FTA in June 2007. This allowed Korean trade negotiators to use technical know-how obtained in these negotiations as an example for an advanced FTA. Effectively, this experience provided a partial template for the Korea–EU FTA. From its side, the EU sought a comprehensive and advanced FTA with Korea, which was at the time its most economically developed bilateral FTA partner to date. Accordingly, the Korea–EU FTA became the most comprehensive FTA ever negotiated by the EU.

The agreement eliminated import duties on nearly all products (97.3 per cent of Korean products for the EU market by number of items) and it liberalised services trade to a greater degree than the KORUS FTA (KORUS-plus) did. Composed of 15 chapters, the Korea–EU FTA includes provisions on investment (termed as 'establishment' due to the fact that the European Commission has an EU mandate in foreign trade policy, not foreign investment policy) both in service and industrial sectors, provisions on intellectual property and competition rules. The Korea–EU FTA is also a pioneering case in that it aims to reduce NTBs and promote a future dialogue on industrial regulation. During the preparatory and implementation period, Korea changed many parts of its domestic laws to be able to implement the KORUS and Korea–EU FTAs. Most of the revisions concern service sectors and intellectual property.[2]

---

2 The Korea–EU FTA had a two-year transition period in order to accommodate market liberalisation and to revise domestic laws. In line with the KORUS FTA, Korea changed 57 Acts, enforcement decrees and rules (as of September 2012). Most changes were relevant to the implementation of the Korea–EU FTA, because it was in part based on the KORUS FTA, in particular its services chapter.

Diverging concerns between Korea and the EU

Two issues delayed the finalisation of the overall negotiation: 1) the duty drawback system (DDS); and 2) rules of origin.[3] Korea and the EU showed a very clear divergence on the DDS from the beginning. For Korea, the DDS is a crucial support system, especially for small and medium enterprises that rely heavily on outsourcing production of intermediate goods to China and Southeast Asia. Without DDS, any kind of FTA would not bring about tangible economic benefits to Korean firms. It seems that European negotiators understood that the DDS is important for the Korean Government not only for economic purposes, but also for political reasons. To gain ground for Korean exporting firms, it was necessary for the Korean Government to maintain the DDS, which dated back to 1964 in the Korean customs system. The problem was that the EU had not included the DDS in its previous three FTAs (i.e. with Chile, Mexico and South Africa). The reason for this can be found in the trade structure of European countries that rely largely on intra-European trade for supplies of intermediate products. More developed Western European firms have taken advantage of the European enlargement towards Eastern Europe in this respect. As a result, they tend to rely to a far lesser extent on outsourcing from outside the EU, so that the DDS is less important for them.

However, this relative indifference of the European Commission on the DDS soon turned into a major preoccupation, when major industrial associations in the EU—especially the association of automobile producers—showed their concerns about Korea's DDS and its positive effect on the price competitiveness of Korean products. The European Automobile Manufacturers' Association (ACEA) strongly opposed Korea's intention to include the DDS in the Korea–EU FTA (ACEA 2009). The ACEA argued that approving the DDS in the framework of the Korea–EU FTA would offer a disproportionate competitive advantage to the Korean auto industry when exporting to the EU. It also insisted that this would set a precedent for other scheduled EU FTAs. In finalising the negotiations, Korea and the EU reached a compromise. In the final deal, the EU agreed to allow Korea to maintain the current DDS (on average 8 per cent) on Korea's exports to the EU for five years from the start of the

---

3   DDS allows an importer to obtain a refund of import duty, if the imported good is subsequently exported. The rules of origin are criteria that specify the degree to which the value of a final product is produced in the exporting country.

FTA implementation. If Korea's imports of intermediate goods increased rapidly after the five-year grace period, the EU would be allowed to limit DDS to 5 per cent.[4]

Setting a threshold for local content in the rules of origin was also an issue for both parties. As with the DDS case, the EU had a precedent that served as a principle: in its FTAs with Chile, Mexico and South Africa, the EU set the minimum percentage of locally produced content in a final product to 60 per cent. This meant that in order to be qualified as 'Made in Korea', at least 60 per cent of the value of a product needed to be produced in Korea. Korea's initial proposal for minimum local content was 35 per cent, as in the KORUS FTA. In the final deal, EU agreed to reduce the local content threshold to 45 per cent.

After more than two years of negotiations, Korea and the EU signed the deal in October 2010 during Korea's presidential visit to Brussels for the 8th Asia-Europe Meeting summit. The agreement was approved in February 2011 by the European Parliament and Korea's National Assembly ratified it in 5 May 2011. With this, all necessary legal procedures were completed and the FTA entered into effect on 1 July 2011.

Four years after implementing the Korea–EU FTA

Trade flow between Korea and the EU after the global financial crisis

In the 2000s, trade between Korea and the EU increased considerably. Korea's exports to the EU soared from US$39.2 billion in 2000 to US$98.4 billion in 2008. Imports from the EU showed a similar increase from US$23.4 billion to US$58.4 billion. In this context, the possibility of FTA implementation raised the prospects for more exports to the EU. Various studies suggested that the Korea–EU FTA would contribute to increasing Korea's exports to the EU, as well as to Korea's gross domestic product (GDP). A 2010 study by the Korea Institute for International

---

4   The Singapore–EU FTA initialled in late 2013 excludes all kinds of drawback of duties for bilateral trade. Given that the FTA with Singapore will undoubtedly serve as a template for FTAs with other ASEAN members, it seems likely that the EU does not want to include the DDS in its future FTAs.

Economic Policy (KIEP) expected that the FTA would increase Korea's exports to the EU by US$2.5 billion per year and, as a result, Korea's GDP would increase by 0.1 per cent in the short term and by 5.6 per cent in the long term (KIEP 2010). Decreux, Milner and Péridy (2010) provided a similar estimation, stating that Korea's export to the EU would increase by up to 5.5 per cent following the implementation of the FTA.

While Korea's trade surplus vis-à-vis the EU reached a record level of over US$19 billion in 2007, it has gradually decreased since then. Korea's imports from the EU increased by 21 per cent per year from 2009 to 2011, while its exports to the EU increased only at an annual rate of 9 per cent in the same period. The reason for the difference between export and import growth rates is the slowdown of the EU's economic growth, which decelerated import demand, and the increase of imports into Korea from the EU due to Korea's rapid economic recovery. In 2011, Korea recorded several monthly trade deficits with the EU, and in 2012 Korea recorded a US$1 billion trade deficit with the EU for the first time since 1998. The deficit expanded further to US$9.1 billion in 2015.

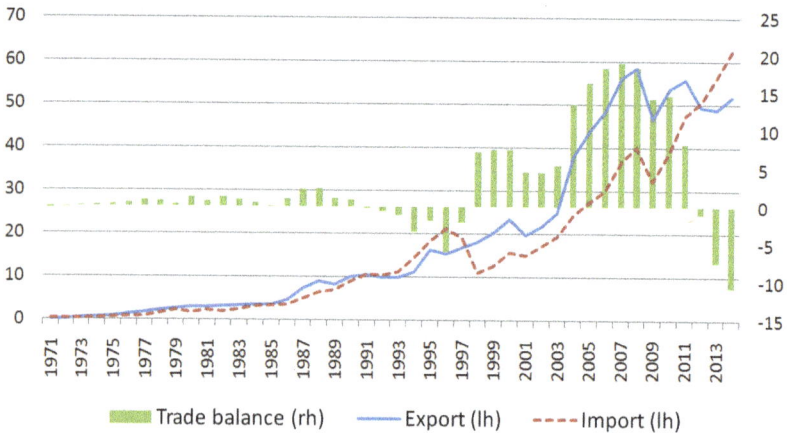

Figure 1. Korea's goods export to and import from the EU, 1971–2014 (US$ billion)

lh, left hand; rh, right hand

Sources: UN Comtrade database, comtrade.un.org/db/; Korean Statistical Information Service, kosis.kr/eng/.

Four years of the Korea–EU FTA

Korea's exports to the EU, which had been recovering following the 2008 global financial crisis, began to decrease in the second half of 2011. For the first year of the FTA with the EU, Korea's exports to the EU decreased 12 per cent compared to the previous year. This result is an exception, given Korea's overall exports to the world increased by 7 per cent in the same period, as shown in Table 2. For Korea, this outcome based on trade statistics is rather disappointing, as most of the previous studies predicted a substantial increase in exports. Moreover, this figure contrasts with Korea's considerable increase in exports to the USA after the KORUS FTA. For the second year, Korea's exports to the EU once again fell, by 4.7 per cent, while it rebounded in the third year, largely due to the base effect.

Table 2. Korea's exports to its trade partners before and after the Korea–EU FTA, 2010–15 (US$ billion)

	One year before	1st year	2nd year	3rd year	4th year	4 years total
EU	57.9	50.8	48.4	51.7	47.6	(–17.7)
		(–12.3)	(–4.7)	(6.7)	(–7.8)	
China	125.6	133.2	140.5	145.8	143.8	(14.5)
		(6.1)	(5.5)	(3.8)	(–1.3)	
USA	54.2	59.1	59.2	64.6	72.1	(33.2)
		(9.1)	(0.2)	(9.2)	(11.7)	
Japan	34.3	40.1	36.6	33.7	29.3	(–14.6)
		(16.8)	(–8.8)	(–7.7)	(–13.1)	
India	12.5	12.5	11.6	11.9	12.5	(–0.1)
		(–0.5)	(–6.8)	(2.4)	(5.2)	
ASEAN	62.2	75.5	82.9	84.4	78.4	(26.0)
		(21.3)	(9.9)	(1.8)	(–7.2)	
Korea's total export	518.7	556.6	549.4	566.4	551.9	(9.7)
		(7.3)	(–1.3)	(3.1)	(–2.5)	

Note: 1) Numbers in parentheses refer to annual percentage change. 2) One year before: July 2010 – June 2011, 1st year: July 2011 – June 2012, 2nd year: July 2012 – June 2013, 3rd year: July 2013 – June 2014, 4th year: July 2013 – June 2014, four years total: change in exports from one year before (July 2010 – April 2011) and the 4th year (July 2014 – June 2015).

Source: Author's calculation based on data from Korea International Trade Association.

In contrast, Korea's imports from the EU increased by 13.1 per cent for the first year of the FTA (Table 3). Given that Korea's overall imports from the world increased by 9 per cent in the same period, the increase in imports from the EU is consistent with the overall trend. However, imports from the EU also increased for a second year by 8 per cent, while Korea's overall imports increased only by less than 2 per cent. During four years of the FTA implementation period, imports from the EU increased by almost 40 per cent and the trade balance turned from a surplus of US$14.5 billion to a deficit of US$12.9 billion. It is clear that the FTA exerted a positive influence on Korea's imports through the tariff-cut effect, given that the growth rate of imports from the EU was four times larger than Korea's overall import growth. However, a question remains regarding the fall in exports to the EU under the 'FTA effect'. In order to understand this change in trade between Korea and the EU, it is necessary to review the economic situation and trade flow in more detail.

Table 3. Korea's imports from its trade partners before and after the Korea–EU FTA, 2010–15 (US$ billion)

	One year before	1st year	2nd year	3rd year	4th year	4 years total
EU	43.5	49.1	53.0	60.0	60.5	(39.5)
		(13.1)	(8.0)	(13.2)	(0.9)	
China	81.0	83.8	81.3	85.9	90.6	(11.9)
		(3.4)	(–2.9)	(5.6)	(5.5)	
USA	42.4	45.7	40.8	43.7	44.2	(4.1)
		(7.8)	(–10.7)	(6.9)	(1.1)	
Japan	67.6	66.8	62.2	56.3	50.8	(–24.9)
		(–1.2)	(–6.9)	(–9.4)	(–9.8)	
India	6.8	7.3	6.6	5.6	4.8	(–29.4)
		(7.0)	(–9.9)	(–14.5)	(–14.4)	
ASEAN	48.8	53.5	51.7	53.8	49.0	(0.5)
		(9.7)	(–3.4)	(4.2)	(–9.0)	
Korea's total import	479.7	513.7	523.2	518.7	485.7	(3.3)
		(9.3)	(1.8)	(–0.9)	(–6.4)	

Note: 1) Numbers in parentheses refer to annual percentage change. 2) One year before: July 2010 – June 2011, 1st year: July 2011 – June 2012, 2nd year: July 2012 – June 2013, 3rd year: July 2013 – June 2014, 4th year: July 2013 – June 2014, four years total: change in imports from one year before (July 2010 – April 2011) and the 4th year (July 2014 – June 2015).

Source: Author's calculation based on data from Korea International Trade Association.

First, there is a stark contrast between Korea's exports to the EU and other regions. Exports to the EU have been decreasing despite the FTA, while its exports to other trade partners have increased considerably. Over the four years since the FTA came into effect, Korea's exports to the EU fell by more than 15 per cent. On the other hand, its exports to the USA, China and the ASEAN countries increased by 14–33 per cent during the same period. The answer to such a difference can be found from a comparative view on exports of other Asian countries to the EU. According to trade data from Eurostat, most East Asian exporting countries—China, Japan and Taiwan—have experienced a sharper decline in their exports to the EU than Korea. While China's exports to the EU increased by 7 per cent, Japan and Taiwan's exports to the EU dropped by 8–20 per cent. Given the continued depreciation of the Japanese yen from late 2012, it is intriguing to see that Japanese exports to the EU have seen the most visible decrease.

It is noteworthy that most East Asian economies experienced a decrease in exports to the EU. They have common features in that they are specialised in exports in manufacturing sectors. The sharp fall in domestic demand in the EU has exerted undoubtedly a very negative influence on exports to the EU of East Asian countries with a high export share in manufacturing industries. In other words, the less-than-expected performance in Korea's exports to Europe should be attributed to weak demand in the EU from around 2008. Indeed, the decline in exports to the EU was common among the exporting countries in Asia.

Second, the fall in exports is salient in ships and electronics, which are Korea's most important export items. For example, ship exports accounted for 28 per cent of Korea's total exports to the EU in 2011. However, its export amount fell by more than 60 per cent since the implementation of the FTA. Exports of mobile phones, LCD televisions and semiconductors were reduced by 15–52 per cent. These products are marked either by general European import market contraction, due to the economic recession, or by relocation of Korean firms to Southeast Asia in order to cut production cost. Because Korean exports to the EU are highly concentrated in these few sectors, their fall creates a more statistically important impact on change in overall exports to the EU. On the other hand, Korea's exports increased for manufacturing items—such as refined oil, automobiles and chemical products—for which the tariff cuts were quite important.

Third, Korea's imports from the EU increased considerably, which had a more important impact on change in the trade balance than the decrease in exports. Imports from the EU increased by almost 40 per cent over four years. This figure is outstanding, given that Korea's total imports only increased by less than 4 per cent during the same period. At the sectoral level, an increase in imports from the EU is identified over a wide range of manufacturing products, from intermediates such as crude oil and refined petrol to machinery, automobiles and luxury items. For instance, Korea's import of both crude and refined oil from the EU (Brent oil) was negligible before the FTA, but its import soared and accounted for 17.2 per cent of Korea's total import from the EU. Instead, imports from Organization of the Petroleum Exporting Countries (OPEC) countries fell, which means the FTA created a trade diversion effect from Korea's main oil resource to the EU—largely the United Kingdom. Some imports from Japan in machinery and industrial equipment were replaced by European products.

Fourth, the weakening value of the Euro (since mid-2011) exerted a positive influence on the EU's exports in that European products became cheaper outside of Europe. The reasons for the weak Euro can be explained by the decline of confidence and economic recession in the Eurozone and the lowest key interest rate since the introduction of the Euro in 1999. As a consequence, the trade balance of crisis-affected European countries improved considerably. For example, Germany recorded its largest-ever trade surplus. It is expected that the Euro will remain weak while the European Central Bank considers an expansionary monetary policy. This will create a favourable trade environment for European exporters.

Korea's exports to the EU turned to positive growth in the third year of the FTA, mainly due to the base effect. As European economies start to lift themselves out of the recession, it is likely that Korea's exports to the EU will increase. However, as the EU is negotiating FTAs with Japan and members of ASEAN, Korea's unique status as the EU's FTA partner in East Asia may become obsolete. All the more, the relocation of Korean firms will be more salient as they try to create supply chains in developing countries. In this context, the role of the FTA in promoting export in statistical terms will meet its limit and a more comprehensive approach will be required to make full use of the FTA.

Conclusion

In summary, this chapter has indicated that Korea enjoys close ties with the EU both in bilateral trade flows and in terms of investment by EU firms in Korea and Korean investment in assembly operations in the EU. Korea's trade and investment relationship with the EU is similar to that with the USA. A factor in the EU giving high priority to Korea, along with ASEAN and Mercosur as a target for a 'new generation' or 'deep integration' FTA following the EU's Global Europe initiative of 2006 was that the USA had already begun FTA negotiations with Korea. The importance of global supply chains, especially in the sourcing of intermediate products from China and Southeast Asia, for the production of final goods, especially cars and consumer electronics, was a major issue for the EU in its FTA negotiations with Korea.

These issues were only settled in the final stages of the negotiations. In the final deal, Korea was able to maintain its DDS for a limited time, and the EU modified its rules of origin requirements by accepting a local content of 45 per cent on Korea's exports to the EU, compared to its customary demand of 60 per cent. In the short period since the Korea–EU FTA entered into force in July 2011, the study of the trade flows implies that the agreement has been somewhat more beneficial to the EU than to Korea. Nevertheless, the high price elasticity of demand of the manufactures that dominate Korea–EU trade can be significantly impacted on by short-term economic circumstances.

The Korea–EU FTA contains a few elements that should be noted. Conventionally, FTAs focus on reducing tariff barriers. However, the role of tariff barriers in trade has become less important, as developed countries have already lowered their tariffs on manufactured goods in the context of General Agreement on Tariffs and Trade (GATT) and WTO. As it has been difficult to progress trade liberalisation in the multilateral context, bilateral FTAs are implemented to advance the agenda. Issues of trade negotiation have therefore shifted from tariff liberalisation to harmonisation and mutual recognition of different regulations. This was also the case in the Korea–EU FTA. During the negotiation of the Korea–EU FTA, different standards between Korea and the EU were highlighted, particularly regulations on the safety certificate procedures in electrical/electronic goods and product standards for automobiles.

The Korea–EU FTA states that both parties establish regular committees on how to reduce trade-impeding regulatory barriers. It is still hard to expect that Korea and the EU can complete a free trade framework equivalent to that of the European Economic Area where most of the trade-related regulations are highly harmonised and mutually recognised. However, as trade and investment relations between the two parties are strengthened by the FTA, the pressure on them to tackle NTB issues will increase. What we will see during the next few years will be policy efforts to coordinate business practice as well as 'regulatory convergence' between Korea and the EU. This will certainly require more time and involve more stakeholders—not only government officials, but also businesses.

Technology cooperation can be another opportunity in the period since the conclusion of the FTA. For example, Korea and the EU could create and activate international technology transfer mechanisms through both public and private initiatives. Small and medium enterprises can experience a number of hardships in the course of doing business, from finding technology to financing. In some cases, it is impossible for small and medium enterprises to independently introduce, apply and spread new technology. As institutional cooperation frames have been consolidated by the Korea–EU FTA and its associated arrangements, it will be more possible to promote cooperation between private firms. Trade associations can find a more important role in this regard.

References

ACEA (European Automobile Manufacturers Association) (2009), 'EU governments must denounce unfair competition to European industries in trade conditions for South Korea', ACEA Press release, 8 July.

Decreux, Yvan, Chris Milner & Nichola Péridy (2010), *The Economic Impact of the Free Trade Agreement (FTA) between the European Union and Korea*, Report for the European Commission (CEPII/ATLASS), May.

Delegation of the EU to the Republic of Korea (2013), *European Union–South Korea: Trade and Investment Relations*, Fact File Edition 2013 (Delegation of the EU to the Republic of Korea: Seoul).

European Commission (2006), *Global Europe: Competing in the World – A Contribution to the EU's Growth and Jobs Strategy*, COM(2006) 567 Final (European Commission: Brussels).

Kang, Moon-Sung (2009), *Korea's Current FTAs and Issues of FTA Strategy*, CFE Report No. 103 (Centre for Free Enterprise: Seoul) (Korean).

KIEP (Korea Institute for International Economic Policy) (2010), 'Economic impact of Korea–EU FTA (jointly conducted with 9 research institutes)', October (Korean).

Lamy, Pascal (2002), 'Stepping stones or stumbling blocks? The EU's approach towards the problem of multilateralism vs regionalism in trade policy', *The World Economy* 25(10): 1399–413. doi.org/10.1111/1467-9701.00498.

Ministry of Foreign Affairs and Trade (2003), cited in Kang, Moon-Sung (2009), *Korea's Current FTAs and Issues of FTA Strategy*, CFE Report No. 103 (Centre for Free Enterprise: Seoul) (Korean).

3

Understanding the EU–Singapore Free Trade Agreement

Deborah Elms

Abstract

Initial negotiations on a free trade agreement (FTA) between the European Union (EU) and the Association of Southeast Asian Nations (ASEAN) began in 2007. Although the quest for a region-wide deal quickly foundered, the EU soon shifted focus to negotiating with key, individual member states in ASEAN. Singapore was targeted to sign the first agreement and negotiations got underway in 2010. The EU–Singapore FTA was completed in 2014, with the remaining issues in the investment chapter finished by May 2015. The final outcome is a relatively high-quality deal, with nearly all tariffs dropped between the two parties, new openings in services markets, some additional rules in areas like intellectual property rights and government procurement, and a robust investment chapter. Implementation of the agreement got delayed, however, pending internal procedures in Europe. Officials are hoping for the deal to enter into force sometime after a ruling from the European Court of Justice, delivered on 16 May 2017.

Rationale for an agreement

In 2007, the EU launched negotiations with ASEAN to create a mega-regional FTA. Such a trade agreement would hook together two large and diverse regional actors—the then 27 members of the EU (EU27) with 10 members of ASEAN (Brunei, Cambodia, Indonesia, Laos, Malaysia, Myanmar, Philippines, Singapore, Thailand and Vietnam).

Taken as a bloc, ASEAN represented a large and growing economic market for the EU, as shown in Figure 1. Trade in goods with ASEAN was larger than trade with Japan, Brazil, India and the Gulf states. Services trade was also significant and growing. Finally, foreign direct investment was substantial. The economic impetus for a deal to more closely connect the two regions was clear.

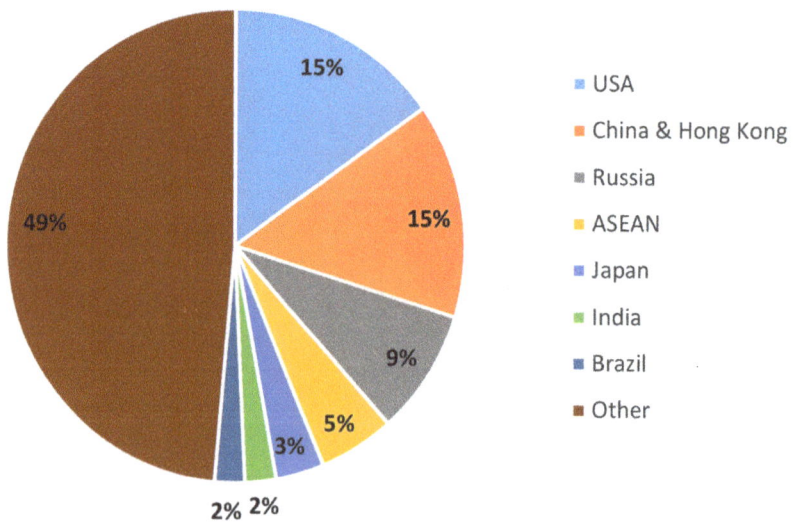

Figure 1. Key EU partners in goods trade (2012)
Source: Eurostat 2013.

However, shortly after negotiations got underway, the Europeans quickly understood that while the EU negotiates as a genuine bloc, ASEAN does not. When negotiating with ASEAN, at least 11 people are seated at the table—one person from each of the member states plus someone from the ASEAN Secretariat. Secretariat staff are largely unable to commit to anything on behalf of their members. Creating an agreement with ASEAN essentially meant creating 10 separate bilateral agreements in key areas (like market access schedules for goods, services and investment) with, potentially, a few common elements across all ASEAN members.

The EU decided that, if it was going to have to negotiate more than one agreement, it might get better terms and an easier negotiating path by starting with key markets on an individual basis. This meant launching bilateral talks with Singapore, Malaysia, Vietnam and Thailand.[1]

EU–Singapore negotiations

On the surface, Singapore did not appear to be a particularly interesting market for Europe. The total population of roughly five million included a substantial number of foreign workers with limited capacity to consume European goods and services. However, this picture does not accurately reflect the actual importance of the Singapore market. Singapore dominated trade within ASEAN vis-à-vis Europe. Figures 2–4 highlight the importance of the Singapore market. For example, Singapore alone accounted for more than €42 billion in exports for European companies, while the region imported €35 billion in goods and services from Singapore. Of equal interest was the substantial stock of foreign direct investment (FDI). Table 1 shows that the EU had more money invested in Singapore (€126 billion) in 2012 than in the United States of America (USA) (€65 billion) by more than double. Singapore's investments into the EU were also significant at €55 billion. The total number of European companies resident in Singapore approached 9,000.

---

1   Of course, the EU was actually composed of 27 distinct members, so the agreement is not technically a 'bilateral' deal between two nations. But the EU effectively negotiates as one, particularly (as noted further below) after the Lisbon Treaty changed competence of investment to the EU level instead of member state levels. This meant that all aspects of trade negotiations could be handled by the European Commission on behalf of its members.

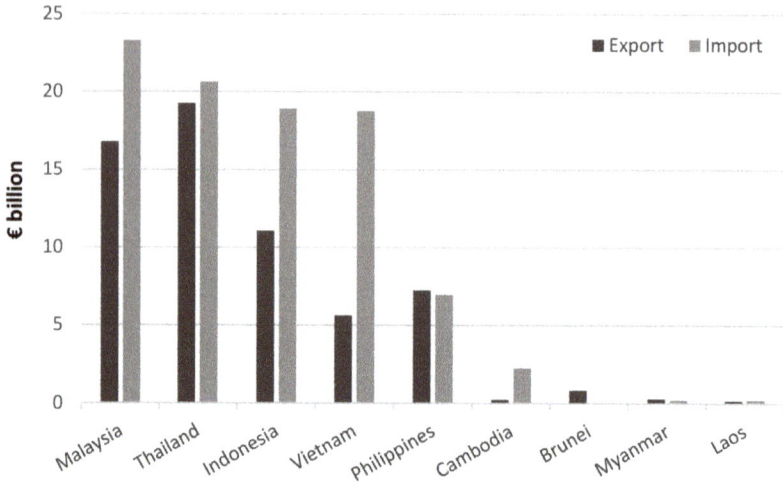

Figure 2. EU trade in goods and services with ASEAN (2012)
Source: Eurostat 2013.

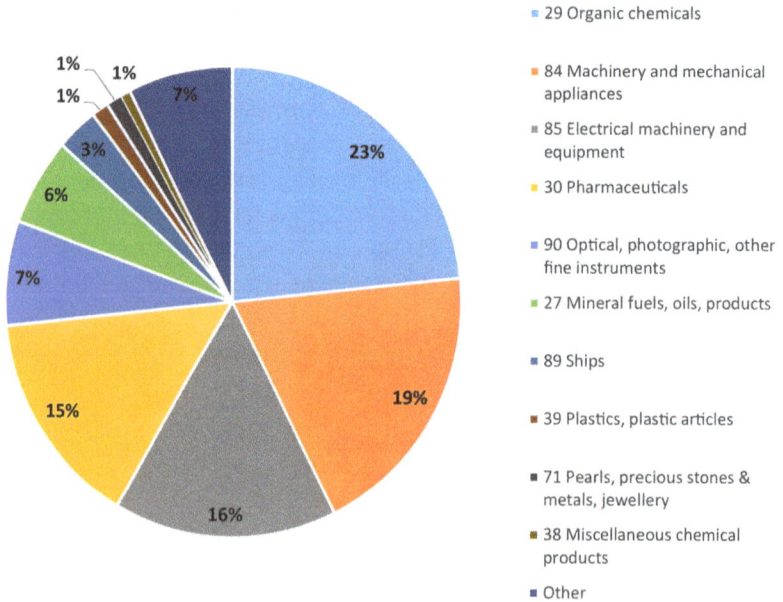

Figure 3. EU27 top imports from Singapore (2012)
Source: Eurostat 2013.

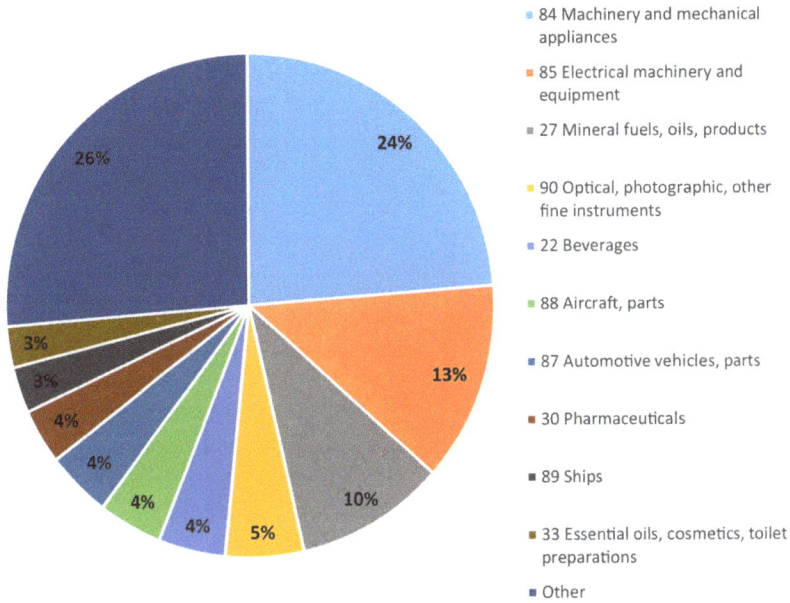

- 84 Machinery and mechanical appliances
- 85 Electrical machinery and equipment
- 27 Mineral fuels, oils, products
- 90 Optical, photographic, other fine instruments
- 22 Beverages
- 88 Aircraft, parts
- 87 Automotive vehicles, parts
- 30 Pharmaceuticals
- 89 Ships
- 33 Essential oils, cosmetics, toilet preparations
- Other

Figure 4. EU27 top exports to Singapore (2012)

Source: Eurostat 2013.

Table 1. Value of foreign direct investment (FDI) in 2011

FDI source	Investment stock into Singapore (€ billion)	Investment stock into the EU (€ billion)
EU	107.3	
Singapore		67
USA	43.1	
Japan	29.1	144
Switzerland	15.9	
ASEAN-9	14.2	
India	13.2	10
Hong Kong	13.0	64
Norway	12.1	
Malaysia	10.3	4
China	8.1	15

Sources: Singapore's figures from Department of Statistics, May 2013; EU from Eurostat 2013.

Hence, Singapore represented an attractive market all on its own as a trade agreement partner. Singapore also had growing interest and experience negotiating FTAs. Much of what the country had promised to the Americans in a 2005 bilateral agreement could potentially be replicated in a negotiation with the EU. This would represent a very high-quality, ambitious FTA for Europe.

Finally, if the EU succeeded in crafting a solid FTA with Singapore, it could serve as the template for a future agreement with ASEAN. The Singaporeans would go first and likely finish negotiating the fastest. Thus an EU–Singapore FTA (EUSFTA) bilateral could serve as a model for negotiations with other countries such as Malaysia and Thailand. Furthermore, keeping consistency across ASEAN-member FTAs could make it easier to combine six agreements into one (with Singapore, Malaysia, Thailand, Philippines, Indonesia and Vietnam). Cambodia, Laos and Myanmar were not invited to join in bilateral negotiations with the EU, but these countries already received preferential access to Europe through 'Everything But Arms' trading schemes. The last ASEAN member, Brunei, was simply not an important enough bilateral partner to warrant separate negotiations. It would have to wait until the regional agreement was ready and be folded in at that time. Hence, by the end of the process, the Europeans could combine enough 'building block' agreements to finally wrap up a region-to-region deal.

Economic benefits of the agreement

Negotiations commenced with Singapore in 2010. The basic framework was finished by 2012, with a few minor issues remaining. As discussed in greater detail below, sticking points included geographical indications, financial services and investment rules. The deal (except for investment) was finished by October 2014. In May 2015, both sides announced the conclusion of the agreement, when the final legal scrubbing was completed for the investment chapter (see Ministry of Trade and Industry, Singapore, 2015). The European Court of Justice (ECJ) decided in May 2017 on whether only the European Parliament must ratify the FTA or whether member states would also have to approve portions of the final agreement. The ruling provided for 'mixed competence', showing that the EU could determine most of the agreement, but some elements, including parts of investment, will require member state approval. The EUSFTA allows for a provisional entry into force once the Court ruling is completed.[2]

Modelling of the economic benefits of the agreement appeared quite lopsided, with the majority of gains flowing to the Singapore side. This reflects the significant differences in economic size between the two parties. The Chief Economist of the European Commission estimated that EU exports to Singapore could increase by €1.4 billion over 10 years while Singaporean exports to the EU could increase by €3.5 billion. Real gross domestic product (GDP) in the EU could grow by €550 million while Singapore could see an increase of €2.7 billion (see Delegation of the European Union to the United States 2015).

Note also that economic modelling usually handles comprehensive FTAs badly. This is because the economic models overemphasise the importance of tariff reductions (which are easy to measure and straightforward to model) and underemphasise the importance of services and investment changes (which are very tricky to measure and hard to model, particularly with knock-on effects likely). In addition, firms are increasingly concerned about the proliferation of non-tariff barriers (NTBs), such as incompatible or complex standards, testing regimes, labelling laws, delays in processing shipments at the border and so forth. NTB reductions are nearly impossible to include in economic modelling. Hence, while economic modelling is a useful exercise and can provide information about the expected direction of economic growth as well as handy figures for political leaders to press for changes, the real-world impact of FTAs can be much greater or different than economic models suggest.

In the case of the EUSFTA, models will likely also fail to capture the potential for increased regional economic growth by European companies using Singapore as a platform for further expansion into ASEAN. Most of the European companies located in Singapore prior to the FTA used the island as a base for regional strategies. There is every reason to expect this pattern to continue and to accelerate after the FTA takes effect.

---

2   For the complete text of the agreement, see European Commission (2015).

Finally, the EUSFTA has always been intended—from the European perspective—to form the basis for the larger regional agreement with ASEAN. Thus, the European Commission and member states have long recognised that while benefits from a bilateral agreement with Singapore may be lopsided, the benefits from the expansion of an FTA to encompass all of ASEAN will likely be substantial for European companies.

Exploring the EUSFTA in detail

So, what happened in the EUSFTA? In brief, the bilateral agreement represents a relatively high-quality outcome. This result was easier to obtain than in many negotiations, given the comparatively open nature of the Singapore market. For example, Singapore's applied tariff rate for all goods (except for six tariff lines for some alcohol products and cigarettes) is zero. This always makes it easier to craft a trade agreement, since Singapore has fewer built-in sensitivities in goods that must be accommodated.

The agreement covers most goods, including a few new provisions on electronics and a consultation process for agricultural trade regulations. Several important sectors have specific coverage under the agreement. Services trade was also opened and liberalised with a clear eye towards crafting an ASEAN-wide deal on services for the future.

The agreement also included provisions on government procurement, new rules on intellectual property rights including a greatly expanded set of covered geographical indications, a chapter on competition, development objectives, labour standards and dispute settlement procedures. Each of these elements is covered in more detail below.

Trade in goods

Given Singapore's duty-free applied access to goods, the EUSFTA binds Singapore tariffs at 0 for European goods imports. The bulk of the negotiations focused on tariff reductions for the European side. Basically, the EU agreed to reduce its own tariffs to match the levels found in the 2011 EU–Korea FTA within 5 years of entry into force. This included dropping tariffs to 0 on entry into force for approximately 75 per cent of tariff lines. Most of the remaining lines were also scheduled to go to 0 across a time period of 3–5 years, with reductions taking place in annual installments.

A goods agreement cannot be evaluated on the basis of tariff line reductions alone, however. Trade between parties is often concentrated, so the bulk of actual trade between members in an FTA might take place in a handful of tariff lines alone. If these lines are not included in the final agreement, a headline figure of even 95 per cent tariff reductions may not translate into meaningful economic outcomes on the ground. However, EU–Singapore trade is relatively widely dispersed, making it more likely that tariff cuts would affect tradeable sectors like machinery, chemicals and pharmaceuticals.

Tariffs also interact with rules of origin. Rules of origin are necessary to ensure that only firms from member countries are eligible to receive the benefits (particularly lower tariff rates) built into the agreement. If any company could take advantage of the deal, it would undermine the specific benefits for members. Hence, every FTA comes with rules of origin to ensure that products claiming preferences are either wholly 'from' members (i.e. grown, produced, mined or extracted from the member without any additional content added from any other member state) or are substantially transformed from their original materials or components into a new type of product within the geographic spaces covered by the FTA.

It is possible to create an agreement with zero tariffs across the board, but make the requirements for receiving duty-free treatment so onerous that almost no firms are able to take advantage of the lower tariff rates. Or, conversely, it is possible to have tariffs drop by less, but make it so easy for firms to use the agreement that nearly all companies participate in the agreement.[3]

There is no agreement among firms on what type of rules are easiest to use. For some companies, blanket rules (such as requiring 40–45 per cent of the content embedded in a product to come from member states) are preferable to more specific rules for each product. These blanket rules can apply to

---

3   Companies never get the benefits of an FTA automatically—each FTA requires firms to certify that they are using an FTA. The method of certification varies, but often FTAs require a certificate of origin to be obtained from a local chamber of commerce or another designated body before customs officers at the border will grant lower tariffs. Without a certificate of origin (or self-certification in some newer generation agreements), products cannot qualify for the preferential rate and are instead charged the most-favoured-nation (MFN) rate. The MFN tariff rate is the tariff charged to all World Trade Organization (WTO) members automatically without requiring any certification of origin. Since more than 160 countries are WTO members, practically speaking, nearly all firms can use MFN rates for their goods shipments. For many firms, unless the preferential benefits of an FTA are substantial, companies often opt to avoid the hassle required in using the provisions of an FTA and ship goods under MFN tariffs.

every item in a firm's inventory, so once a company works out the value of the content for each product, it can determine easily which will be allowed to claim preferences and which (absent reformulation or shifts in the supply chain) cannot. However, some firms prefer more specific rules. Product-specific rules grant less flexibility to customs officials in evaluating products at the border. Product-specific rules can also be subject to fewer disputes and may be less at risk to shifting prices in raw materials, components, labour and even exchange rate fluctuations (since products that reach, for example, 43 per cent value content today may be only 38 per cent value content tomorrow if the prices shift in determining the product values).

The EUSFTA contains mostly product-specific rules of origin. The agreement includes some co-equal rules (which allow firms to use one *or* the other of two calculation methods to prove sufficient content). The agreement is effectively a bilateral agreement between the EU (counting EU members as if they were one) and Singapore. Hence, the agreement does not allow content from across ASEAN to count towards content. This can be a problem for Singapore, since the country has very few indigenous items to add to a product's content. Singapore's major exports to the EU include oil and oil-related products, manufactured goods (especially electronics), and pharmaceuticals. With raw materials, parts and components usually coming from overseas, it is not always possible to reach high levels of locally added content, absent the ability to add up, or cumulate, content from elsewhere. Nevertheless, as the EU moves towards incorporating all the bilateral trade agreements into one region-wide ASEAN agreement, it is likely that ASEAN cumulation rules will be built in the future.

The EU did not pledge to reach duty-free status in all products. The EUSFTA left some items that will not be subject to tariff elimination including some fish products (tilapia, catfish, salmon in vegetable oil, bonito and surimi); as well as chemically pure fructose; and sweetcorn and maize.

Specific customs duties will remain for some vegetable and fruit products imported into Europe, including vegetables (fresh or chilled tomatoes, cucumbers, globe artichokes and courgettes); citrus (including fresh sweet oranges, clementines, monreales and satsumas, mandrins and wilkings, tangerines and lemons); and fruits (including table grapes, apricots, sour cherries, nectarines and plums).[4]

---

4   For the specific exceptions, please see the market access schedules of the EU found in Annex 2-A of European Commission (2015).

Other goods provisions

The agreement included an additional chapter on what are called technical barriers to trade. These are largely regulatory and standards-based rules that govern specific types of goods. The EUSFTA sets up a rudimentary structure to strengthen cooperation in regulatory areas in the future, as well as better procedures for exchanging information and streamlining regulations between the parties.

One exception to the largely generic nature of the technical barriers to trade rules can be found in an annex on electronics. Singapore has an unusually complex system of testing in this sector. The agreement contains promises to use conformity assessments and international standards bodies as much as possible.

Another chapter covers rules for food and food safety. The sanitary and phytosanitary chapter codified that both sides could have import requirements for food and food stuffs. Imports can be stopped and checked for compliance with relevant sanitary and phytosanitary rules, under a set of procedures that was tightened and clarified with specific timelines for inspections. The agreement sets out a variety of committees and consultations to take place around sanitary and phytosanitary issues in the future.

Finally, the agreement also sets out four sector-specific provisions. For motor vehicles, Singapore agreed to recognise EU standards and testing regimes for cars and car parts. The agreement also has language on green rebates for more environmentally friendly motor vehicles. A second section covers electronics, where Singapore agreed to gradually replace third-party testing of products (particularly to accept suppliers' declarations of conformity that are widely used inside the EU). A third sectoral element of the EUSFTA looked at pharmaceuticals where the primary pledge calls for greater transparency in pricing structures. Finally, the agreement has a section on green technology: both sides pledged to allow renewable energy equipment to move between the EU and Singapore with national treatment (foreign products granted the same treatment as locally produced comparable items) and no additional conformity tests.

Trade in services

While the agreement covers trade in goods, the primary offensive objective of the EU was to improve access to Singapore's services markets. Services could include financial services, insurance, banking, brokerage, accounting, design, architecture, legal, management, food and beverage, travel and tourism and so forth. For most developed economies, services can represent the bulk of economic activity. Even in manufactured goods, the services content of goods in cross-border supply chains can be 40–70 per cent. Hence, greater access and better protections of these key sectors were important objectives for both sides.

The EU claimed to have given Singapore levels of access comparable to the EU–Korea FTA in telecommunications, financial, computer, transport, environmental and some business services. The sections of the agreement covering postal services, the EU argued, went beyond what Korea got.

Both parties agreed that the governments may not use licensing requirements as a mechanism to obstruct entry into services markets. While licensing is not a particularly serious barrier to entry in either the EU or Singapore, this remains a favoured mechanism in many ASEAN countries to restrict foreign firm competition. Hence, the inclusion of clauses on licensing for services in the EUSFTA is primarily a marker for future ASEAN and ASEAN-wide agreements.

To ensure that both parties maintain the very best access to each other's services markets going forward and to capture whatever gains come from future negotiations with other partners, the parties agreed to include a most-favoured-nation (MFN) ratchet clause into the agreement. This means that the EU automatically receives new, matching benefits if Singapore ever negotiates an improved services agreement in any other format and vice versa for Singaporean firms entering the EU.[5]

---

5   This is, frankly, a terrible idea, but it is currently wildly popular with trade officials all over the globe who worry about losing ground to new players in future agreements. The problem with ratchet clauses is that they tie your government and markets into provisions that you had zero input in negotiating and could potentially cause harm in ways you cannot imagine. The easiest way to see the dangers is to imagine one party signing an agreement in the future with a small country in the Pacific Ocean (for example) where the economic stakes seem so modest that the agreement can afford to be incredibly ambitious. Suddenly, your own country has granted the same access through the ratchet to far more competitive firms in the partner country that could ultimately threaten domestic firms.

The services chapter does not cover all services. Carved out of the deal are audio-visual services; national maritime cabotage; air transport; and mining, manufacturing and processing of nuclear materials.[6] The Europeans were not terribly successful in getting new market access to Singapore's financial services sector.[7]

Services were negotiated on the basis of a 'positive list'. This is a typical negotiating style for the EU. Under a positive list approach, only the services sectors and subsectors specifically listed are opened for competition from firms in the partner country. Any new services sectors developed in the future (such as the whole industries of services generated by new technologies) are not opened unless the parties specifically negotiate such an opening in the future.[8] The positive list is currently easier for the EU to use, since the individual member states can be very clear about what sorts of commitments in which subsectors they are willing to promise. Everything else not specifically noted is not opened for competition from partner firms.

In services, like in goods, an agreement includes two parts. The first is a set of rules and regulations governing the sector. The second are specific market-access promises made by each side, broken down by 12 sectors and 160+ subsectors. In addition, in the EUSFTA, the European-side commitments are split into horizontal commitments (to apply across all subsectors in a sector), as well as establishment promises for the subsector and specific pledges on what is called mode 4 (temporary movement of personnel).

The EUSFTA opens up competition in postal services. These are services that are often considered sensitive by many governments with extensive restrictions for entry into the market.

---

6   As an example of the dangers of the ratchet, if not done carefully, future deals on either side could open the audio-visual sector or lead suddenly to open skies if a future agreement on either side grants such provisions (and the ratchet in the EUSFTA contains any ambiguities that would let these new rules flow through the EUSFTA). Clever lawyers can find all sorts of ways to make mischief.

7   The goal was to get comparable coverage to what the Americans received in their bilateral agreement with Singapore. But the EU was not successful in meeting this objective. See Singapore's specific commitments on financial services in Annex 8B-2 of European Commission (2015).

8   The contrasting approach is called a 'negative list'. The Trans-Pacific Partnership (TPP) and all American FTAs include a negative list. Under this style of negotiating, all services sectors *except* for those listed are opened to competition. This includes all future and new sectors and subsectors that are automatically opened unless the parties agree in a negotiation to close them to competition. Singapore, which has agreements with the USA and is a TPP member, negotiates services agreements using both positive and negative approaches. ASEAN, as a whole, has always used positive lists.

Both sides agreed that telecommunications has a vital role to play in business today. They agreed to respect the confidentiality of information and to require firms to provide services on non-discriminatory terms, conditions or rates. The agreement also outlined competitive safeguards for major suppliers of telecommunications services. While the agreement does not break new ground on e-commerce, it does pledge cooperation between both sides. Both sides agreed to avoid imposing unnecessary restrictions or regulations on e-commerce activities. The agreement recognises the importance of the free flow of information and commits both sides to uphold international standards of data protection.

Other new areas of coverage

Meat

One issue of concern for Europe was Singapore's complex system of approval for meat imports. Under the EUSFTA, Singapore agreed to remove a requirement that meat products should be individually inspected and approved by the Agri-Food and Veterinary Authority (AVA) in Singapore. Going forward, Singapore agreed to set up an auditing system and allow inspections only when triggered by the auditing system.

Government procurement

Both Singapore and the EU are signatories to the Agreement on Government Procurement (GPA) at the World Trade Organization (WTO). In 2017, 19 parties are signatories.[9] Under the GPA, members agree to allow certain government contracts for goods and services to be opened to firms from member states under competitive bidding.

Since both parties are included in the GPA, the EUSFTA extended the coverage areas under which tenders are to be accepted. The EU agreed to include EU central government entities, public works concessions such as railways, and some additional utilities. In addition, the EU dropped the threshold levels for bidding by Singaporean firms.

9   Counting the EU as one. www.wto.org/english/tratop_e/gproc_e/memobs_e.htm (accessed 14 May 2017).

Geographical indications

Although the EUSFTA includes other elements in the intellectual property rights chapter, nearly all the focus was on geographical indications (GIs). This issue nearly derailed the entire negotiations and largely held up the conclusion of the agreement for nearly two years.

The basic problem is that the EU is the world's staunchest supporter of GIs, while Singapore has been generally hostile to the idea. To complicate matters further, Singapore was simultaneously negotiating an FTA with the USA and other parties in the Trans-Pacific Partnership (TPP). The TPP specifically did not include GIs, and TPP members were extremely uncomfortable with reconciling the two agreements at the end.[10]

A GI is a specific type of product protection. Put simply, a GI suggests that products are unique largely due to specific conditions, reputations and traditions surrounding their creation. These products cannot be recreated elsewhere and should not be allowed to bear similar names. To allow similar names is to confuse consumers who are not receiving benefits from all the specific aspects of a good.

The term originally came from wine (and subsequently spirits) production. Champagne grown in Champagne, France, is assumed to carry elements of the specific soil, weather conditions, growing traditions and bottling procedures. These elements cannot be replicated in a place like California. Whatever product gets produced in California should be called something other than champagne, such as sparkling wine, to avoid misleading consumers.

The EU has pushed for the inclusion of GIs in FTAs and has expanded the list of products beyond wines and spirits (many of which now have protections at the global level under the WTO) to items like cheeses and meats.[11] Once a product receives GI protections, no other similar product

---

10   The resolution of this issue in the aftermath of Singapore's commitments in the EUSFTA for the TPP has been to allow GIs for 'compound names'. In general, such product designations require two names. Thus, 'feta' cheese is considered generic (and not protected). But 'Wisconsin cheddar' might qualify.

11   In the EU–Korea FTA, the GIs annex runs to 22 pages and includes a wide range of products including a host of different types of mushrooms. The EU's internal register of these products includes more than 1,000 food items and 3,000 different types of alcohol. The USA, by contrast, prefers to give products protection under trademarks, if the products meet the necessary criteria for trademark protection.

can use the same product terms even if the label makes origin explicit. The EU tries to stop firms from producing products made 'like' or 'in the style of' or using a 'method'.

Singapore had no list of GI protections and no products that it wanted included on a list. After heated negotiations, Singapore developed a list of 196 products to be granted GI protections in the marketplace. Recognition was therefore not automatic, but subject to negotiation and approval from the regulatory authorities in Singapore. The Singapore list is particularly heavy on compound names (not just parmesan cheese, but Parmesan-Reggiano cheese or not just ham but Parma Ham) and items already protected with trademarks. In general, the stance of the Singaporean Government was to add products to the list only after determining whether such product names were viewed in Singapore as a 'generic' name. If so, products could not be granted GI protection.

Singapore added another wrinkle to the negotiations by insisting in a side letter that the entire agreement would not go into force until the GI procedures were sorted out and the list of protected GIs was confirmed by the Singapore Parliament. The bill was passed in April 2014.

Competition chapter

The agreement includes a chapter on competition policy. Both Singapore and the EU already have in place laws that are designed to prevent the growth and spread of monopolies. Hence, the chapter starts at a deeper level and commits both parties to enforcing their own respective laws on competition. The chapter also urges both sides to address the horizontal and vertical agreements between undertakings that might distort competition.

The chapter does, however, explicitly allow for public undertakings with special or exclusive rights and to maintain state monopolies. Finally, the chapter includes provisions that clarify procedures around subsidies. The agreement allows for subsidies for things such as serious disturbances to the economy; the coal industry; social character; natural disasters; economic development for abnormally low areas; certain economic activities such as research and development (R&D), environment and supporting small and medium-sized enterprises; culture; and regional interest projects.

Trade and sustainable development

All European agreements include a chapter on trade and sustainable development, including the EUSFTA and EU–Korea FTA. The primary purpose in these two agreements is to include binding commitments on domestic levels of environmental and labour protections consistent with core international standards and agreements.

The deal has provisions for corporate social responsibility activities, as well as conservation efforts. Fish and logging are specifically called out in the texts.

This chapter includes information about the procedures for stakeholder engagement and consultation with civil society. Finally, the chapter comes with its own dispute mechanism.

Labour standards in the EUSFTA

The agreement gives each party the right to establish their own levels of labour protection. Both sides also have the right to adopt or modify relevant laws or policies on labour. Finally, both sides committed to upholding the 1998 International Labor Organization (ILO) Declaration. Under this provision, parties agreed to the freedom of association, and effective recognition of the right to collective bargaining; elimination of all forms of forced or compulsory labour; effective abolition of child labour; and elimination of discrimination in respect of employment and occupation.

Dispute settlement and management

The agreement spells out the procedures for handling disputes. Complaints are to be handled by an arbitration panel if necessary.

The EUSFTA also sets out a strong institutional structure of committees and working groups for implementation.

Obstacles to entry into force: Who is responsible for investment now?

Officials negotiating the agreement considered the possibility that ratification in 27 (now 28) member states might be a lengthy process. The deal allows provisional implementation to take effect during ratification by individual member states.

The effective date of the agreement, however, was thrown into turmoil by an unexpected European obstacle. The EUSFTA was the first agreement negotiated by the EU after the Lisbon Treaty took effect.

Lisbon moved competence over investment from individual member states to the European level (Meunier-Aitsahalia 2014). But it did so in a relatively unusual way. As Sophie Meunier relates, five words ('*and on foreign direct investment*') were added in a very late review session for the treaty that could change the way Europe deals with investment issues. Prior to this session, individual member states in Europe had their own responsibility for managing investment. Most member states had an extensive network of existing bilateral investment treaties (BITs) spanning the globe.

But once the relevant section of the Treaty on the Functioning of the European Union (TFEU or the Lisbon Treaty) came into force on 1 December 2009, the European Commission argued that responsibility for investment moved to the European level and was no longer to be handled by individual member states directly. Articles 206 and 207 of the TFEU include the phrase 'the progressive abolition of restrictions on international trade and on foreign direct investment'. Changes to the treatment of investment could be quite challenging to manage.[12]

After the conclusion of the treaty, some member states in the EU objected to an expansive definition of this phrase, which saw the European Commission suddenly taking over the task of handling investment negotiations as well as broader trade issues. Some members suggested that investment—at best—ought to be considered an area of 'shared

---

12   But a great boon to an army of consultants, lawyers and scholars to sort out in the coming years. The fate of other agreements, such as the FTA between Canada and the EU as well as ongoing early negotiations with China over a BIT, are also stuck in limbo.

competence' with the European Commission and individual member states involved in any agreements that covered the gamut of potential investment issues like those usually handled inside an FTA or a BIT.

The EUSFTA does include broad coverage of investment. The negotiated rules cover expropriation, national treatment, fair and equitable treatment for investors from member countries, full protection and security, and free capital movements and payments. These clauses are, by now, fairly typical for recent FTA agreements between developed economies. The EUSFTA chapter will replace 12 existing BITs between Singapore and European member states.

One wrinkle in a standard investment treaty comes from Europe's status as 'not a state', which makes it ineligible for investor–state dispute settlement under the International Centre for Settlement of Investment Disputes (ICSID). Therefore, the EUSFTA provides additional venues for settling disputes over investment such as an additional facility at ICSID, the United Nations Commission on International Trade Law, and any other forum designated by the parties to a dispute. The rules allow tribunals to dispose of claims that are 'manifestly without legal merit' and 'unfounded as a matter of law'. The agreement contains three annexes that outline a mediation alternative, give a code of conduct to arbitrators, and cover procedures for transparency and access to the public of the dispute proceedings (see Shepherd 2014).

The investment chapter of the EUSFTA was handed over to the European Court of Justice to revise on 30 October 2014. The European Court of Justice delivered its ruling on 16 May 2017, and the expectation is that the agreement will now progress to ratification.[13]

Conclusions

The signing of the EUSFTA was a key first step on the pathway to a larger regional agreement linking Europe with ASEAN. Once the agreement clears the European Court of Justice and then the European Parliament, it will set up additional opportunities for European economic activity with Singapore and allow Singaporean companies expanded access into

---

13   ECJ Opinion 2/15 (Full Court), curia.europa.eu/juris/document/document.jsf;jsessionid=9ea
7d2dc30d6b9fc7709f4e94ae5a2948b05c7a3a370.e34KaxiLc3qMb40Rch0SaxyLb3r0?text=&docid
=190727&pageIndex=0&doclang=EN&mode=req&dir=&occ=first&part=1&cid=470866.

European markets. For both sides, the agreement also includes a wide range of rules and regulations that bring greater certainty and increased transparency to business operations.

References

Delegation of the European Union to the United States (2015), 'EU and Singapore Present Text of Comprehensive Free Trade Agreement'. Available at www.euintheus.org/press-media/eu-and-singapore-present-text-of-comprehensive-free-trade-agreement/, last accessed 15 July 2015.

European Commission (2015), 'EU–Singapore Free Trade Agreement: Authentic Text as of May 2015', 29 June. Available at trade.ec.europa.eu/doclib/press/index.cfm?id=961, last accessed 15 July 2015.

Eurostat (2013), Eurostat online database. Available at ec.europa.eu/eurostat/data/database.

Herbert Smith Freehills (2014), 'European Commission requests European Court of Justice Opinion on competence to enter into EU-Singapore FTA', 6 November. Available at hsfnotes.com/publicinternationallaw/2014/11/06/european-commission-requests-european-court-of-justice-opinion-on-competence-to-enter-into-eu-singapore-fta/, last accessed 15 July 2015.

Meunier, Sophie (2017), 'Integration by Stealth: How the European Union Gained Competence over Foreign Direct Investment Policy'. *Journal of Common Market Studies* 55(3): 593–610. doi.org/10.1111/jcms.12528.

Ministry of Trade and Industry, Singapore (2015), 'Singapore and the European Union Initial the Investment Protection Chapter', Press release, 22 May. Available at www.mti.gov.sg/NewsRoom/SiteAssets/Pages/Singapore-and-the-European-Union-Initial-the-Investment-Protection-Chapter-/Press%20release%20on%20EUSFTA%20IPC%20Initialling.pdf, last accessed 15 July 2015.

Shepherd, Jordan (2014), 'EU–Singapore FTA Concluded, but EU Ratification May Be Delayed', Lexology, 19 December. Available at www.lexology.com/library/detail.aspx?g=4e5fc749-bbb0-4bb1-9ee2-473a302877e1, last accessed 15 July 2015.

4

Is the CETA a Road Map for Australia and the EU?

Annmarie Elijah

Introduction

Canada and the European Union (EU) reached agreement on key aspects of the Comprehensive Economic and Trade Agreement (CETA) in October 2013. The full text was released to the public in September 2014 before undergoing a legal 'scrub' ahead of ratification across the jurisdictions. The CETA was signed in October 2016 and approved by the European Parliament in February 2017.

For the EU the CETA is the first trade agreement with a Group of Eight (G8) country and a significant plank in its post-2006 'Global Europe' trade strategy, which moved the focus of EU trade policy towards bilateral deals. For Canada it represents an attempt to cement political and economic ties with the EU and diversify its trade profile, which is otherwise heavily dominated by the United States of America (USA).

In a joint statement at the time of its release, the EU and Canada referred to the CETA as an 'ambitious and ground-breaking' agreement. It is a complex and lengthy text that took almost five years to negotiate. The agreement is a good example of the 'new generation' of trade agreements that seek to address both traditional market access issues and 'behind the border' impediments to trade.

The CETA includes chapters on market access; rules of origin; trade remedies; technical barriers to trade; sanitary and phytosanitary measures; customs and trade facilitation; subsidies; investment; cross-border trade in services; temporary entry; mutual recognition of professional qualifications; domestic regulation; financial services; international maritime transport services; telecommunications; electronic commerce; competition policy; state enterprises; monopolies and enterprises; government procurement; intellectual property; sustainable development; labour; the environment; and regulatory cooperation.

It includes protocols on conformity and manufacturing practices and a number of joint declarations and understandings, some of which serve to incorporate former agreements into the new framework. Multiple annexes set out reservations to the agreement. It contains robust administrative and institutional provisions and sets out the parameters for dialogue and further bilateral cooperation between the EU and Canada. It thus constitutes a 'living agreement' in the sense that obligations among the parties may be expected to change in coming years.

The starting question for this chapter was whether the CETA might constitute a 'road map' for a possible trade agreement between Australia and the EU, with particular reference to the role of sub-national governments; mutual recognition of qualifications; government procurement; and institutional provisions. The chapter proceeds with a history and context, before outlining findings in the specific areas, and drawing lessons for Australia. With some important qualifications, the research confirms the usefulness of the CETA as a recent indicator of the EU's likely position in any forthcoming negotiations. The concluding section argues that the CETA provides grounds for cautious optimism about prospects for an Australia–EU agreement, noting the different context of the bilateral relationships.

History and context

Notwithstanding some clear historical parallels in the bilateral relationships, a survey of existing political and economic cooperation between Canada and the EU compared with Australia and the EU reveals a 'thicker' transatlantic relationship. Canada has a longer and stronger record of cooperative action with the EU, including a less acrimonious trading relationship since establishment and more cooperative agreements in place. In the postwar years, economic ties with European countries waned in favour of strong Canada–USA ties (Deblock & Rioux 2010). Canada did, however, maintain significant member state relationships with both the United Kingdom and France, a fact that became relevant in the trade negotiations.

The formal history of the CETA commenced in 2007 at the Canada–EU Summit in Berlin when the parties announced that joint work would be undertaken on the potential benefits of an agreement. However, a Canada–EU trade agreement was debated and even pursued much earlier. There was an attempt to institutionalise economic cooperation in the late 1990s with the EU–Canada Trade Initiative. In the early 2000s, a parliamentary report suggested a trade agreement to address the 'steady downward spiral' of Canada–Europe economic relations (see especially Dymond & Hart 2002) and Prime Minister Jean Chrétien was instrumental in launching the Trade and Investment Enhancement Agreement (2002). There was little enthusiasm on the EU side, however, with the main emphasis still on multilateral trade negotiations at that time (Hage 2011). Canada–EU economic cooperation remained largely superficial.

In Canada, the debate over enhanced ties with the EU is always conducted with reference to the concentration of trade with the USA: the EU is necessarily cast as an 'alternative' partner, and in some cases a solution to 'stagnating' North American economic integration (DeBardeleben & Leblond 2010). However, Canada has faced difficulties in terms of leverage. Although political and economic ties between the EU and Canada were sound, for many years Canada 'did not constitute a priority for Europe' (Deblock & Rioux 2010).

In the event, it was a provincial premier who raised the political profile of a possible trade agreement in both Canada and the EU. Arguably, Quebec Premier Jean Charest was uniquely placed in this regard. His work in championing an agreement at home and abroad (including with the French Council presidency of 2008) coincided with extremely slow progress multilaterally and a changed set of EU trade policy priorities (Hage 2011). After a joint study that promised benefits in both the EU and Canada, the negotiations were formally launched in May 2009.

Like other potential trade agreement partners for the EU, Canada was obliged to put in train a treaty-level political agreement in tandem with the economic negotiations. The Strategic Partnership Agreement was concluded in 2014. The form of wording in the agreement includes a satisfactory outcome on the so-called linkage issue, whereby agreements with the EU are connected with each other and subject to human rights clauses. The wording had previously caused consternation over the EU's political agreements with Canada, Australia and New Zealand.

The CETA negotiations took five years, not including the 'scoping' period preceding the formal launch in 2009 or the legal scrub, multiple translations and ratification currently underway. The time that would be required to complete the CETA was repeatedly underestimated by analysts and governments throughout the negotiations (see, for example, Deblock & Rioux 2010: 39) and few anticipated the EU's internal political difficulties of October 2016 when the government of the Belgian region of Wallonia threatened to veto the CETA immediately prior to its signature.

At the completion of the CETA text, the agreement was recognised by the EU and Canada as a new phase in bilateral relations and 'a vehicle to create new prosperity' on both sides of the Atlantic (Government of Canada & European Union 2014). In terms of traditional market access the CETA results in clear gains for both parties, with liberalisation (tariff reductions and quota increases) occurring upon entry into force and at three, five and seven years thereafter. The European Commission describes the elimination of customs duties for goods originating in the EU and Canada as applying to 'almost all goods' (European Commission 2014a). Carve outs (exclusions and longer transitional arrangements) remain in sensitive areas.

In relation to services and investment, the CETA 'constitutes the most comprehensive trade agreement the EU has ever concluded' (European Commission 2014a). Given that the projected gains from the agreement rely heavily on trade in services, this is significant. The chapters relevant to trade in services are numerous and not all aspects are covered here. A key point is that the EU was persuaded to enter into a 'negative list' for services, widely regarded as being a more liberalising instrument, since parties are required to list reservations and exceptions and include all other trade.

The way this has been handled in the CETA is a complex two-tiered system of annexes. Annex I lists existing measures and restrictions that parties wish to maintain, with no other restrictions to apply and 'no risk of rollback' (European Commission 2014a). This is considered especially important to provide certainty to business. Annex II lists further measures but makes no commitment on whether parties will adopt new, different or potentially more restrictive measures in the future. The annexes on services run to more than 300 pages. The full implications of the CETA and its treatment of trade in services will not be known for some time.

The role of sub-national entities

Negotiations for the CETA were genuinely 'multilevel'. While the interests of the EU's member states (and for that matter its sub-national entities) were represented by the European Commission, the Canadian provinces and territories were directly involved in the negotiations. This was the first—and so far only—time that the provinces were 'at the table' for a trade deal.[1] This involvement was at the request of the EU, which sought 'buy-in' at a sub-national level (Fafard & Leblond 2013).

Projected gains from the CETA are substantially attributed to 'behind borders' liberalising measures. The changed nature of trade agreements— often referred to as 'second generation' agreements—has involved sub-national entities more than previously, as issues under negotiation impact on policy competences not held exclusively at the national level.

The need for province and territory commitment to the CETA was most obvious in relation to government procurement, but sub-national involvement was by no means limited to Chapter 19. It was estimated in 2012 that the provinces and territories were actively involved in more than half of the negotiating committees on the CETA (Fafard & Leblond 2012). Further, as negotiations progressed it was clear that different regions stood to gain (or lose) to different degrees from the proposed deal. The negotiations underlined the need for effective coordination among the Canadian provinces and territories and with the federal government, which has the authority to negotiate, sign and ratify international treaties.

---

1   This negotiating model has not been replicated in other trade negotiations that Canada has since commenced; for example, the Trans-Pacific Partnership (TPP) negotiations, which Canada formally joined in October 2012.

This is not to suggest that the CETA was the first time that Canadian provinces and territories were involved in international negotiations. Consultation and information-sharing mechanisms had existed since the negotiations of the (then) Canada–USA Free Trade Agreement (1989) and later the North American Free Trade Agreement (NAFTA). Established 'C-Trade' meetings took place quarterly and more often as appropriate. Existing coordination mechanisms, however, were challenged by the CETA. Proponents of the deal—such as the former Premier of Quebec, who saw himself as a key player—sought additional involvement. Other provinces and territories were vocal in their opposition. Particularly where provincial interests did not align with likely outcomes, the difficulty of maintaining 'one voice' was an ongoing challenge for the Canadian government.

Notwithstanding the difficulties, the Canadian rationale for including the provinces and territories in the negotiations may have been twofold. First, it met the need to assure the EU of provincial commitment to the agreement. Second, it served as a neat precursor to the domestic reforms that will need to occur to implement the CETA—some of which are long overdue. Here the recognition of occupations and professions is a good example, where domestic impediments to movement across provinces has become a significant problem. In this case, the CETA has provided impetus to a domestic reform process.

Since the CETA's conclusion and its release in September 2014, the complex nature of provincial commitment to the agreement has become publicly apparent. Based on a dispute over compensation for fisheries, Newfoundland has first, threatened to withdraw support for the CETA and second, raised its concerns directly with EU institutions and the member states. This is notwithstanding considerable effort on the part of the Canadian Government to maintain a unified negotiating position and adequate buy-in from provinces and territories. It is unclear whether these late objections will have any impact on implementation of the agreement. In the event, it was the role of EU sub-national entities that proved politically salient immediately prior to the CETA's signature in late 2016.

Mutual recognition of professional qualifications

A stated objective of the CETA is to increase the flow of professionals between the EU and Canada. Chapter 10 (temporary entry) clarifies and simplifies provisions relating to short-term business visitors with the aim of facilitating trade and investment. It includes the aim of visa-free travel for EU and Canadian citizens in the near future (Government of Canada & European Union 2016).

Provisions for mutual recognition of professional qualifications appear in Chapter 11 and a related annex. The European Commission Directorate-General for Trade's assessment of this chapter is that the CETA has 'broken new ground' (European Commission 2014a). The institutional innovation here is to enable relevant authorities and professional bodies in the jurisdictions to work with government in establishing a mutual recognition agreement (MRA) in a given area.

The chapter establishes a joint committee that will oversee cooperation on the recognition of qualifications. The committee will assess proposals on the basis of criteria including industry needs, potential economic benefit, and compatibility of licensing and qualifications requirements for that sector before a sector-specific MRA is signed and implemented. These provisions are potentially liberalising but must be seen as a starting point for a forthcoming, potentially lengthy, process of assessment across different sectors.

Ultimately, when specific MRAs are concluded, EU professionals would have their qualifications recognised in Canada, and vice versa. Much may depend on relevant authorities or professional bodies driving the process. In some cases professional bodies appear to have begun their work in anticipation of institutional mechanisms that would enable mutual recognition. Engineers and architects are apparently advanced in negotiations, and in these cases the measures will most likely prove successful in enabling people movement.

In other areas sustained attention to implementation and uptake will be required to make best use of the measures. This can best be described as a cautious or 'managed' form of mutual recognition that will be applied on a case-by-case basis.[2] Economic gains from mutual recognition provisions in the CETA may therefore be limited in the short term. The Joint Committee on Mutual Recognition will meet within a year of the entry into force of the CETA and report back to the CETA committee on progress in relation to MRAs. Built-in transparency provisions (Article 11.5(e)) should enable progress on MRAs to be monitored.

Government procurement

The European Commission summary of the CETA states that the EU achieved 'a very positive result, fully in line with the EU interests and negotiation requests' on government procurement (European Commission 2014a). The provisions of Chapter 19 refer to reciprocal bidding rights inside the EU member states and the Canadian provinces and territories. This may include federal entities, provincial and territorial ministries, most agencies of government, crown corporations, regional, local and municipal governments and entities.

Certain thresholds and exemptions remain in place to address provincial interests, for smaller contracts and non-urban areas in Canada.[3] However, Chapter 19 is seen by the EU as a significant win in terms of access, particularly in relation to municipalities, academic, school boards and hospitals (known as MASH), which have not previously been included in any Canadian trade agreement. According to the Directorate-General for Trade the 'opening to European bidders is unprecedented' (European Commission 2014a).

The CETA text on government procurement is compatible with—and indeed derived from—the World Trade Organization's (WTO) Agreement on Government Procurement (GPA), a plurilateral agreement aiming to ensure fairness and transparent conditions of competition on procurement. Signatories commit to the GPA with schedules detailing market access. In the revised GPA (finalised in April 2014) the parties undertook to revisit the agreement and negotiate on extended coverage within three years. WTO dispute resolution mechanisms

---

2   These provisions in no way resemble the mutual recognition provisions implemented by Australia and New Zealand in the 1990s. In that case all registered occupations (except medical practitioners) were deemed mutually recognised among Australian jurisdictions and New Zealand upon entry into force of the agreement. See the Trans-Tasman Mutual Recognition Arrangement (1998).
3   For example, exceptions were made for some energy suppliers in Ontario and Quebec.

apply to the GPA. The CETA further builds on GPA commitments by institutionalising Canada–EU cooperation through a government procurement committee, which will report to the CETA committee.

Importantly, Canada has committed to a level of openness in the CETA that it did not in the GPA context. While both the EU and Canada are signatories to the GPA, the EU has committed to coverage across central, sub-central and 'other entities'. Canada committed only to coverage at the level of central government. On the basis of lack of reciprocity, the EU did *not* extend access to procurement to Canada under its GPA commitments. The 2008 joint study commissioned by the Canadian Government and the Directorate-General for Trade estimated that only 10 per cent of procurement in the EU and Canada was subject to any GPA commitments at that time (European Commission & Government of Canada 2008).

Thus, the benefits from Chapter 19 accrue to both European and Canadian companies, which will upon ratification have unprecedented access to procurement across levels of government, with certain exceptions. For obvious reasons, the ongoing commitment of sub-national entities in both Canada and the EU will be crucial to successful implementation of the procurement measures. This goes some way to explaining the EU's enthusiasm for having Canadian provinces and territories 'at the table' for the negotiations.

On close inspection, the procurement situation inside the EU is also complex. Notwithstanding claims from the European Commission about the EU being substantially open to outside bidders already, analysts have recently highlighted the inadequacy of procurement data internationally. This makes claims about openness difficult (if not impossible) to substantiate. The CETA does include transparency provisions (Article 19.19) requiring the collation of statistics and that parties report annually to the committee, which may help in time to understand procurement in the bilateral relationship.

Researchers also found in 2012 that openness varied significantly across EU member states, and that there may be non-tariff barriers (NTBs) at work in procurement in both the internal market and for foreign suppliers (Messerlin & Miroudet 2012a, 2012b). This issue was also highlighted in the annual US report on trade barriers, which newly singled out Poland and Slovakia, and identified further issues in countries listed previously, such as the Czech Republic, France, Italy and Romania. US trade negotiators have pointed to issues ranging from widespread corruption to transparency issues, inadequate law enforcement and inefficiencies in government as trade barriers (Inside US Trade, 8 April 2015). Procurement has been a vexed issue in the EU–USA negotiations for a Transatlantic Trade and Investment Partnership (TTIP).

It is worth noting that government procurement across the EU single market is a work in progress, with a recent law reform taking place in 2014 and still being implemented across the member states. For the moment it is safe for trade partners and foreign bidders to assume that the 28 member states (EU28) are not all equally accessible in terms of procurement.

Institutional provisions

Institutional provisions governing how the CETA will work are found predominantly in Chapter 26 (administrative and institutional provisions). These are straightforward and complement existing mechanisms for bilateral dialogue. The CETA Trade Committee will oversee a number of specific committees tasked with monitoring chapters of the agreement (for example, on mutual recognition and government procurement). Dispute settlement mechanisms (Chapter 29) provide for consultation, mediation and intergovernmental bargaining among the parties should differences of opinion arise. These exist alongside existing recourse to the WTO but aim to resolve issues much faster. In general, the institutional provisions for the CETA are robust. Given that much work remains to be done—for example, in working together on closer regulatory regimes, and finalising MRAs—it is imperative that the CETA is a 'living agreement'. Progress in bringing Canada and the EU economically closer will depend greatly on the effectiveness of these committees.

Strong review mechanisms no doubt reflect EU and Canadian intentions to fully implement the CETA. The mechanisms also reflect the fact that neither party yet knows the outcomes of the TTIP during negotiations. An indicative example can be found in Chapter 4 on technical barriers to trade, which has an annex entitled 'Cooperation in the field of motor vehicle regulations'. Annex 4-A of the annex is a revision clause that enables the parties to revisit the terms of the deal relating to motor vehicle regulations, in a long-standing area of disagreement between the EU and the USA. It is entirely possible that aspects of the CETA could be refined or reviewed if the TTIP were to proceed in some form. Institutional provisions reflect this.

Bilateral negotiations between Canada and the EU on a Strategic Partnership Agreement were conducted in tandem with the CETA negotiations and concluded in September 2014. The agreement aims to enhance bilateral cooperation on a broad range of issues.

The Strategic Partnership Agreement is relevant here in that it contains provisions relating to the 'linkage issue', which arises in EU agreements. The linkage clauses knit together bilateral agreements between a third country and the EU. Further, at the insistence of the European Parliament, framework and partnership agreements with the EU necessarily contain clauses relating to human rights. The upshot of the linkage clauses and the human rights inclusions is that in the event of a breach by a partner government, the EU could effectively suspend *all* bilateral agreements with that partner, including trade and economic agreements. Among developed economies this is considered an unlikely event; nevertheless, the clauses have been a sticking point in agreements with a number of countries negotiating with the EU, including Canada, Australia and New Zealand. The form of words agreed in the SPA has effectively provided an institutional workaround for this longstanding irritant.

An aspect of the CETA that has not yet been explored in any detail is the implications of the agreement for third countries. These will be most apparent in relation to the USA to the extent that the CETA impinges on North American economic integration. However, the third country implications will not be limited to the USA. Institutional provisions include a joint declaration (Chapter 30) towards the end of the CETA text, which encourages Canada to begin negotiations as soon as possible with countries who have an existing customs union with the EU and 'whose products do not benefit from the tariff concessions under this Agreement' (European Union & Government of Canada 2016). Canada may need to add further trade deals to its current negotiating list.

Implications for Australia

Preliminary work on a possible Australia–EU trade agreement is being undertaken in both Canberra and Brussels. However, the case for such an agreement is still being made. Current indications are that the agreement will be launched in late 2017. In this context, the final terms of the CETA take on particular relevance for Australia.

Kenyon and van der Eng have previously established the economic comparability of Canada and Australia in terms of suitability for an EU trade agreement (Kenyon & van der Eng 2014).[4] Adams et al. concur, noting that the two share 'substantial economies, similar economic structures and similar trade profiles with the EU' (Adams, Brown & Wickes 2013). Without rehearsing this argument in full, if anything, this case has recently strengthened. Canada remains the larger economy, but the gap has narrowed.

The two countries' top 10 export commodities continue to bear a striking resemblance. Trade in services—and the EU's role in that sector—remains crucially important to both economies. Total services trade has been growing, basically doubling in value between 2000 and 2012 for both countries (UN Comtrade 2015a, 2015b). Canada is rated 22nd in the most recent Ease of Doing Business Survey and Australia is rated 15th (World Bank 2016). Recent figures confirm that investment is the strongest dimension of the economic relationship for both Canada and Australia (see especially EU Delegation to Australia 2016).

A key difference in the trade profiles between the two countries is the relative diversity of the Australian economy. Merchandise exports are *moderately* concentrated among partners for Australia, with the top nine partners accounting for 80 per cent or more of exports in 2013. Exports are described as *highly* concentrated among partners for Canada, with the USA accounting for almost 75 per cent of Canadian exports in 2013. Australian imports are even more diversified whereas Canadian imports are also concentrated (UN Comtrade 2015a, 2015b). The importance of the USA to the Canadian economy can hardly be overstated, and this alters the context of Canada's trade negotiations significantly.

---

4   See especially Table 2 on page 236, which sets out a comparison of economic indicators.

The history of Australian–EU relations also differs in important respects to Canadian–EU relations. Australia and Canada have achieved a similar set of cooperative agreements with the EU, although Canada has often been ahead. It was the first country to achieve an agreement with Euratom (1959) and the first industrialised country to arrive at a Framework Agreement on Economic Cooperation (1976). It can be no surprise that Canada was regarded by the EU as a suitable candidate for comprehensive trade negotiations.

With these issues in mind and drawing on analysis of the CETA in the chapters outlined above, this section begins to draw out the possible implications for Australia in any forthcoming negotiation with the EU. In general terms, the CETA does provide some clues for Australia: it confirms, for example, that enhanced market access to the EU is possible in sectors such as agriculture, and that the EU would bring to the negotiating table a high level of ambition in relation to 'behind borders' measures.

The role of sub-national entities

The CETA raised unprecedented issues relating to the involvement of Canadian provinces and territories in trade agreements. While there are important differences in the functioning of the Canadian and Australian federations, it is clear that an Australia–EU agreement would raise many of these same issues.

The first set of questions for Australia are about whether the EU would seek state and territory representation at the negotiations, and whether the Australian Government would accept this. Either way, the states and territories (and perhaps even local governments) would need to be involved in some form, and the importance of early and effective engagement on a possible agreement can hardly be overstated. This engagement would need to go beyond consultation to secure political commitment and ensure successful ratification and implementation. It is worth noting that the entire process may take some years. Further, if the EU was assured of successful Australian internal coordination on trade policy, the perceived need for direct involvement in the negotiations could perhaps be overcome. As negotiations progress, the Australian Government will need to be prepared to give specific details of how the proposed trade agreement will benefit Australian states and territories,[5] and how any negative implications will be dealt with. In the Canadian case, this meant federal government compensation in some sectors to secure provincial agreement.

Mutual recognition of professional qualifications

Specifically in relation to the provisions on mutual recognition of professional qualifications, the CETA measures in their current form constitute no obvious difficulty for the Australian Government. The question here is whether a higher level of ambition would be warranted, rather than case-by-case painstaking construction of specific MRAs by sector. If the CETA provisions were replicated for Australia, it is likely that well-organised industry and/or professional bodies would be able to pursue mutual recognition in specific instances to good effect. It may take some time. On the other hand, in sectors where there has already been significant domestic and/or trans-Tasman efforts made, mutual recognition could potentially proceed faster.

Government procurement

On government procurement it is safe to assume that the EU would bring the same or similar negotiating requests to the table in the first instance, and that increased access would be pursued aggressively. The European Commission has stated that their demands were successful in the CETA (European Commission 2014a). This same ask would place new demands on Australian authorities.

In the event that the Australian Government proceeds with plans to move from observer status to a member of the GPA (The Hon Andrew Robb AO MP, Minister for Trade and Investment, 2014) EU expectations could potentially line up with current Australian policy intentions in this sector. Recent changes to the GPA (2014) appear to be better aligned with Australian policy objectives.

The openness and barriers in the Australian procurement market are well summarised in recent WTO reviews. Recent European Commission reports on potentially trade-restrictive measures identify certain Australian procurement policies (at federal and state levels) as problematic

---

5   See the Canadian Government's breakdown of benefits by jurisdiction at www.international.gc.ca.

(European Commission 2013, 2014b). The *Buy Australian at Home and Abroad* and the *Plan for Australian Jobs* packages both feature, as do minimum local content targets, 'buy local' campaigns, and small and medium enterprises measures. These issues are likely to be raised in negotiations.

Negotiations on government procurement would also draw attention to new opportunities inside the EU market for Australian companies. As outlined above, existing research shows that sound data around government procurement is scarce. Claims about the openness of the EU market should be carefully evaluated across the 28 member states. Claims that GPA membership (and commitments across all levels of government therein) somehow equate to open procurement markets should also be scrutinised.

The procurement issue places state and territory involvement front and centre in any negotiations, and has the potential to raise the political profile of a potential agreement. One critical report argues that the CETA:

> will substantially restrict the vast majority of provincial and municipal government bodies from using public spending as a catalyst for achieving other societal goals (Sinclair, Trew & Mertins-Kirkwood 2014).

The issue of 'green procurement' also came to the fore in the course of the negotiations (Hubner 2010). Similar political sensitivities can be expected in the Australian context.

Institutional provisions

On the face of it, the institutional provisions present no special problem for the Australian Government. Robust review mechanisms and the prospect of a 'living agreement' are consistent with the approach taken in other bilateral deals. The principal institutional impediment to an Australia–EU trade deal was the incomplete framework agreement, which is now finalised.

Conclusions

So, is the CETA a 'road map' for Australia and the EU as a trade agreement, as canvassed in Canberra and Brussels? The answer is yes, and no. In many ways the CETA provides a suitable comparison for any agreement between

Australia and the EU. In the CETA, Canada and the EU were able to secure increased market access and progress a raft of 'behind the border' measures. Australia and Canada are similarly attractive as trade partners for the EU, and the two countries face similar asymmetrical difficulties in dealing with the EU28.

In the CETA chapters examined in detail here, the agreement is an excellent guide as to what the Australian Government could expect in a negotiation. An optimistic assessment might conclude that an Australia–EU agreement would yield a negative listing for trade in services (with significant reservations); improved access to government procurement markets for both parties; managed mutual recognition provisions on qualifications leading to greater people movement; and a set of institutional provisions enabling long-term economic cooperation to flourish. Impact on the states and territories would be significant, in a range of areas.

Yet, offensive and defensive interests in a trade negotiation are unique to each bilateral relationship, and outcomes will differ. Australia and the EU have a more troubled, less institutionalised, history. Canada and Australia operate in different regional contexts and have adapted accordingly. The overwhelming importance of the USA in Canada's trade profile cannot be overlooked. Considering the EU's stated intention to negotiate a comprehensive trade deal with the USA, it is impossible to escape the conclusion that both parties conducted the CETA negotiations with one eye on the TTIP. It is clear that the TTIP and the CETA are connected from the EU perspective. Prospects for the TTIP's conclusion are presently poor, and the internal EU controversy relating to CETA has not helped.

This dynamic is not at work in the Australian case, and it changes the negotiating context significantly. The EU arguably has a 'defensive interest' in a trade agreement with Australia because of the Trans-Pacific Partnership (TPP) negotiations (Adams, Brown & Wickes 2013), but this may not raise Australia as a priority for the EU—in terms of starting negotiations, or successfully completing them. Bauer et al. have argued that the EU should seek to address the 'blind spot' of Australia and New Zealand to advance its priorities in the Asia-Pacific, and there is a case to be made for this approach (Bauer et al. 2014).

The timing of negotiations also matters a great deal, especially on traditional market access issues. Adams, Brown and Wickes pointed out in 2013 that if the TTIP suddenly progressed the USA could 'strip the EU's cupboard bare' on agriculture in particular (Adams, Brown & Wickes 2013). A transatlantic deal looks increasingly unlikely, however the progress of other trade deals, and their implications for Australian trade with the EU has not escaped the attention of Australian exporters (Condon 2014). The advancement (or otherwise) of the mega-regionals may therefore impact prospects for an Australia–EU agreement.

References

Adams, Mike, Nicolas Brown & Ron Wickes (2013), *Trading Nation: Advancing Australia's Interests in World Markets* (UNSW Press: Sydney).

Bauer, Matthias, Fredrick Erixon, Martina Ferracane & Hosuk Lee-Makiyama (2014), 'Trans-Pacific Partnership: A challenge to Europe', *ECIPE Policy Brief*, no. 9/2014.

Condon, Jon (2014), 'BeefEx: Are There Risks Ahead for Australia's Grainfed Beef Access to the EU?', Beef Central, 23 October. Available at www.beefcentral.com/features/beefex-2014/are-there-risks-ahead-for-australias-grainfed-beef-access-to-the-eu/.

DeBardeleben, Joan & Patrick Leblond (2010), 'The other transatlantic relationship: Canada, the EU, and 21st-century challenges', *International Journal* 66(1): 1–7. doi.org/10.1177/002070201106600101.

Deblock, Christian & Michèle Rioux (2010), 'From economic dialogue to CETA: Canada's trade relations with the European Union'. *International Journal* 66(1): 39–56. doi.org/10.1177/002070201106600104.

Dymond, William & Michael Hart (2002), 'A Canada-E.U. FTA is an awful idea', Policy Options Politiques, 1 July. Available at policyoptions.irpp.org/issues/public-policy-2002/a-canada-eu-fta-is-an-awful-idea/.

EU Delegation to Australia (2016), 'Australia and the EU: Economic relations'. Available at eeas.europa.eu/delegations/australia/610/australia-and-eu_en#Economic+relations, last accessed December 2016.

European Commission (2013), 'Tenth Report on Potentially Trade Restrictive Measures, Identified in the Context of the Financial and Economic Crisis, 1 May 2012 – 31 May 2013', DG Trade.

European Commission (2014a), 'CETA – Summary of the Final Negotiating Results'. Available at trade.ec.europa.eu/doclib/docs/2014/december/tradoc_152982.pdf.

European Commission (2014b), 'Eleventh Report on Potentially Trade Restrictive Measures, 1 June 2013 – 30 June 2014', DG Trade.

European Commission & Government of Canada (2008), 'Assessing the Costs and Benefits of a Closer EU – Canada Economic Partnership: A Joint Study by the European Commission and the Government of Canada'. Available at trade.ec.europa.eu/doclib/docs/2008/october/tradoc_141032.pdf.

European Union & Government of Canada (2014), 'Consolidated CETA Text'. Available at trade.ec.europa.eu/doclib/docs/2014/september/tradoc_152806.pdf.

Fafard, Patrick & Patrick Leblond (2012), 'A Comprehensive Economic and Trade Agreement (CETA) between Canada and the European Union: Challenges for Canadian Federalism', *Federal News* 3(1), January (The Federal Idea: Montreal).

Fafard, Patrick & Patrick Leblond (2013), 'Closing the deal: What role for the Provinces in the final stages of the CETA negotiations?' *International Journal: Canada's Journal of Global Policy Analysis* 68(4): 553–59. doi.org/10.1177/0020702013509319.

Government of Canada & European Union (2014), 'Declaration by the Prime Minister of Canada and the Presidents of the European Council and European Commission'.

Government of Canada & European Union (2016), 'Text of the Comprehensive Economic and Trade Agreement'. Available at www.international.gc.ca/trade-commerce/trade-agreements-accords-commerciaux/agr-acc/ceta-aecg/text-texte/toc-tdm.aspx?lang=eng.

Hage, Robert (2011), 'Changing Canada: Canada-European Union Free Trade', *CETA Policy Brief*, May (Canada-Europe Transatlantic Dialogue: Ottawa). Available at www.canada-europe-dialogue.ca.

Hübner, Kurt (2010), 'CETA: Stumbling blocks in ongoing negotiations', *CETA Policy Brief*, May (Canada-Europe Transatlantic Dialogue: Ottawa). Available at www.canada-europe-dialogue.ca.

Kenyon, Donald & Pierre van der Eng (2014), 'Defining the relationship between Australia and the European Union: Is the Framework Treaty enough?' *Australian Journal of International Affairs* 68(2): 225–42. doi.org/10.1080/10357718.2013.840558.

Messerlin, Patrick & Sébastien Miroudet (2012a), 'EU Public Procurement Markets: How Open Are They?', *Groupe d'Économie Mondiale Policy Brief*, 10 August. Available at gem.sciences-po. fr/content/publications/pdf/Messerlin-Miroudot_EU_public_ procurement072012.pdf.

Messerlin, Patrick & Sébastien Miroudot (2012b), 'Public Procurement Markets: Where Are We?' Vox CEPR's Policy Portal.

Robb, Andrew, MP Minister for Trade and Investment (2014), 'Government Sets Its Sights on New Trade Deal', Media Release, 14 November. Available at trademinister.gov.au/releases/Pages/2014/ ar_mr_141114a.aspx.

Sinclair, Scott, Stuart Trew & Hadrian Mertins-Kirkwood, eds (2014), *Making Sense of the CETA: an analysis of the final text of the Canada-European Union Comprehensive Trade and Economic Agreement* (Canadian Centre for Policy Alternatives: Ottawa), September.

UN Comtrade (2015a), 'Country Profile: Australia'. Available at comtrade.un.org/.

UN Comtrade (2015b), 'Country Profile: Canada'. Available at comtrade. un.org/.

World Bank (2016), 'Economy Rankings'. Available at www.doing business.org/rankings, last accessed December 2016.

WTO (World Trade Organization) (2015), Trade Policy Review, Report by the Secretariat: Australia, 21 July. Available at www.wto.org/ english/tratop_e/tpr_e/tp_rep_e.htm, last accessed December 2016.

Section 2

5

The Changed Architecture of the EU's Agricultural Policy Over Four Decades: Trade Policy Implications for Australia

Alan Swinbank and Carsten Daugbjerg

When the European Economic Community (EEC)—today's European Union (EU)—created its common agricultural policy (CAP) in the 1960s and 1970s it paid scant regard to the interests of other nations. That 'old' CAP attempted to increase farm incomes by manipulating farm-gate prices, while a nascent, but rather ineffectual, structural policy sought to improve the competitive structure of European agriculture. Details differed from one product to another, but market price support meant in the main that imports were heavily taxed, exports subsidised and intervention stocks accumulated. When, in 1973, the EEC was enlarged with the accession of Denmark, Ireland and the United Kingdom (UK)—the latter a major importer of agricultural products from world markets—trade diversion was inevitable, and Australia in particular found its agricultural products displaced from the UK market. The CAP's escalating budgetary costs in the 1980s led to some half-hearted attempts at reform, but it was the Uruguay Round of trade negotiations under the auspices of the General Agreement on Tariffs and Trade (GATT) that triggered a succession of 'reforms' that significantly changed the CAP's policy mechanisms, while retaining its core focus of farm income support (Daugbjerg & Swinbank 2009, 2011, 2016). The latest recalibration of the CAP, in 2013, established the policy framework for the period 2014–20. The aim of this chapter is to briefly explain the succession of policy changes of the last four decades and how it has changed the policy context within which a free trade area agreement with Australia has to be considered.

Accession of the UK to the CAP of the 1970s

By the time of the UK's accession to the EEC in 1973, the main outlines of the old-style CAP were firmly in place (see Box 1; and Harris, Swinbank & Wilkinson 1983). In the late 1960s, the then European Commissioner for Agriculture, Sicco Mansholt, had attempted a CAP reform, arguing that support prices were too high, and that significant structural change, and investment, was needed to improve the competitive position of European agriculture; but his efforts were rebuffed and for his pains he was dubbed the 'peasant killer' ('Bauernkiller') amid angry street protests (Merriënboer 2011: 511–8). All that was achieved was the adoption in 1972 of three rather ineffectual 'structural directives', which had the objective of improving the efficiency of European agriculture (Harris, Swinbank & Wilkinson 1983: 222–4).

> **Box 1. The terminology of price support**
>
> The language differed from product to product, and has subsequently varied over time, but in the cereals regime, for example, the EEC's institutions fixed an *intervention price*—at which the member states would purchase grain to add to intervention stocks. To stop cheaper imports from undercutting the higher EEC market price, at the border a *threshold price* was fixed, and a *variable import levy* was payable on imports to bridge the gap between the lower world market price and this threshold price. As the EEC's level of self-sufficiency increased, exports became necessary if intervention stocks were not to continue increasing; but private traders would only export if they were paid subsidies to do so. Thus, *export refunds* were required. The costs of intervention, and export subsidies, were borne by the EEC's budget. In 1995 the Uruguay Round's Agreement on Agriculture placed a cap on subsidised exports, limited the extent to which domestic market prices could be supported, and through a process referred to as *tariffication* converted most border measures, such as variable import levies, into fixed tariffs, which were then reduced (Daugbjerg & Swinbank 2009: 54).

The world food crisis of the early 1970s, together with the opening of the UK's food market for surpluses from the European continent, meant that any internal constraints on generous increases in support prices in the annual farm price review could, for the moment, be ignored. The Dillon (1960–62), Kennedy (1964–67) and Tokyo (1973–79) Rounds of multilateral trade negotiations in the GATT had little impact on the CAP, as did attempts by the United States of America (USA), Australia and others to challenge aspects of the CAP through GATT's dispute settlement procedures (Daugbjerg & Swinbank 2009: 76–80). Academics had criticised the CAP, and suggested alternative approaches (e.g. Corbet & van Riemsdijk 1973), but their comments were largely ignored. Consumer interests and, at the time, the environmental lobby had very little influence over the design of EEC farm policy; but with lower world market prices, and the increase in EEC production outpacing consumption, by the early 1980s the budget cost was beginning to bite (Moyer & Josling 1990: 24–7).

The frustrations felt by Australia at the time were forcibly expressed by Australia's Minister for Special Trade Representations in the House of Representatives in March 1978. He declared that trade was 'causing great strains between Australia and the EEC'. A major problem was the CAP:

> We are efficient producers of agricultural products … Yet the EEC is denying us the opportunity, the right, to compete in its markets. Worse, the EEC is disposing of the surpluses caused by its policies at heavily subsidised prices on third markets in which we would otherwise sell our products (Garland 1978).

In particular, he claimed that 'Australia is the country worst affected by the enlargement of the EEC and its common agricultural policy'. He asserted that exports of beef had been badly affected 'as a result of the imposition of increasingly protective mechanisms', and that the 'application of the EEC's common agricultural policy to United Kingdom imports has wiped out our trade in sugar and butter to the EEC' (Garland 1978). The Australian Government commissioned its own research to demonstrate the follies of the CAP (e.g. Bureau of Agricultural Economics 1985) for presentation at workshops in Europe.

A brief history of CAP reform

The CAP of the mid-2010s is significantly different from the 'old' CAP of the 1970s and '80s, as described above. In particular, it can be claimed with some justification that it is much less trade distorting, that the costs it imposes on European consumers (and the economy as a whole) are much reduced, and that more care is taken to ensure that its environmental impact is benign. This section outlines the policy changes that have brought this about, while highlighting the international trade dimension.

Budget pressure in the 1980s prompted the first policy changes. In 1984, milk quotas were introduced to curb the upward trend in milk production, much of which was surplus to the EU's requirements and had been converted into butter and skim milk powder for sale to intervention. Although a temporary measure, milk quotas lasted until 2015. Then in 1988, with the budgetary costs of the CAP still increasing, partly because of the need to subsidise a growing surplus of cereals, a new system of agricultural stabilisers was introduced. Limits were placed on the growth in the CAP budget—although no policy mechanisms would be directly triggered if the limit was breached—and for key commodities such as cereals the intent was that automatic reductions in support prices would apply if production exceeded a maximum guaranteed quantity (Swinbank & Tanner 1996: 85–6).

The changes introduced in 1992 were far more significant. Although prompted in part by a continuing budget crisis, in reality the major problem that the EU had to address was the stalemate over agriculture in the Uruguay Round negotiations. The Uruguay Round had been launched in 1986 as a *single undertaking*, in which nothing was agreed until everything was agreed. The USA had demanded sweeping changes in the rules governing farm support, with the Australian-led Cairns Group playing a mediating role (Kenyon & Lee 2006).

The EU had been reluctant to make significant concessions on agriculture, but in the lead-up to the ministerial meeting at the Heysel conference centre in Brussels in December 1990—initially arranged to ceremonially close the Round—it became obvious that the EU would have to reform its CAP if it were to achieve its wider ambitions for the Uruguay Round. Following the breakdown of the Heysel ministerial meeting, the European Commissioner for Agriculture, Ray MacSharry, launched his CAP reform plan. Agreement was secured in May 1992 with the Portuguese farm minister, Arlindo Cunha, chairing the Council of Agricultural Ministers. As Cunha has noted, 'after the Heysel deadlock, GATT negotiations and CAP reform were inevitably linked, despite the *politically correct* official line of denying such a link in public' (Cunha & Swinbank 2011: 82).

The MacSharry reform began the *decoupling* of support for European farmers. The core agreement concerned cereals. Here support prices were cut by a third. Furthermore, they were fixed in nominal terms for an indefinite period: no longer would an annual price review result in inflationary increases in intervention prices. To compensate farmers for the implied loss in revenue they could claim an arable area payment.

Thus, the incentive to increase yields, or even harvest the crop, was lessened. The per hectare payment was based on a regionally determined historic yield, multiplied by the reduction in support prices. Larger farm businesses had to set aside (i.e. not use) 15 per cent of their arable area, although the arable area payment was still payable on the land set aside (Swinbank & Tanner 1996: 94–5). The oilseed, beef and sheep meat regimes were also amended, and provisions for support for environmental policies were introduced.

A critical juncture in the two negotiations came in the spring of 1992 when it became clear that the USA would accept the concept of a *blue box* of domestic support into which the area and livestock payments being negotiated in the CAP reform could be slotted (Cuhna & Swinbank 2011: 83).[1] This encouraged ministers to press ahead with CAP reform, which was an important step in enabling the Uruguay Round negotiations on agriculture to be concluded satisfactorily. Thus, not only did the Uruguay Round negotiations put pressure on the EU to reform its agricultural policy (Kenyon & Lee 2006), but as Tanner (1996: 31) has pointed out, within the Uruguay Round's 'consensus framework, the pace of change [was] determined by the extent to which the most recalcitrant participant [was] prepared to proceed'. Thus, 'the imprint of the European Union's domestic reforms [was] clearly stamped on the final agricultural outcome'.

Moreover, as Tangermann (2004: 40) highlighted, the Uruguay Round 'also affected the nature of the policy debate in agriculture. The WTO has become a relevant factor in agricultural policy making'. Thus, it was in the Agenda 2000 reform of 1999, and the Fischler reforms of 2003–04, that the EU sought to anticipate the likely future outcome of trade negotiations in what was now the World Trade Organization (WTO), and was obliged to make changes to its sugar policy to bring its sugar exports into conformity with a ruling from the WTO's Dispute Settlement Body in a case brought by Australia, Brazil and Thailand (Daugbjerg & Swinbank 2009: 114–5).

---

1   For developed economies the final agreement made provision for three categories of domestic support. Support deemed to be decoupled, with 'no, or at most minimal, trade-distorting effects or effects on production', and as defined in Annex 2 to the Agreement on Agriculture (the *green box*), would not be subject to reduction commitments. *Blue box* measures—direct payments under production-limiting programmes—such as the EU's area and livestock payments, were also exempt from reduction commitments. All other 'domestic support measures in favour of agricultural producers'—the *amber box*—would, after a transitional period, be limited to 80 per cent of the support granted in a historic base period (Daugbjerg & Swinbank 2009: 54).

The Agenda 2000 CAP reform was negotiated in the run-up to the WTO ministerial meeting in Seattle, at which it was thought a Millennium Round of trade negotiations might be launched. The EU at the time was of the view that any agreement on agriculture in a Millennium Round could be limited to a further tranche of reductions (to import tariffs, domestic support and export subsidies) similar to those agreed in the Uruguay Round. But the EU was worried about its ability to abide by the existing export subsidy limits on cereals. It was also keen to appeal to the Uruguay Round agreement's reference to the need to respect the *non-trade concerns* of WTO members, particularly the *multifunctionality* of European agriculture (Daugbjerg & Swinbank 2009: 157–9).

The Agenda 2000 package was also concerned with establishing a new Financial Framework for the 2000–06 planning period, a reform of the structural funds, and preparation for enlargement to embrace up to 10 former communist regimes from Central and Eastern Europe (Cunha & Swinbank 2011: 107).

With regard to the CAP market price regimes, Agenda 2000 resulted in a further decoupling of farm support. This involved another cut in support prices for cereals and beef, and one for butter and skim milk powder to apply from 2005, with partially offsetting increases in area and livestock payments, and a new blue box payment for milk producers. Support for environmental enhancement on farms, investment in restructuring European agriculture, and a new dimension of rural development were packaged together as the second pillar of the CAP, although the budget devoted to the second pillar remained small in relation to first pillar expenditure on market price support and direct payments. In a further effort to enhance the CAP's green credentials, member states had the option of introducing *cross-compliance*, making full disbursement of area and livestock payments conditional upon the farmer having complied with a number of environmental conditions. But few did. Although the package covered the period until 2006, a little noticed provision provided for a *mid-term review* in the early 2000s.

In his second term as European Commissioner for Agriculture and Rural Development, Franz Fischler took the opportunity of turning this mid-term review into another substantial reform of the CAP in 2003 and 2004: the Fischler reform. This resulted in more decoupling of support, in two respects. First, all the direct payments that had been introduced by the MacSharry and Agenda 2000 reforms, but that were still linked to areas planted or the number of livestock kept, were transferred into the new single payment scheme. Although farmers had to have agricultural land at their disposal on which to claim their entitlement, and this land had to be kept in good agricultural and environmental condition and other cross-compliance conditions respected, in the main the link with *production* was broken. For example, ex-dairy farmers could continue to claim a payment in compensation for the cuts in milk support, but they no longer had to keep cows, and could instead engage in other agricultural activities. Second, in 2004 and subsequent years, the decoupled single payment scheme was extended to other products that had not been touched by the MacSharry and Agenda 2000 reforms, such as olive oil, processed fruit and vegetables, and hops (Swinbank & Daugbjerg 2006).

Although some member states engaged in the full-decoupling allowed under the single payment scheme, others opted for only partial decoupling. For example, member states had the option to link 25 per cent of the displaced area payment for cereals to continued planting of a cereal crop. Most of these residual partial decoupling options were, however, removed by the Health Check of 2008 (Daugbjerg & Swinbank 2011).

At the outset of the Doha Round in 2001 the EU had been on the defensive, still seeking to defend the CAP and limit the impact of any new agreement on agriculture. But CAP reform and WTO negotiations interacted, and the Fischler reform allowed the EU to adopt a more proactive stance. Franz Fischler claimed, after the reform package had been agreed in June 2003, that:

> Today marks the beginning of a new era. European agricultural policy will change fundamentally. In future, our products will be more competitive, and our agricultural policy will be greener, more trade-friendly and more consumer-oriented. …

> The reform's message to the world is clear: today we have largely said goodbye to an old system of support which distorted trade. The new agricultural policy is trade-friendly, particularly as regards its effects on developing countries.

> This will put us on the offensive at the WTO negotiations in Cancún in September (Fischler 2003).

The WTO ministerial meeting in Cancún in September 2003, however, failed to conclude the Doha Round.

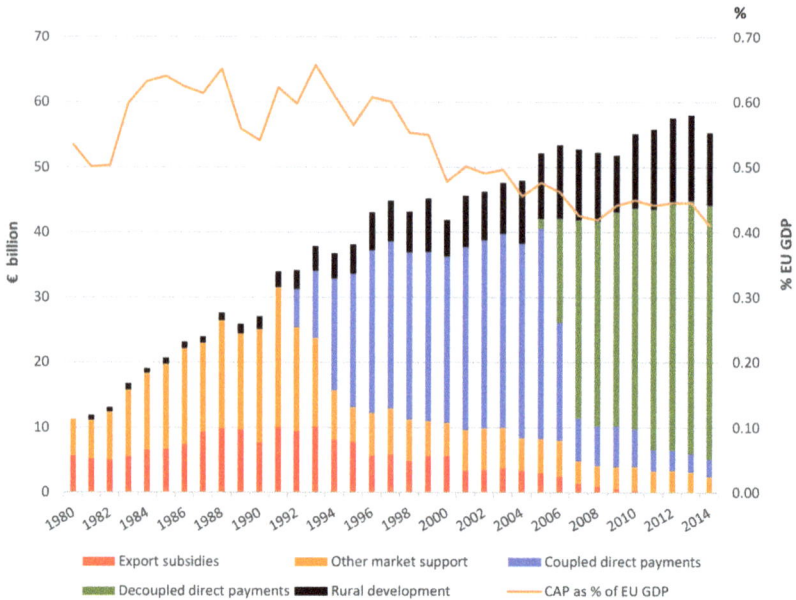

Figure 1. EU budget expenditure on the CAP, 1980–2014, in € billion and as a percentage of EU GDP, current prices

Source: Data compiled and supplied by the EU's Directorate General for Agriculture and Rural Development.

Figure 1 shows the evolution of EU budget expenditure on the CAP from 1980 to 2014, through the MacSharry, Agenda 2000, Fischler and Health Check reforms, and as it enlarged from nine to 28 member states. For the last decade the level of expenditure has been more or less constant in nominal terms (and thus has declined in real terms), while falling as a percentage of the EU's gross domestic product (GDP). In the 1980s, under the 'old' CAP, expenditure on market support (e.g. intervention) and export subsidies dominated, and the 'rural development' budget was poorly developed.

The 1992 MacSharry reform (and Agenda 2000) reduced expenditure on the area labelled 'other market support' in Figure 1, with an offsetting increase in coupled direct payments. In the WTO, these area and livestock payments were declared as blue box measures, with a corresponding decrease in amber box support. Then the Fischler reforms of 2003–04, and subsequent changes, switched most of the coupled direct payments, and some expenditure on market support, into the decoupled single payment scheme—labelled 'decoupled direct payments' in Figure 1. These were declared as green box expenditure in the WTO.

Another notable development was the decrease in the use of export subsidies. In the early 1980s, half of the EU agricultural budget was spent on export subsidies while they only accounted for a small fraction in the late 2000s. This development was partly a result of the MacSharry and Agenda 2000 reforms, which lowered internal support prices. With a smaller price difference between EU internal and world market prices, less subsidisation was needed to compensate exporters for the price difference. Improved world market prices further contributed to the decrease in the use of export subsidies.

Thus by 2010 export subsidies were largely a matter of the past. Indeed, the EU had already agreed to ban their use in the context of an overall agreement to the Doha Round. Then, at the Ministerial Conference in Nairobi in December 2015, it was decided that 'Developed Members' would eliminate their remaining export subsidy entitlements for most products with immediate effect, with the remainder to go by the end of 2020 (WTO 2015: paragraph 6). Australia, however, continues to monitor the export of sugar from the EU (Swinbank 2015), and is entitled to do so until the EU's quota regime for sugar expires in 2017.

Although some analysts have queried how decoupled the EU's policies really are, particularly in the aggregate, the declarations of domestic support to the WTO have not been seriously challenged. The numbers suggest that the decoupling of the CAP over the period 1992 to 2008 meant that no further changes would be required to meet the stricter limits on domestic support that were envisaged in the *Revised Draft Modalities for Agriculture* circulated in 2008 (Swinbank 2015; WTO 2008).

What these policy reforms have not done, however, is change the EU's protective tariff regime. Tariffs remain at the levels established in the Uruguay Round, and it is unlikely that the EU will agree to reductions except in the context of a multilateral agreement in the WTO (although temporary suspensions have applied in response to high market prices). Thus, for example, the most-favoured-nation (MFN) tariff on white sugar remains at €419 per tonne despite the fact that the 2006 sugar reform reduced the support price from €631.9 to €404.4 per tonne (Noble 2012: 12–13). High tariffs have a particular significance when considering free trade areas, such as that being considered between Australia and the EU; this is discussed below.

Multifunctionality

In the run-up to the Seattle ministerial meeting, the EU and its allies ('the friends of multifunctionality') were keen to stress that in the densely populated Old World the use of agricultural land had a wider social and environmental dimension than the simple provision of agricultural products. Thus, European agriculture sustained a diverse fauna and flora, a treasured landscape, cultural diversity, and so on. Furthermore, if these alleged *public goods* were to be produced in the future, then the farm sector had to be protected, or else overseas producers who were not expected to meet the same environmental norms (those located in the New World in particular) could flood the European market with lower-cost produce, and Europe's multifunctional agriculture would be threatened. Although the European Commission soon desisted from using the term 'multifunctionality' in Geneva, because of the adverse reaction of its trading partners, the basic idea still pervades much European thinking about agriculture.

Critics suggest that the public goods associated with the concept of multifunctionality could be delivered on the basis of a series of contracts between the EU and individual farmers. Thus, for example, Anderson (2000: 491) concluded that the WTO's green box provisions 'are adequate for dealing with the main issues raised'. However, there is a trade-off between the administrative costs of negotiating, and monitoring, tens of thousands of contracts with individual land managers for the delivery of environmental services, and a more generic approach in which the expectation is that land managers will produce a multifunctional agriculture although, in strictly contractual terms, not required to do so. In the 2013 recalibration of the CAP, and the so-called *greening* of direct payments, this broad-brushed approach prevailed, as discussed below.

The single market and its regulatory provisions

Although a number of regulatory provisions relating to European agriculture are governed by national rules—taxation of farm business profits, landlord–tenant relations, land zoning and planning laws, for example—the opposite is the case for legislation that might affect the free movement of goods within the EU's single market. Thus, geographical indications of origin, wine denominations, food law, plant health and veterinary rules are either regulated by EU legislation, or the principle of mutual recognition that guarantees the free movement of goods between member states provided fundamental public safety provisions are not compromised. One prominent domain in which this basic single-market concept is potentially threatened relates to the use of genetically modified products in animal feed and human food (Agra Facts 2015).

The concept of a single market is very important to EU policy makers, and it extends beyond the territorial domain of the EU. Countries such as Norway that are not members of the EU, but are members of the European Economic Area (in essence a 'GATT-plus' FTA), have to apply the EU's single-market regulatory provisions just as they would were they EU member states. Similarly, as the EU has extended its web of FTAs around the world, so it has attempted to extend its regulatory regimes, particularly geographical indications, to its FTA partners (Kerr & Hobbs 2015).

The post-2013 CAP

The 2003 (Fischler) and 2008 (Health Check) reforms had not been linked to the determination of the periodic financial frameworks that the EU had been operating for two decades, but it was agreed that the CAP budget (and thus the CAP itself) would be reviewed in establishing the 2014–20 financial framework. That review was concluded under the second College of Commissioners headed by José Manuel Barroso, with Dacian Cioloş serving as European Commissioner for Agriculture and Rural Development.

Circumstances had changed. One consequence of the price gyrations experienced on world commodity markets since the mid-2000s was that a number of EU governments and members of the European Parliament were extremely wary of a neo-liberal approach to agricultural policy, canvassed for a 'strong' CAP, and expressed concerns about food security. The near collapse of the world financial system following the Lehman Brothers debacle of 2008, the sovereign debt crisis and austerity budgets experienced by many EU member states, and the stark suggestion that one or more countries might have to abandon their use of the euro, suggested to others that the CAP budget should be reduced to reflect the straightened circumstances of the time: if social welfare programs were being cut why should CAP income support be spared?

Following ratification of the Lisbon Treaty, the European Parliament had enhanced decision-making powers over the CAP—it had become the co-legislator with the Council of Ministers—boosting the power of the European Parliament's Committee on Agriculture and Rural Development (COMAGRI). Moreover, the new member states that had acceded in 2004 and 2007 were expressing more forcibly their criticism of a system of farm income support that they believed disadvantaged their farmers in favouring those in most of the old member states. And the Doha talks remained in deep freeze.

The recalibrated CAP that emerged after an extended negotiation is, in its broad outlines, not hugely different from its pre-2013 predecessor, but the detail is exceedingly complex (despite the declared objective of simplification!), and member states have considerable discretion in how they apply important provisions.

The trade regime is unaltered. As in previous reforms the EU's import tariffs have not been touched, and legislation would still have allowed the use of export subsidies. The residual elements of domestic market price support have not, in substance, been changed; although milk quotas were abolished in 2015 and sugar quotas will go in 2017, both of which may affect the EU's net trade balance.

The European Commission proposed a CAP budget for 2014–20 more or less unchanged from 2013 in nominal terms, although declining in real terms, and this was accepted with some modification by the co-legislators. It is widely believed that Commissioner Cioloş had argued in the College of Commissioners that a substantial budget was needed to enable the CAP to face the challenges of climate change. Whether the outcome of the reform matched that expectation is not explored here. Despite the environmental and greening rhetoric, there was no marked switch in the budget from Pillar 1 (market price and income support) to Pillar 2 (rural development), but in drawing up their rural development plans member states have had to pay more attention to promoting a low-carbon and climate-resilient economy.

On direct payments (the successor to the previous single payment scheme) there are a number of changes, three of which are highlighted here. First, most noticed in the media was the decision to devote 30 per cent of the direct payments budget to a new greening component. What is now known as the *basic payment* will be claimed and paid annually as under the old single payment scheme: farm businesses have to have enough agricultural land at their disposal to match, hectare by hectare, their basic payment entitlements, and cross-compliance means that a number of environmental, food safety, and animal welfare provisions must be observed if payments are to be received in full. In addition, to claim the greening component on their land a series of requirements will apply, outlawing, for example, mono-cropping on larger arable farms.

Whether these measures in a cost-effective way will help retain soil carbon and combat global warming, and enhance environmental provision, are questions under debate in Europe. The European Commission offered little evidence to support its contention that greening would achieve significant environmental benefits, and the Council of Agricultural Ministers and the European Parliament significantly watered down the Commission's initial intent in legislating for the post-2013 CAP (Hart 2015). The green box status in the WTO of these greening payments might also be queried (Swinbank 2015).

Second, in addition to the need to meet the new greening requirements, some of Europe's farmers will find that the level of their payments changes significantly. There is a limited redistribution of funds between member states, boosting payments, for example, in the Baltic States where payments were seen to be significantly below the EU norm. Elsewhere, if member states had not already moved to a flat-rate per hectare payment on a regional basis, they will now be obliged to do so. Farmers who, for a variety of reasons, had accumulated large payment entitlements on their farms may now see their payments decline to the regional average, while others gain.

Third, member states now have a variety of options to recouple part of the basic payment to specific production activities; known as *voluntary coupled support* (Daugbjerg & Swinbank 2016). Some member states have announced that they will make little use of this provision; others plan to do so to the maximum extent permitted. Overall, the European Commission (2015: slide 19) believes that 10 per cent of the direct aid budget will now be coupled—more than was the case in the pre-2013 CAP, but less than was allowed following the 2003 reform. The change will not jeopardise the EU's ability to meet its current domestic support commitments in the WTO, but international observers might have noted that the French farm minister referred to 'an historic turning-point that breaks with the process of decoupling aid that has prevailed since 1992' (Embassy of France 2013).

Free trade area agreements and the CAP

The EU is proud of its achievements in liberalising the import of agricultural products from selected developing countries. Thus, under its Everything but Arms (EBA) initiative it offers duty- and quota-free access for products originating in the least developed countries (LDCs), and it is party to a series of free trade area agreements—known as Economic Partnership Agreements (EPAs)—with African, Caribbean and Pacific Group of States (ACP) countries (Daugbjerg & Swinbank 2009: 162–3). Both allow for the free importation of white sugar, and raw cane sugar for refining, for example. Agreements with states around the Mediterranean Basin give access for fruit and vegetables, olive oil and other Mediterranean products.

Given the failure to progress the Doha Round, attention has refocused on bilateral trade deals—FTAs—with non-LDC and non-ACP developing countries in Asia and South America, and with developed economies such as Australia, Canada and the USA. Negotiations on a Comprehensive Economic and Trade Agreement (CETA) with Canada, for example, began in 2009 (Kerr & Hobbs 2015: 437), but the European Parliament's approval was only secured in February 2017.

When countries form an FTA they are supposed to ensure that 'duties and other restrictive regulations of commerce … are eliminated on *substantially all the trade* between the constituent territories in products originating in such territories' (GATT Article XXIV: 8, emphasis added). Despite an attempt in the Uruguay Round to clarify what 'substantially all the trade' meant, it remains an unclear, and untested, provision. It seems doubtful, however, that an entire sector such as agriculture could be excluded, as had been the case prior to 1995. As the Commission of the European Communities (1995: 4) commented at the time: 'To date, the free trade agreements concluded by the Union have been restricted in terms of product coverage. In particular, they have generally excluded all or most agricultural trade'. With exceedingly high import tariffs on, for example, sugar, beef and dairy products, and the 'old' CAP's support arrangements designed to keep EU prices well in excess of those prevailing on world markets, it was indeed difficult to see how the EU's protected agricultural sector could be included in an FTA with a competitive agricultural exporter.

Despite the changes to the CAP over the last two decades—the MacSharry, Fischler and other reforms—the tariffs on many agricultural products remain stubbornly high. Thus, a competitive supplier of sugar or beef, for example, might aspire to the inclusion of these products in an FTA with the EU, while EU producers can be expected to object. If one competitive supplier gains entrée in this way, others will want to negotiate (or renegotiate) their own FTAs to gain comparable access to the EU's protected market: *precedents do matter*. Thus, as Kerr and Hobbs (2015) document, 'sensitive' agricultural products tend to be excluded from the draft Canada–EU CETA, or—like European cheeses into the protected Canadian market, or Canadian beef (but hormone free) into the EU—are granted restricted access based on tariff rate quotas. As Commissioner Cioloş (2014) acknowledged, 'the EU capacity to absorb additional concessions in the beef sector is limited … The composition and size of tariff quotas are most relevant in this respect'. Moreover, he noted:

> [b]eef was one of the most important elements for Canada in this negotiation, and this concession should be seen as part of a wider agricultural package: The EU obtained results on its offensive interests in agriculture including protection of Geographical Indications and very significantly improved market access for key products including dairy.

The willingness of the EU to open its market for increased beef imports—a politically sensitive issue—may indicate that agriculture is not a deal-breaker to the extent that it was in the past. Nonetheless, Kerr and Hobbs (2015: 454) conclude, perhaps overly pessimistically: 'The sub-sectors of agriculture in each market that were heavily protected prior to the CETA remain heavily protected at the conclusion of the negotiations. No areas of substantial liberalisation in agri-food trade are included in the text of the CETA'. Whether Australia could do better remains an open question.

In 1973, Australia's agricultural exports were adversely affected by the UK's accession to the then EEC. The world has moved on, and agricultural markets are significantly different now to what they were then. The CAP has changed, but many of the EU's agri-food sectors are still protected by prohibitively high MFN tariffs. An FTA with the EU that incorporates these products in a meaningful way is an outcome to be prized by a competitive agricultural exporter, even if it means incorporating some of the EU's regulatory measures, such as recognition of the EU's geographical indications, into the free trade area agreement.

The result of the UK's June 2016 referendum on EU membership, and the government's subsequent decision to trigger the withdrawal process ('Brexit'), could well mean that the UK will have left the EU by the end of March 2019 (Swinbank 2017). Is it an FTA with the remainder of the EU that the Australian farm sector would want to secure, one with the UK, or perhaps with both?

Concluding comments

This chapter has acknowledged that the 'old' CAP of the 1970s was highly protectionist, causing significant distortions to world trade, particularly for efficient agricultural exporters such as Australia. However, it has also sought to show that the policy has changed significantly, and that its distortions to international trade are much reduced (although there has been no attempt here to demonstrate this empirically). A number of pressures have borne down on EU policy makers that help explain this policy shift, but international pressure exerted through the GATT/WTO has—the authors believe—been crucial. This is why we deplore the failure to conclude the Doha Round, which would have the effect of locking in past CAP reforms. Despite the policy changes, the high tariffs on agri-food products established by the EU at the conclusion of the Uruguay Round remain in place—another reason to deplore the international community's failure to conclude the Doha Round. But this does mean that an FTA with the EU that effectively sidesteps these trade barriers is potentially important for an efficient agricultural exporter.

References

Agra Facts (2015), 'Commission Tables Plan Allowing Countries to Ban Use of GM Animal Feed', *Agra Facts* No. 31–15, 22 April: 1.

Anderson, Kym (2000), 'Agriculture's "multifunctionality" and the WTO', *Australian Journal of Agricultural and Resource Economics* 44(3): 475–94. doi.org/10.1111/1467-8489.00121.

Bureau of Agricultural Economics (1985), *Agricultural Policies in the European Community: Their Origins, Nature and Effects on Production and Trade*, Policy Monograph No. 2 (Australian Government Publishing Service: Canberra).

Cioloş, Dacian (2014), Answer given by Mr Cioloş on behalf of the Commission, 18 September, Written Question E-006196-14, European Parliament. Available at www.europarl.europa.eu/sides/getAll Answers.do?reference=E-2014-006196&language=EN, last accessed 3 June 2015.

Commission of the European Communities (1995), *Free Trade Areas: An Appraisal*, SEC(95)322 (Commission of the European Communities: Brussels).

Corbet, Hugh & J. F. van Riemsdijk (eds) (1973), 'Wageningen memorandum on the reform of the European Community's Common Agricultural Policy', *European Review of Agricultural Economics* 1(2): 151–60. doi.org/10.1093/erae/1.2.151.

Cunha, Arlindo with Alan Swinbank (2011), *An Inside View of the CAP Reform Process: Explaining the MacSharry, Agenda 2000, and Fischler Reforms* (Oxford University Press: Oxford).

Daugbjerg, Carsten & Alan Swinbank (2009), *Ideas, Institutions, and Trade: The WTO and the Curious Role of EU Farm Policy in Trade Liberalization* (Oxford University Press: Oxford). doi.org/10.1093/ acprof:oso/9780199557752.001.0001.

Daugbjerg, Carsten & Alan Swinbank (2011), 'Explaining the "health check" of the Common Agricultural Policy: Budgetary politics, globalisation and paradigm change revisited', *Policy Studies* 32(2): 127–41. doi.org/10.1080/01442872.2010.541768.

Daugbjerg, Carsten & Alan Swinbank (2016), 'Three Decades of Policy Layering and Politically Sustainable Reform in the European Union's Agricultural Policy', *Governance* 29(2): 265–280. doi.org/10.1111/ gove.12171.

Embassy of France in Washington (2013), 'CAP reform. Communiqué issued by the Ministry of Agriculture, the Food Industry and Forestry. Paris, March 26, 2013'. Available at ambafrance-us.org/spip. php?article4468, last accessed 19 September 2013.

European Commission (2015), *The CAP towards 2020. Implementation of the New System of Direct Payments. MS Notifications* (European Commission: Brussels).

Fischler, Franz (2003), 'The New, Reformed Agricultural Policy', Final Press Conference After the Decision at the Council on Agriculture, Luxembourg, 26 June, Speech/03/326 (Commission of the European Communities: Brussels).

Garland, (Ransley) Victor (1978), 'Australia's Trade Relations with the European Economic Community. Ministerial Statement', Thursday, 16 March (House of Representatives: Canberra).

Harris, Simon, Alan Swinbank & Guy Wilkinson (1983), *The Food and Farm Policies of the European Community* (John Wiley & Sons: Chichester).

Hart, Kaley (2015), 'The fate of Green Direct Payments in the CAP Reform negotiations' in Johan Swinnen (ed.), *The Political Economy of the 2014–2020 Common Agricultural Policy: An Imperfect Storm* (Rowman & Littlefield International: London), 245–76.

Kenyon, Don & David Lee (2006), *The Struggle for Trade Liberalisation in Agriculture: Australia and the Cairns Group in the Uruguay Round*, The Foreign Affairs and Trade Files No. 4 (Department of Foreign Affairs and Trade: Canberra).

Kerr, William A. & Jill E. Hobbs (2015), 'A protectionist bargain?: Agriculture in the European Union–Canada Trade Agreement', *Journal of World Trade* 49(3): 437–56.

Merriënboer, Johan van (2011), *Mansholt: A Biography* (P.I.E. Peter Lang: Bruxelles).

Moyer, H. Wayne & Timothy E. Josling (1990), *Agricultural Policy Reform: Policy and Process in the EC and USA* (Harvester Wheatsheaf: Hemel Hempsted).

Noble, Joan (2012), *Policy Scenarios for EU Sugar Market Reform*, PE 495.823 (European Parliament: Brussels).

Swinbank, Alan (2015), 'The WTO: No longer relevant for CAP Reform?', in Johan Swinnen (ed.), *The Political Economy of the 2014–2020 Common Agricultural Policy: An Imperfect Storm* (Rowman & Littlefield International: London), 193–213.

Swinbank, Alan (2017), World Trade Rules and the Policy Options for British Agriculture post-Brexit, UK Trade Policy Observatory Briefing Paper 7 (University of Sussex: Falmer). www.sussex.ac.uk/webteam/gateway/file.php?name=briefing-paper-7-final.pdf&site=18.

Swinbank, Alan & Carsten Daugbjerg (2006), 'The 2003 CAP reform: Accommodating WTO pressures', *Comparative European Politics*, 4(1): 47–64. doi.org/10.1057/palgrave.cep.6110069.

Swinbank, Alan & Carolyn Tanner (1996), *Farm Policy and Trade Conflict: The Uruguay Round and CAP Reform* (The University of Michigan Press: Ann Arbor).

Tangermann, Stefan (2004), 'Agricultural policies in OECD countries ten years after the Uruguay Round: How much progress?', in Giovanni Anania, Mary E. Bohman, Colin A. Carter & Alex F. McCalla (eds), *Agricultural Policy Reform and the WTO: Where Are We Heading?* (Edward Elgar: Cheltenham), 15–42.

Tanner, Carolyn (1996), 'Agricultural trade liberalisation and the Uruguay Round', *Australian Journal of Agricultural Economics* 40(1): 1–35. doi.org/10.1111/j.1467-8489.1996.tb00726.x.

WTO (World Trade Organization) (2008), *Revised Draft Modalities for Agriculture*, TN/AG/W/4/Rev.4 (WTO: Geneva).

WTO (2015), *Export Competition*. Ministerial Decision of 19 December 2015, WT/MIN(15)/45, WT/L/980, 21 December (WTO: Geneva).

6

Agriculture in the Australia–EU economic and trade relationship

Karen Hussey and Carl Tidemann

Introduction

Following the collapse of the Doha Development Agenda, two dominant trends have emerged in the international system of trade. The first is the proliferation of bilateral and regional free trade agreements[1] (FTAs) as an 'operational second best' approach to multilateral regulation (Bonciu & Moldoveanu 2014). Such agreements are second best because they impose significant transaction costs on the international system of trade (i.e. exporters can be forced to handle sometimes dozens of different regulatory regimes concurrently), and they only occasionally produce significant trade gains in those areas that are particularly sensitive such as in agriculture and labour-intensive manufactured products (WTO 2013; Viju & Kerr 2011). Despite these drawbacks, hundreds of FTAs have been negotiated over the last two decades and some optimism is warranted; at the very least, the size of the markets and the number of countries covered by some FTAs suggest that it may eventually be easier to return to the World Trade Organization (WTO) for a truly global trade

---

1   Such agreements are also called preferential trade agreements (PTAs), for example by the WTO, but in this chapter we will use the more commonly used term free trade agreement.

agreement because some regulatory reform under FTAs are intrinsically non-discriminatory, leading to a de facto most-favoured-nation dividend (WTO 2013: 24).

The second trend in recent years has been the rise of non-tariff barriers (NTBs) as impediments to trade between nations. Other than to tell us what they are not, the term NTB itself does not reveal any of the details of what they include. Nevertheless, they are, generally, all measures other than tariffs that restrict or otherwise distort trade flows (OECD 2005). More broadly, such measures could be customs rules and procedures, competition-related restrictions on market access, public procurement practices, or internal taxes or charges. Specifically, they may relate to requirements around labelling, certification, packaging, and health and safety standards. The challenge for the international system of trade governance is to balance the imperative of free trade with legitimate domestic concerns and expectations relating to social and environmental public good outcomes, a challenge acknowledged by the WTO:

> While a convergence of public policy design would facilitate matters from a purely trade perspective, we recognise that respect for differing social preferences is paramount. We must work towards a shared understanding of what constitutes a level playing field (WTO 2013: 29).

Establishing 'convergence of public policy design' is where regional and bilateral agreements can be very useful. Despite the fact that high tariffs are still evident in key product areas, including agricultural products, more than four-fifths of international trade flows take place on a non-discriminatory basis, which means that regulations are far more important as potential trade barriers and sources of discrimination (WTO 2013: 25–6). Thus, while such FTAs can never achieve the same gains as multilateral agreements, they do nevertheless provide significant opportunities for trading partners to forge ahead in reducing traditional trade barriers as well as behind-the-border trade barriers (Hussey & Kenyon 2011). In very recent years there has been a revival in *anti*-free trade sentiment, most vehemently in the United States where vocal members of both the Republican and Democrat parties have objected to US ratification of the 12-nation Trans-Pacific Partnership Agreement and negotiations for the Trans-Atlantic Trade and Investment Partnership (Irwin 2015). Similar sentiments are also evident in parts of Europe, and the BREXIT 'Leave' campaign based at least some of their campaign on the perception that free trade between the EU and UK had failed to deliver promised gains.

However, those sentiments notwithstanding, the opportunities that an EU–Australia FTA offer are the motivation for the recent announcement on 15 November 2015 by the Australian Prime Minister, together with the President of the European Council and the President of the European Commission, to start the process towards a 'comprehensive and high-quality' FTA (DFAT 2015). As a bloc, the European Union (EU) is Australia's second-largest trading partner and largest source of foreign investment: in 2014, the EU's FDI in Australia was valued at A$169.6 billion and Australian FDI in the EU was valued at A$83.5 billion (DFAT 2015).

For Australia, a bilateral agreement with the EU could provide better access to over 500 million consumers and help it to attract additional investment, technology, and skilled workers from Europe. However, as was the case in the Canada–EU negotiations towards the Comprehensive Economic and Trade Agreement (CETA, see Chapter 4 in this volume), some of the predictable, sensitive issues that will challenge the Australia–EU negotiations relate to agriculture. They include tariffs and quotas, but negotiators will also have the opportunity to deal with a range of NTBs, including packaging, labelling, certification (technical barriers to trade—TBTs), and health and safety standards (sanitary and phytosanitary—SPS standards) (Viju & Kerr 2011).

The objective of this chapter is to assess the major challenges that Australian and European negotiators will face in tackling the agricultural trade barriers that exist between the two trading partners. The asymmetry of the relationship prompts us to take a largely Australian perspective on the benefits to be gained in the agricultural sector from an Australia–EU FTA. This chapter is informed by statistical analysis of the current trading relationship; 15 interviews with key industry peak bodies and government departments; analysis of previous FTAs involving Australia and the EU; submissions to government enquiries; and the peer-reviewed academic literature. It begins by outlining the agri-trade relationship between Australia and the EU, then assesses the extent of traditional barriers that exist in agricultural trade between the two markets. It analyses the range of NTBs that currently impinge on the trading relationship and which could therefore usefully form the focus of trade negotiations, and proposes a number of ways forward to achieve greater convergence and coherence between the EU's and Australia's trade rules and the policies, norms and standards in other areas of public policy that create NTBs.

Agricultural trade between Australia and the EU

The EU and Australia have a long economic and diplomatic history governed most recently by the 1997 Australia–EU Partnership Framework, the 2008 Wine Agreement and a mutual recognition agreement (MRA) relating to industrial products. However, the relationship has historically been characterised by a high level of antagonism, caused by, on the one hand, the EU's trade-distorting policies under the common agricultural policy (CAP) and their immovable stance on geographic indicators (see Chapter 7 in this volume), and on the other hand, Australia's strict quarantine and biosecurity regimes (Kenyon & Lee 2006; Kenyon & Kunkel 2005). However, iterative reform of the CAP throughout the 1990s, and especially since 2003, introduced a number of important innovations including a fundamental change to the decoupling of income support payments to farmers freeing them up to produce for the market and not for subsidies (i.e. a less trade-distorting approach) (Costa et al. 2009; and for further detail see Chapter 5 in this volume).

Two further reforms included the introduction of cross-compliance to ensure that farmers only receive financial support if they meet minimum good agricultural, animal welfare and environmental practices; and a shift from market support to rural development objectives (i.e. building capacity and diversification in regional areas, retaining young farmers on the land etc.). In the following years, those sectors still considered to be in surplus (e.g. sugar, fruit and vegetables and wine sectors) were also reformed, and a new rural development policy for the financial period 2007–13 was prepared. The 'heat' in the relationship has also lessened owing to a shift in focus by Australian exporters to growing markets in Asia and the Middle East, and a relative decline in Australia's market share to the EU due to increased competition from Brazil, China and South Africa—the same dynamics that saw the United States of America (USA) share of the EU market decline.

Despite the rise of Asia and the Middle East as key trading partners, at the time of writing the EU is second only to China as Australia's largest trading partner (DFAT 2017b). The EU is the third-largest export market for Australian goods behind China and Japan, and is the largest source of Australia's imports ahead of both China and the USA. But the relationship is an entirely asymmetrical one: Australia represents just 1.7 per cent of the

EU's export market and a mere 0.5 per cent of EU imports (DFAT 2017a). Imports from the EU are made up almost completely of manufactured goods as well as medicines and pharmaceutical products (Figure 1).

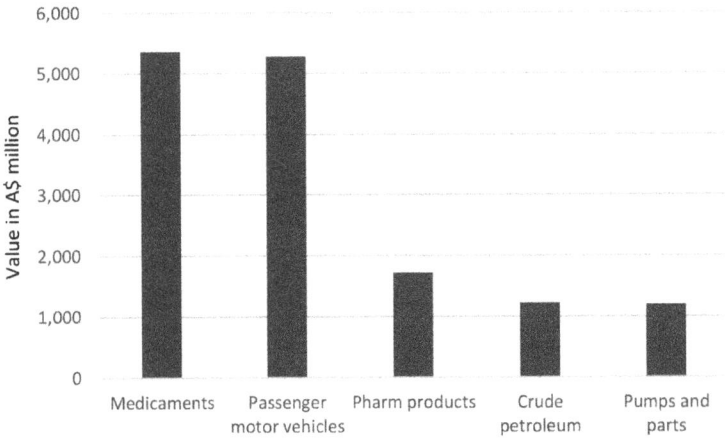

Figure 1. Top five Australian imports from the EU
Source: DFAT 2017a.

Australia's agricultural exports to the EU represent 18 per cent of all exports to the EU, with a total value of A\$2.77 billion (coal is Australia's second-largest export commodity to the EU at 15 per cent) (ABARES 2014; DFAT 2017b). Figure 2 shows the key agricultural export commodities.

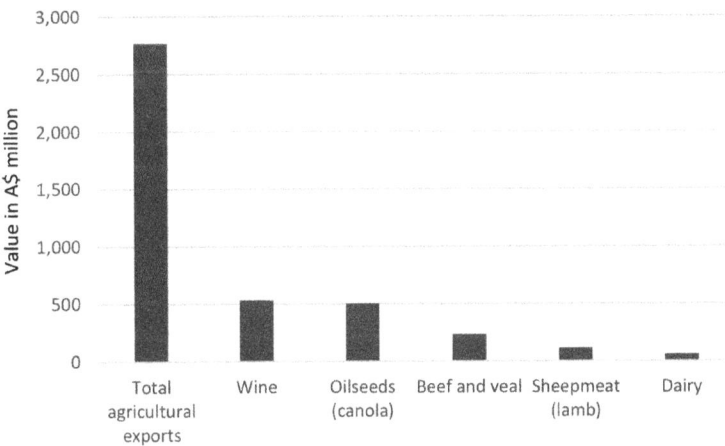

Figure 2. Value in AUD of Australian exports of key agricultural products to the EU in 2013–14
Source: ABARES 2014.

However, like the USA and Japan, the EU employs strict quotas and high tariffs for a number of agricultural products that act as significant barriers to Australia's exports. Figure 3 compares the extent of tariff measures in both Australia and the EU for key agricultural commodities.

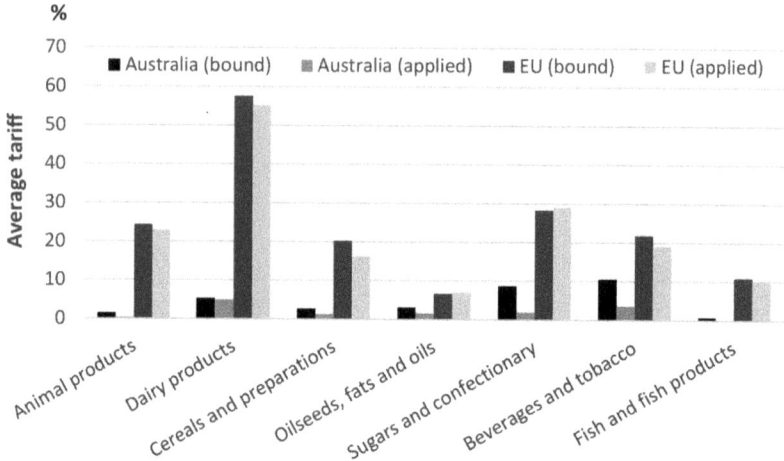

Figure 3. Average bound and applied tariffs for Australia and the EU of selected trade categories
Source: WTO 2014.

As well as tariffs and quotas, the EU continues to subsidise its agricultural sector in a complicated system of payments, governed by the CAP. Since 1986–88, the EU has worked to reduce its level of agricultural support, which now sits at 19 per cent as measured by the percentage producer support estimate (PSE),[2] declining from a rate of 39 per cent—the Organisation for Economic Co-operation and Development (OECD) average sits at 18 per cent (OECD 2014). Though the EU's level of support to farmers is declining, that support remains high when compared with Australia's rate of PSE of just 2 per cent (Table 1). The EU's above average support highlights that even beyond the considerable reforms of the CAP, support to European farmers continues to be a trade barrier. Conversely, Australia places no tariffs on fresh or unprocessed products. There is, however, a flat rate of 5 per cent on almost all processed agricultural products (PAPs) of which the EU is a large exporter.

2   The percentage producer support estimate (PSE) represents policy transfers to agricultural producers, measured at the farm gate and expressed as a share of gross farm receipts.

Table 1. Level of agricultural support in Australia and the EU

Country/ Customs area	Product support estimate (%)	Highly trade distorting (%)	Price differential – country to border	TSE* as per cent of GDP	Single commodity transfer (%)	Key commodities subsidised (%)
Australia	2	11	1	0.1	None	None
EU	19	27	1.05	0.8	26	Sugar (13), beef and veal (24), poultry (12)

* TSE = total support estimate
Source: OECD 2014.

Much of the consternation surrounding the CAP also relates to the EU's use of export subsidies, even though these have also been significantly reduced in recent years. In 2014, export subsidies were €12 million, compared with €67 million in 2013, and €3.7 billion in 2004 (OECD 2014). The EU continues to use trade-distorting subsidies, with average prices received by EU farm producers remaining 5 per cent above world prices, compared to Australia where farmers receive average prices that are at par with world prices (OECD 2014). Overall, while the EU market has declined in importance for Australian agricultural producers, there is still an opportunity and appetite to negotiate reforms to the tariff and quota arrangements of the EU in some key markets: oilseeds, beef and veal, lamb and mutton, dairy and wheat—each explored in turn now.

The EU is a very significant market for Australian oilseeds, with canola alone making up 18 per cent of all agricultural exports to the EU. Demand for that product has skyrocketed since 2006–07. The EU Renewable Energy Directive (2009) further intensified demand, with canola being used in the production of biodiesel. The market is not subject to tariffs or quotas, but reflecting the product's use in biodiesel, there are two significant European certification schemes for sustainable production that Australian exporters are required to adhere to. In essence, those schemes enforce sustainability standards in the production of canola along the whole supply chain—'from the paddock to the Peugeot'—with current requirements demanding a 35 per cent reduction in greenhouse gas emissions in comparison to fossil fuels[3] (EC 2015). Those standards will increase to a minimum 50 per cent reduction in 2017 and 60 per cent reduction in 2018. However, based on current scientific evidence, Australian producers are likely to meet those thresholds. Somewhat ironically, it is unclear whether European oilseed producers will be able to do the same. While the EU market pays a premium price for Australian canola, almost two-thirds of the certification schemes' criteria are irrelevant for the Australian environment so there are significant opportunities for negotiators in this sector.

Beef and veal exports have also enjoyed strong recent growth between 2007–08 and 2013–14, with exports to the EU more than tripling from 7.3 thousand tonnes to 22.8 thousand tonnes, including an extraordinary 33 per cent increase from 2013 to 2014. The continued growth in grain-fed beef shipments has allowed Australia to diversify its markets in the EU, with further growth in exports to Italy (up 9 per cent), the Netherlands (up 29 per cent) and Denmark (up 12 per cent) (MLA 2015). Australian beef and veal, though they face no in-quota tariff, are restricted by two major quotas, the high-quality beef (HQB) Hilton quota (Australia's share of this quota is 7,150 tonnes swt/year) that has a utilisation average from 90 per cent to 100 per cent, and the HQB grain-fed quota (48,200 tonnes swt/year—on a 'first come first served' import allocation).

To put this in perspective, Australia exported over one million tonnes of beef and veal globally in 2013–14 (ABARES 2014), so the EU quotas are hugely restrictive. Nevertheless, the EU remains the highest value market for Australian beef on a per tonne basis, averaging A$10,550/metric tonne in 2014 (MLA 2015). Australia's access to the HQB Hilton quota and grain-fed HQB quota means that the majority of cuts exported to the EU are high quality and subsequently of high value (MLA 2015), and the fact that the quota is almost always filled suggests there would be significant gains for Australian exporters if that quota could be increased. In contrast to US and Canadian beef, Australian beef does not contain hormones and is therefore not subject to the EU's ban on hormone-treated beef.

---

3   To be considered sustainable, biofuels must achieve greenhouse gas savings of at least 35 per cent in 2015 in comparison to fossil fuels, 50 per cent in 2017, and 60 per cent in 2018, but only for new production plants; cannot be grown in areas converted from land with previously high carbon stock such as wetlands or forests; and cannot be produced from raw materials obtained from land with high biodiversity such as primary forests or highly biodiverse grasslands.

The Australia–EU relationship in the dairy sector has been strained for the better part of four decades. In contrast to Australia, New Zealand dairy producers have enjoyed privileged access to the EU for New Zealand butter and cheese dating back to the United Kingdom's (UK) accession to the EU in 1973. At that time, New Zealand's access to the UK market was safeguarded on the grounds that New Zealand's economy was so utterly dependent on it. For similar reasons those privileges were subsequently extended to an EU-wide bound commitment in the Uruguay Round negotiations (Kenyon & Lee 2006). No such privileges were afforded to Australian producers—then or since—with the result that dairy exports to the EU have been limited.

The Australian dairy industry faces perhaps the most restrictive barriers with quotas and in-quota tariffs existing for most products: butter is limited to 10,000 tonnes from all third parties and an in-quota tariff of €950 per tonne; cheddar, of which Australia is a large exporter, is limited to 15,000 tonnes from all third parties and an in-quota tariff of €210 per tonne; all other cheeses are limited to 19,500 tonnes from all third parties with in-quota tariffs ranging from €690 to €1,060 per tonne, depending on the variety of cheese. Not surprisingly then, dairy exports from Australia have declined in all categories since 2007–08 and the main market for Australian exports—the sale of cheese to the UK—has also declined over recent years.[4] The EU accounts for just 2 per cent of Australia's exports, and in-quota tariffs are partly to blame. However, of all the agricultural commodities exported to the EU, the dairy industry is arguably most affected by NTBs, especially in the areas of environmental standards and geographic indicators. On the latter there is little prospect that the EU will soften its stance in the foreseeable future (see below).

Interestingly, as with dairy products, NZ exports of lamb were similarly privileged after the UK's accession to the EU and again Australian producers enjoyed no such access. Today, lamb and mutton exports to the EU are limited by a 19,186 tonne carcass weight equivalent tariff rate quota (TRQ)—a quota that is almost always filled. When compared with New Zealand's quota (just over 228,000 tonnes), it is clear just how significant New Zealand's privileged market access is. Indeed, the volume of lamb exports to the EU has increased slightly since 2006–07, with the main market being the UK. Importantly, the value of lamb exports

---

4   This correlates with a reduction in production of dairy product in Australia between 2007–08 and 2013–14, though average export unit values have continued to increase over time.

has almost doubled in the last five years, with the UK and EU attracting high-end, high-value lamb exports from Australia. At the other end of the value spectrum, mutton exports to the EU have also increased but neither the volume nor the value is very significant. Nevertheless, as is the case with beef exports, any leeway made in relation to lamb quotas would see considerable benefits accrued to Australian exporters, although New Zealand exporters might be less than enthusiastic about such an outcome.

Like lamb and dairy exports, Australian sugar exports to the UK had a similar (but sadder) history with the demise of the Commonwealth Sugar Agreement in 1973 when the UK joined the EU. Again, the Uruguay Round failed to deliver similar market access arrangements for Australian sugar, and that sector has been exposed to significant tariffs and quotas in almost all major foreign markets as a consequence of the EU and USA in particular being major sugar producers themselves. Australian exports face a quota of just below 10,000 tonnes and an in-quota tariff of €98 per tonne; the quotas of Brazil (334,000 tonnes) and Cuba (69,000 tonnes) as well as all other third parties (254,000 tonnes) dwarf the Australian figure. In recent years, sugar exports decreased between 2006–07 and 2011–12, though they have rebounded since. Exports to the EU are statistically insignificant, but for reasons mentioned above they will likely prove to be a sticking point in trade negotiations not least owing to the controversies of the Australia–United States Free Trade Agreement (AUSFTA) negotiations. In that case, the sugar industry was assured of positive outcomes but in reality was completely removed from the agreement.

Australian wine exports to the EU have decreased significantly with the volume of imports into the major markets—Germany, Ireland, the Netherlands, and the UK—more than halved since 2006–07. However, the value of these exports remains very high. Tariffs on Australian wine are at 3 per cent—described by one interviewee as 'a nuisance more than anything else'—and the treaty-level Australia–EU wine agreement has established an effective forum in which to resolve emerging issues. Indeed, while the EU's regulations relating to geographic indicators and environmental sustainability (and associated labelling) are still problematic for Australian wine producers, both bilateral and multilateral dialogues are effective in addressing them, thus limiting the value of including wine in negotiations for an EU–Australia FTA.

Less significant markets for Australian agricultural products include fish and seafood exports and wheat. However, the EU is a net exporter of both commodities, so the potential to increase market share in those products is limited, with two exceptions. The first is the opportunity to expand exports of specialised grains, building on Australia's reputation for producing high-quality durum wheat for use in pasta production. The second opportunity lies in the area of plant energy systems. However, in both cases the EU's standards in relation to environmental sustainability and genetic modification could prove to be prohibitive to trade.

Expectations from an Australia–EU FTA

As the previous section indicated, despite the gains made from the Uruguay Round of General Agreement on Tariffs and Trade (GATT) and reforms to the EU's CAP, significant trade barriers continue to impede trade in agricultural products between the EU and Australia. Certainly, the existence of highly restrictive tariffs and quotas in the EU suggests that trade negotiators could reasonably be expected to begin negotiations there. But the experience of other FTAs is sobering. In the lead-up to the AUSFTA, for example, it was predicted that there would be significant gains for the Australian agricultural industry as the USA maintained some of its highest trade barriers for agricultural goods (Krever 2006). The outcomes were far from ideal. Though there were seemingly positive changes made with respect to in-quota tariff removals in beef and dairy, safeguards were included by the USA ensuring that tariffs would remain in place in case of declines in the domestic value of those commodities (Clarke & Gao 2007; Krever 2006). Sugar was excluded from the agreement altogether. In Australia's FTA with Japan, most Australian tariff lines will be reduced to zero. However, for cheese, various vegetables and a number of fresh and dried fruits, tariffs remain and they are not trivial. With respect to NTBs, in the Australia–Japan FTA little progress was made, with the text simply stating that each party shall not implement a measure unless it is allowable under the WTO and that such measures need to remain transparent.

In contrast, CETA did deliver significant tariff reductions on agricultural products, with almost all tariff eliminations to be undertaken immediately. However, a key difference with the case of Australia mutes one's optimism: the EU has been a significant *net agricultural exporter* to Canada for a number of years (Viju & Kerr 2011), which is a fundamentally different relationship to that enjoyed by Australia and the EU. Success in agriculture in an Australia–EU FTA will almost certainly rely on Australia's willingness to offer concessions in other sectors.

In reality, the major opportunities for trade liberalisation in agricultural trade between Australia and the EU lie in the area of NTBs. These can be divided into technical and nontechnical measures and they are regulatory in nature (WTO 2013: 25).

> Technical measures include SPS standards (covered by the SPS agreement); rules for product weight, size or packaging; ingredient or identity standards; mandatory labelling; shelf-life restrictions; and import testing and certification procedures. Nontechnical measures include bureaucratic restrictions, subsidies or other legal measures that hinder trade, such as failure to provide adequate and effective intellectual property protection (Nathan Associates 2013: 2).

Both types may have legitimate purposes, especially in the eyes of enforcers, but both can also be misused to covertly impede trade. They may be designed to limit trade or they may have that effect because of the way they are implemented, either with a lack of transparency, inefficiency or corruption.

Estimating the costs of NTBs is therefore understandably complex (Boza 2013), but estimates run into the millions per annum. Beghin and Melatos (2012) examined the impact of Australia's quarantine regime on pig meat imports. They concluded that the effects on welfare and trade of the Australian quarantine regime were very significant and estimated that the withdrawal of the regime resulted in a staggering welfare gain to consumers of A$409 million and the expansion of revenue to three exporting nations of A$479 million.

The WTO's Sanitary and Phytosanitary and Technical Barriers to Trade agreements do allow countries to adopt appropriate measures to protect human, plant and animal health, but to reduce compliance costs and minimise disputes, countries are encouraged to base their domestic technical regulations or standards on those developed by international organisations, including the Joint FAO/WHO Codex Alimentarius Commission (Codex) for food safety; the Office International des Epizooties (OIE) for animal health; and the International Plant Protection Convention (IPPC) for plant health (WTO 2010). However, member states are allowed to impose more stringent guidelines under the GATT if a risk assessment—supported by sufficient scientific evidence—deems such an approach to be justified.

When third countries question those more stringent guidelines, they raise a specific trade concern (STC) with the appropriate committee. If the number of bilateral STCs raised in the WTO is any indication of the level of NTBs used by countries, then the EU and Australia have much to gain by exploring opportunities for regulatory cooperation. Figures from Horn et al. (2013: 737) (Figure 4) illustrate that the EU and Australia received the greatest number of STC notifications in relation to SPS issues, while Figure 5 illustrates the same statistics for STCs relating to TBTs. Clearly, both jurisdictions have imposed barriers to trade that third countries find worrisome. Somewhat ironically, the fact that both the EU and Australia impose comparatively stringent regulations on imports suggests that they may have more in common than either side cares to admit.

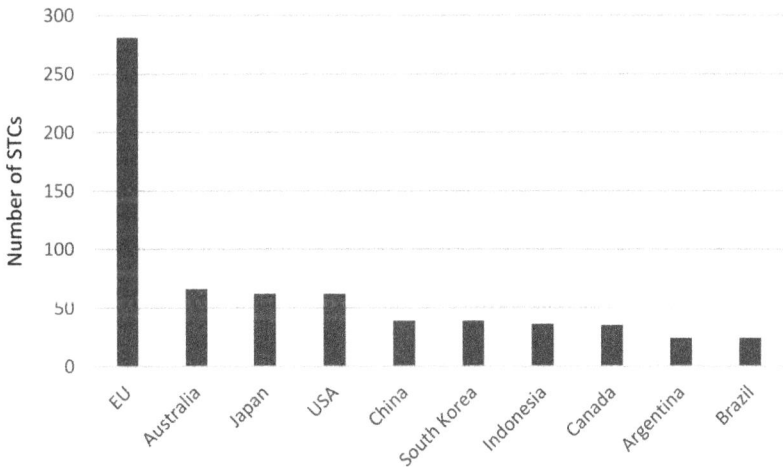

Figure 4. Members that most frequently face SPS 'Bilateral' STCs
Source: After Horn, Mavroidis & Wijkstrom 2013: 737.

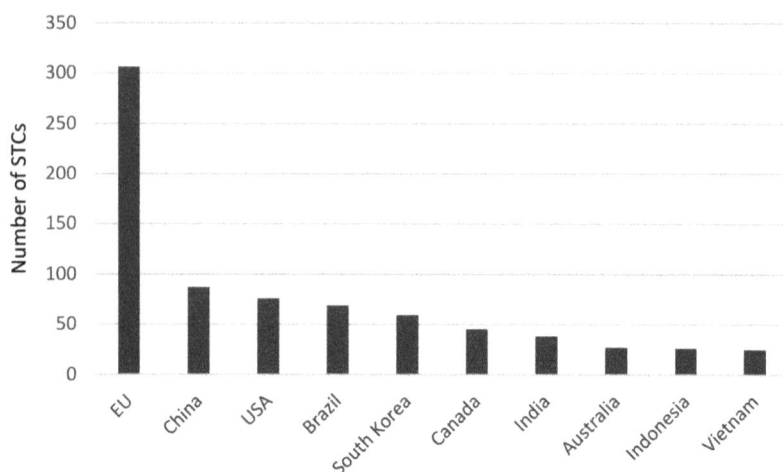

Figure 5. Members that most frequently face TBT 'Bilateral' STCs
Source: After Horn, Mavroidis & Wijkstrom 2013: 737.

Increasingly, NTBs reflect with public policy objectives and consumer preferences and they therefore raise issues of far greater complexity than tariffs. As Philip Stephens of the *Financial Times* put it:

> The nature of free trade deals has changed. They used to be about tariffs. Now they focus on regulatory standards and norms, intellectual property rights, data privacy and investment protection. These are issues that cut deep across national political and cultural preferences. Lowering import duties is one thing; persuading voters to relax the rules on data protection or accept new rules on food safely is another (Stephens 2016).

Furthermore, while the purpose of some NTBs is very specifically to restrict trade—for example in the prohibition of harmful products— often that restriction is an unintended, perverse consequence of pursuing a given public policy objective. As the WTO phrased it:

> [d]ivergence can occur for different reasons. It may be a reflection of different social preferences and values. In this case, the notion of 'levelling the playing field' in trade relations takes on an additional layer of complexity – the search cannot be for uniformity in cases where an attempt to homogenize societal preferences would be an intrusive step too far. Cooperation in this case can only be about avoiding unnecessary friction or unwarranted discrimination (WTO 2013: 25).

Where do NTBs exist in the Australia–EU agri-trade relationship? The following issues all impede trade to varying degrees on either side of the relationship:

- custom surcharges
- high level of food and safety standards resulting in high SPS measures that are more stringent than international standards or that are not relevant to the exporting environmental conditions
- long and difficult authorisation procedures
- labelling requirement laws
- direct and indirect government support through tax relief and concessions or protective legislation to EU farmers
- traceability and labelling of biotechnology foods
- maximum limits on mycotoxins for a variety of foodstuffs (including cereals, fruit and nuts)
- product process, production or labelling requirements relating to the classification of 'organic' foods.

Following Berden et al. (2009), NTBs and regulatory divergence can have two main effects:

a. Those NTBs that increase the cost of doing business for firms result in increased commodity prices for end users, because firms increase prices to cover the higher cost of doing business, which constitutes a welfare loss to society.

b. Those NTBs that restrict market access for firms increase the market concentration and economic power (and thus revenue profits) of companies in the importing country, with the result that commodity prices may increase anyway—reducing welfare gains overall—and welfare is redistributed away from consumers towards domestic producers (i.e. protecting them, not consumers).

NTBs can be especially cumbersome for small and medium-sized enterprises in exporting countries, which lack the resources to deal with multiple regulatory regimes in multiple markets (noting that when dealing with the EU, sometimes there are multiple regimes at the level of member states).

An oft-suggested method of overcoming these barriers is mutual recognition of regulations in exporting and importing countries (see, for example, Nicolaidis & Shaffer 2005; Trachtman 2007; and Kerber & van den Bergh 2008). Mutual recognition across different regulatory jurisdictions assumes an equivalence of regulatory and public policy goals across jurisdictions but accepts that there are differences in regulatory approach or detail in how those goals are met; in this way, it is possible to 'mutually recognise' (usually with exceptions) each other's regulation so as to facilitate trade. Kerber and Van den Bergh (2008: 447) suggest 'mutual recognition is often recommended as a nearly ideal solution for removing obstacles to free trade without embarking on a pathway to harmonisation'.

Mutual recognition has been a part of trade negotiations and bilateral agreements for some time; however, this has generally been limited to conformity assessment procedures and, more often than not, specifically excludes SPS measures (see, for example, the multiple MRAs of the EU, the Australia–Singapore MRA, CETA and the China–Australia FTA). Conformity assessment measures in these agreements have always related to technical products or medicines (e.g. telecommunications and electronics) whereby a consumer may be at risk or a product may simply not work when imported. However, there is precedent for mutual recognition to spread beyond simply technical measures to those measures affecting agricultural products (see, for example, the Trans-Tasman Mutual Recognition Arrangement (TTMRA) between Australia and New Zealand).

The arguments against using mutual recognition centre on fears that regulatory competition can undermine public interest concerns such as health and safety standards and environmental goals, and lead to lowest-common-denominator outcomes or a 'race to the bottom'. It follows, therefore, that the acceptance of 'equivalence' in regulation between jurisdictions demands a high degree of trust between trading partners. Arguably, this was particularly problematic in the context of the WTO's multilateral trade negotiations, but there is some justification for suggesting that it is less of a problem when states negotiate bilateral or plurilateral trade agreements. In the case of an FTA between Australia and the EU, the potential to embark on significant arrangements to mutually recognise each other's regulatory frameworks is, arguably, very large, for three reasons.

First, the underlying *intent* of many of the NTBs in the agricultural sector in both jurisdictions is the same. Australia and the EU have similar, very stringent, robust regulatory frameworks governing the agricultural sector. Whether in the area of waste management, water and air pollution control, management of non-point source pollution, tracing systems, or even occupational health and safety requirements, the objectives of the respective frameworks are very similar. Moreover, the high level of institutional capacity in both markets ensures that the regulatory regimes are upheld, thus providing the necessary trust for a form of mutual recognition. Nevertheless, there have been some major disagreements between Australia and the EU regarding the use of sanitary measures since the WTO SPS agreement came into force.

As has been the case in disputes between the EU and Canada, these disagreements relate to both the science itself and whether or not science should be the sole, or a contributing, factor in the establishment of sanitary import regulation (Viju & Kerr 2011). For example, Woolcock (2007: 6) suggests:

> [owing to] shifts in European consumer preferences in favour of higher food safety and environmental standards, the EU has sought to use the precautionary principle in the regulation of risk which implies an approach that views science-based risk assessment as an important but not the only criterion.

Another source of tension is the 'blanket' approach of some of the EU's import requirements aimed at sustainability objectives. In many cases, those requirements are irrelevant to the Australian landscape. Australia could, for example, seek agreement from the EU that a thorough review of EU schemes for Australia be undertaken, so that at the very least those conditions that do not affect Australia could be excluded.

Second, the gains from cooperating on regulatory divergence accrue to both sides of the trade, particularly for NTBs in the agricultural sector. As Figure 4 demonstrated, the EU and Australia are both onerous in their regulatory regimes in the eyes of rest of the world. Thus, there is much to be gained from exploring opportunities to cooperate. In contrast to the situation with tariffs and quotas, regulatory cooperation on NTBs would deliver welfare gains to all.

The third reason relates to the increased influence the EU and Australia would be able to exert in non-trade forums if they could cooperate more on NTBs, especially in emerging issues. There is no point in pursuing public policy objectives in one forum, if they are going to be undermined by WTO trade rules; this is particularly the case in the 'trade environment' domain:

> Convergence between trade and public policy NTBs requires greater coherence between trade rules and policies, norms and standards in other areas of international cooperation (WTO 2013: 7).

If the EU and Australia—two jurisdictions with very high levels of SPS protection—were to establish common ground at an early stage in the trade of new products, they could possibly prevent NTBs from setting in.

For example, momentum is building internationally to address climate change, and domestic regulation to mitigate greenhouse gas emissions has already been brought in front of the WTO dispute settlement panel. Four WTO disputes have been filed since 2010 that challenge government programs supporting renewable energy, and a number of related disputes have yet to reach the WTO (Meyer 2013). Other emerging areas relate to environmental tariffs at the border, particularly in the area of border carbon adjustments to 'level the playing field' between those countries or regions that have a robust climate mitigation policy, vis-à-vis those without one. What is almost certain is that the conflation of environmental concerns with international trade is likely to increase in the coming years, but the WTO Committee on Trade and Environment is unlikely to find meaningful solutions in the foreseeable future.

Another potential future NTB to trade and investment is 'nanotechnology'. Berden et al. (2009: 85) suggest that 'while the technique itself is not being challenged, the regulatory, trade and investment consequences of introducing nanotechnology can potentially lead to high NTBs, especially in the food-producing and processing sectors'. Further advancements in the area of genomics, as well as increasing pressure from consumers and/ or companies in relation to the traceability of agricultural products, are other areas of potential future tension. To the extent that bilateral and plurilateral FTAs can be used to mitigate such disputes, they should be.

Conclusion

Given the failure of the Doha Development Agenda to secure the further reduction of tariffs in the agricultural sector, or to overcome some of the complex extant issues in the SPS and TBT agreements, it is hardly surprising that OECD countries quickly found an alternative mechanism through which to pursue trade liberalisation. The fact that so many bilateral and regional FTAs have been concluded in recent years is testament to the fact that the gains must surely outweigh the significant transaction costs that so many simultaneous negotiations incur. Indeed, the capacity for these agreements to tackle the 'new trade agenda' issues that this volume examines—the expansion of services trade, the rise of TBTs and the shifting geopolitical sands in the international system of trade—has no doubt spurred the announcement of the Australia–EU FTA negotiations. However, as our analysis above illustrates, the potential for an Australia–EU FTA to deliver significant market access concessions in agriculture is limited; gains in relation to tariffs and quotas are likely to be sector specific and limited. Nevertheless, there are significant opportunities in the negotiations to overcome many of the NTBs that plague the relationship, in both the SPS and TBT domains.

The reasons lie in the fact that Europe and Australia are more similar than either would care to admit: both have strong regulatory regimes relating to biosafety and environmental sustainability and as a result both enjoy enviable reputations for clean and green agricultural sectors; both have strong institutional arrangements to ensure risk frameworks are enforced; and both would prefer to see a gradual return to the WTO for all matters trade. And with the rise of Asia and the Middle East as export markets, politicians and bureaucrats in Brussels and Canberra have been allowed to settle into a comfortable détente, in the knowledge that they now have more in common than ever before. These factors combined mean that a comprehensive and considered review of where regulatory coherence could be achieved in agriculture is both desirable and feasible. As the reforms of Australia's biosafety regime relating to pork demonstrated, the welfare gains that arise from removing TBTs can be enormous.

That said, there have been and remain profound differences in the way the EU and Australia reconcile public policy objectives with trade liberalisation. One area that is likely to prove particularly divisive in the negotiations is that of geographic indicators. Past FTAs have indicated that the EU has very little motivation to concede on geographic indicators, but Australian negotiators will need to be careful to ensure that tensions over geographic indicators don't scupper market access gains in other areas from being realised. In short, we are cautiously optimistic.

References

ABARES (Australian Bureau of Agricultural and Resource Economics and Sciences) (2014), *Agricultural Commodity Statistics* (ABARES: Canberra).

Beghin, John & Mark Melatos (2012), 'The trade and welfare impacts of Australian quarantine policies: The case of pigmeat', *World Economy*, 35(8): 1006–21. doi.org/10.1111/j.1467-9701.2012.01459.x.

Berden, Koen G., Joseph Francois, Martin Thelle, Paul Wymenga & Saara Tamminen (2009), *Non-Tariff Measures in EU–US Trade and Investment—An Economic Analysis* (ECORYS Nederland BV: Rotterdam). Available at trade.ec.europa.eu/doclib/docs/2009/december/tradoc_145613.pdf.

Bonciu, Florin & Marcel Moldoveanu (2014), 'The proliferation of free trade agreements in the post-Doha Round period: The position of the European Union', *Procedia Economics and Finance*, 8: 100–105. doi.org/10.1016/S2212-5671(14)00068-9.

Boza Martínez, Sofia (2013), 'Assessing the Impact of Sanitary, Phytosanitary and Technical Requirements on Food and Agricultural Trade: What Does Current Research Tell Us?', SECO / WTI Academic Cooperation Project Working Paper Series, no. 2013/02. Available at dx.doi.org/10.2139/ssrn.2614352.

Clarke, Andrew & Xiang Gao (2007), 'Bilateral free trade agreements: A comparative analysis of the Australia–United States FTA and the forthcoming Australia–China FTA', *UNSW Law Journal* 30(3): 842–54.

Costa, Catherine, Michelle Osborne, Xiao-guang. Zhang, Pierre Boulanger & Patrick Jomini (2009), *Modelling the Effects of the EU Common Agricultural Policy*, Staff Working Paper (Productivity Commission: Melbourne).

DFAT (Department of Foreign Affairs and Trade) (2015), 'Australia-European Union Free Trade Agreement'. Available at dfat.gov.au/trade/agreements/aeufta/Pages/aeufta.aspx, last accessed 2 December 2015.

DFAT (2017a), 'EU Economy Factsheet'. Available at dfat.gov.au/geo/europe/european-union/Pages/european-union.aspx.

DFAT (2017b), *Composition of Trade 2014* (DFAT: Canberra).

EC (European Commission) (2015), 'Sustainability Criteria'. Available at ec.europa.eu/energy/node/73, last accessed 7 December 2015.

Horn, Henrik, Petros C. Mavroidis & Erik N. Wijkstrom (2013), 'In the shadow of the DSU: Addressing specific trade concerns in the WTO SPS and TBT committees', *Journal of World Trade* 47(4): 729–60.

Hussey, Karen & Donald Kenyon (2011), 'Regulatory divergences: A barrier to trade and a potential source of trade disputes', *Australian Journal of International Affairs* 65(4): 381–93. doi.org/10.1080/1035 7718.2011.586668.

Irwin, Douglas A. (2015), *Free Trade under Fire*, 4th edition (Princeton University Press: New Jersey). doi.org/10.1515/9781400866182.

Kenyon, Donald & John Kunkel (2005), 'Australia and the European Union in the World Trade Organisation: Partners or adversaries?', *Australian Journal of International Affairs* 59(1): 55–69. doi.org/10.10 80/1035771042000332048.

Kenyon, Don & David Lee (2006), *The Struggle for Trade Liberalisation in Agriculture: Australia and the Cairns Group in the Uruguay Round* (Department of Foreign Affairs and Trade: Canberra).

Kerber, Wolfgang & Roger van den Bergh (2008), 'Mutual recognition revisited: Misunderstandings, inconsistencies, and a suggested reinterpretation', *KYKLOS* 61(3): 447–65. doi.org/10.1111/j.1467-6435.2008.00412.x.

Krever, Tor (2006), 'The US–Australia free trade agreement: The interface between partisan politics and national objectives', *Australian Journal of Political Science* 41(1): 51–69. doi.org/10.1080/10361140500507286.

Meyer, Timothy (2013), 'Energy subsidies and the World Trade Organization', *ASIL Insights* 17(22). Available at www.asil.org/insights/volume/17/issue/22/energy-subsidies-and-world-trade-organization.

MLA (Meat and Livestock Australia) (2015), 'Overseas markets – Europe and Russia'. Available at www.mla.com.au/Prices-markets/Overseas-markets/Europe-Russia?&session-id=af3d341e31b1449cbb 82d2de37174092, last accessed 10 December 2015.

Nathan Associates Inc (2013), 'Nontariff Barriers to Trade: Regional Agricultural Trade Environment (RATE) Summary. USAID Maximizing Agricultural Revenue through Knowledge, Enterprise Development and Trade (MARKET) Project', Submitted to USAID Regional Development Mission for Asia. Available at www.nathaninc.com/sites/default/files/Nontarriff_barriers.pdf.

Nicolaidis, Kalypso & Gregory Shaffer (2005), 'Transnational mutual recognition regimes: Governance without global government', *Law and Contemporary Problems* 68(3/4): 263–317.

OECD (Organisation for Economic Cooperation and Development) (2005), *Looking Beyond Tariffs- The Role of Non-Tariff Barriers in World Trade* (OECD Publishing: Paris). Available at www.oecd-ilibrary.org/trade/looking-beyond-tariffs_9789264014626-en, last accessed 2 December 2015.

OECD (2014), *Agricultural Policy Monitoring and Evaluation 2014: OECD Countries* (OECD Publishing: Paris). dx.doi.org/10.1787/agr_pol-2014-en.

Stephens, Philip (2016), 'US politics is closing the door on free trade', *The Financial Times*, 8 April. Available at next.ft.com/content/41fd9efa-fbee-11e5-b3f6-11d5706b613b, last accessed 8 April 2016.

Trachtman, Joel P. (2007), 'Embedding mutual recognition at the WTO', *Journal of European Public Policy* 14(5): 780–99. doi.org/10.1080/13501760701428373.

Viju, Crina & William A. Kerr (2011), 'Agriculture in the Canada-EU Economic and Trade Agreement', *International Journal: Canada's Journal of Global Policy Analysis* 66(3): 677–94. doi.org/10.1177/002070201106600310.

Woolcock, Stephen (2007), European Union policy towards Free Trade Agreements, *ECIPE Working Paper*, no. 03/2007. Available at ecipe.org/publications/european-union-policy-towards-free-trade-agreements/.

WTO (World Trade Organization) (2010), *Sanitary and Phytosanitary Measures*, The WTO Agreements Series (WTO: Switzerland). Available at www.wto.org/english/res_e/booksp_e/agrmntseries4_sps_e.pdf.

WTO (2013), *The Future of Trade: The Challenges of Convergence: Report of the Panel on Defining the Future of Trade* (WTO: Geneva). Available at www.wto.org/english/res_e/publications_e/future_of_trade_e.htm.

WTO (2014), 'Tariff Profiles'. Available at stat.wto.org/TariffProfile/WSDBTariffPFHome.aspx?Language=E, last accessed 13 September 2014.

7

Geographical Indications: An Assessment of EU Treaty Demands[1]

Hazel Moir

Introduction

Modern 'trade' treaties cover a wide range of market interventions and regulations. The five post-2006 Global Europe treaties are no exception.[2] As with US trade agreements they all include intellectual property (IP) regulations. IP regulations sit uneasily in a trade agreement as their purpose is to limit competition, not to increase it. The major benefits from trade agreements are through their impact on increasing competition.

The European Union (EU) and the United States of America (USA) failed to achieve their full IP agenda in the Uruguay Round. Undaunted, both have been pursuing their unmet IP goals through a series of bilateral and regional agreements, often with quite small trading partners. This chapter focuses on the issue that most distinguishes EU IP demands: geographical indications (GIs) for foodstuffs. GI demands are often

---

1   The discussion in the earlier sections of this chapter draws on two more detailed papers on geographical indications (Moir 2015a, 2015b).
2   The sixth—with Vietnam—was agreed on 2 December 2015.

referred to as a deal-breaker. All five post-Global Europe agreements include GI provisions, and it is unlikely that any EU agreement could proceed without at least some coverage of this area.

This chapter commences by reviewing the provisions on GIs in the Agreement on Trade-Related Aspects of Intellectual Property Rights (TRIPS), and then turns to how GIs have been implemented in the EU in the period since the Uruguay Round negotiations began. The discussion of the EU's experience allows a focus on the rationales that have been put forward for the GI intervention in the market. These rationales are critically assessed. This provides essential background to the final section of this chapter—evaluating the EU's GI demands in bilateral trade agreements, and Australia's potential responses.

TRIPS and GIs

GIs are about what things can be called. They are about *labelling, packaging and marketing*. Nothing in GI rules prevents any producer anywhere from using the techniques specified as being associated with the GI name. But they may not use the name to communicate the production techniques they have used.

GIs are collective marks signalling the region from which a product comes. The product characteristics *must* derive from the land and climate (the *'terroir'*). GIs originated in Europe and are currently available only for agricultural products.

TRIPS makes only modest provisions for GIs and provides substantial protection for trademark owners (Articles 22 to 24). Both from the perspective of the EU and major New World agricultural exporters, such as Australia, the TRIPS outcome was a compromise (Geuze 2009).

In TRIPS, the EU gained 'strong-form' GIs for wines and spirits. With strong-form GIs, no producer from outside the designated region may use the protected name, even with qualifiers. While an identical product may be produced, any reference to a protected name—for example, 'champagne-style wine, product of Australia'—is not allowed.

For all other products, TRIPS mandates only 'weak-form' GIs. Countries are free to determine the form GIs take. New World countries have generally used a trademark system of collective and/or certification marks. This allows producers from outside the named region to use labels such as 'Parmesan-style cheese, made in New Zealand'.

TRIPS has substantial 'grandfathering' safeguards[3]—even strong-form GIs do not have to be adopted. TRIPS safeguards generic names and existing trademarks, protecting the community and trademark owners from expropriation. Article 24 provides that those with existing trademarks, or having used a name continuously for at least 10 years, may continue to use those names, with no provisos, even if they are for wines or spirits.

Nonetheless, some countries have signed EU wine and spirit agreements, adopting strong-form GI privileges in exchange for improved access to EU wine and spirit markets. Australia was one of the first countries to sign a wine agreement with the EU, in 2004. The EU also has wine agreements with other New World countries.[4] The improved market access provisions of these agreements effectively compensated wine producers for their re-labelling and associated marketing costs. Because GI issues on wines have been largely settled through these agreements, this chapter concentrates on GIs for foodstuffs.

EU GI policy for foodstuffs

The EU framework for the protection of GIs for foodstuffs was established in 1992,[5] building on earlier systems in place in a few member countries. The system was revised in 2006[6] following a dispute brought against the EU by Australia and the USA to the World Trade Organization (WTO).[7]

---

3   A provision in which an old rule continues to apply to some existing situations while a new rule will apply to all future cases.

4   See ec.europa.eu/agriculture/wine/third-countries/index_en.htm.

5   Council Regulation (EEC) No. 2081/92 of 14 July 1992 (eur-lex.europa.eu/legal-content/EN/TXT/PDF/?uri=CELEX:31992R2081&from=EN).

6   Council Regulation (EC) No. 510/2006 of 20 March 2006 also incorporated some other changes, including dropping the requirement for a published list of generic names (see Profeta et al. 2009: 633) (europa.eu/legislation_summaries/internal_market/businesses/intellectual_property/l66044_en.htm).

7   WTO dispute DS290, EC – Trademarks and Geographical Indications (www.wto.org/english/tratop_e/dispu_e/cases_e/ds290_e.htm).

It was revised again in 2012.[8] The system identifies three separate types of designation: protected designation of origin (PDO), protected geographical indication (PGI), and traditional specialty guaranteed (TSG). TSGs are little used at present and are not further discussed in this chapter. They provide few difficulties for competition policy because production need not take place in the specified geographical area. Recently, the EU has begun to consider extending GIs to non-agricultural products.[9] This issue too is beyond the scope of this chapter, which looks only at GIs for agricultural products and foodstuffs.

While the privileges provided by PDOs and PGIs are identical—in neither case may a competitor from outside the designated region use the name, even with clear qualifiers—the requirements are very different. PDOs have strict production controls and the key ingredients must, in theory, be produced within the designated area.[10] In contrast, PGIs are far more flexible in terms of the sourcing of inputs, and seem to be able to have limited association with the designated region. Indeed, issues have been raised that this flexibility in the origin of materials for PGI products can make such labelling misleading for consumers (London Economics 2008: 86–91).

There have been a number of initiatives to promote the use of GIs within the EU,[11] and there have been impressive increases in the number of registered PDOs and PGIs; from 1993 to the end of 2012, PDOs

---

8   Regulation (EU) No. 1151/2012 of 21 November 2012 (eur-lex.europa.eu/legal-content/EN/TXT/PDF/?uri=CELEX:32012R1151&from=en) followed a rather poor-quality evaluation of the GI program, largely because of the absence of relevant data. The EU's Impact Assessment Board considered that the added value of the GI schemes had not been demonstrated (European Commission 2010a: 6).

9   The two EU studies are at trade.ec.europa.eu/doclib/docs/2011/may/tradoc_147926.pdf and ec.europa.eu/internal_market/indprop/docs/geo-indications/130322_geo-indications-non-agri-study_en.pdf. France has recently promulgated regulations for non-agricultural GIs (www.inta.org/INTABulletin/Pages/France_7015.aspx).

10   In practice, raw materials can come from a far wider area for PDOs registered before May 2004 (Calboli 2014).

11   A special fast-track registration system was initially used to encourage GI applications, but in 2003 this was abandoned in favour of financial incentives (Evans & Blakeney 2006: 584). Some member states provide direct financial and administrative assistance for producer groups to establish GIs (London Economics 2008: 118–19).

increased by 19 per cent and PGIs by 40 per cent (Figure 1).[12] The initial set of GIs, with 369 PDOs and 281 PGIs, were largely names transferred from national registers to the EU register.

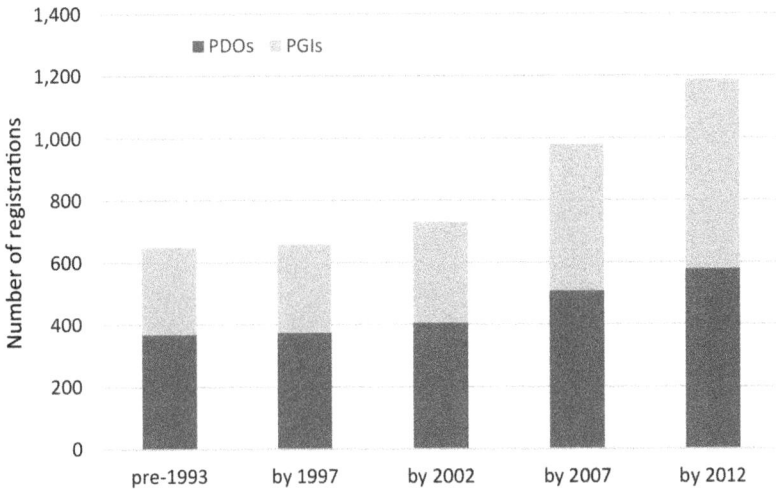

Figure 1. Growth in EU-registered GIs
Source: Author analysis from data from the DOOR database.

Of the 1,188 registrations filed by end 2012, 75 per cent (887) were owned by France, Greece, Italy, Portugal and Spain. These five countries had 87 per cent of initial PDO registrations and still have 85 per cent of such registrations. They had 75 per cent of initial PGI registrations, but this share had fallen to 64 per cent by the end of 2012.

London Economics (2008) has noted that the countries dominating the GI system have large agricultural sectors. Other relevant variables to benchmark the relative use of GIs are population and size of the total economy, variables that reflect aspects of consumer demand. These benchmarks put the dominant use of GIs by France, Italy and Spain into perspective. The three right-hand columns of Table 1 provide summary indicators of whether a country has more or fewer GIs than would be expected simply on the basis of population, gross domestic product (GDP) or agricultural value added shares.

---

12   Data are from the DOOR database (ec.europa.eu/agriculture/quality/door/list.html). Data were downloaded on 6 July 2015 and are analysed by application year (the point at which the decision to seek registration of a GI is first recorded). All applications from EU member states registered by 6 July 2015 are counted. Unless otherwise specified, data in all tables and figures are from this source.

Table 1. Percentage shares of GIs, GDP, population and agricultural value added

	Share of EU total (percentage)				Over or under-representation of GIs vis-à-vis indicator		
	GIs by 2012 (%)	Population, 2012 (%)	GDP (PPP)* 2012 (%)	Agricultural value added, 2000–07 (%)	Population (%)	GDP (%)	Agricultural value added (%)
Germany	6.8	16.0	20.0	10.6	0.4	0.3	0.6
France	18.1	13.1	14.0	18.3	1.4	1.3	1.0
United Kingdom	4.6	12.7	13.4	7.6	0.4	0.3	0.6
Italy	22.3	11.9	11.9	14.9	1.9	1.9	1.5
Spain	14.9	9.3	8.6	13.3	1.6	1.7	1.1
Greece	8.5	2.2	1.6	3.9	3.9	5.3	2.2
Portugal	11.0	2.1	1.5	2.0	5.2	7.1	5.6

* PPP = purchasing power parity

Sources: GI data from the DOOR database; GDP and population figures from knoema.com; agricultural value added figures (for 2000–07 in € millions) from London Economics 2008: 52.

On an agricultural value added basis, the proportion of GIs owned by France is what one would expect were GI ownership based solely on agricultural value added. Similarly, Spanish GI ownership is only 10 per cent higher than expected. But Italian GI ownership is 50 per cent greater than would be expected on the basis of the size of its agricultural sector, and 90 per cent higher than expected based on population or GDP share (Table 1).

The two countries that are truly over-represented in terms of GI ownership are Greece and Portugal. The proportion of GIs owned by Greece is more than twice what one would expect based on the size of the agricultural sector, more than five times as large with respect to GDP share and nearly four times as large based on population. Portugal's over-representation in terms of GI share is even more striking—between five and seven times larger than expected. In contrast, Germany and the United Kingdom are substantially under-represented in terms of the share of registered names.

What these data do not tell us is how important GI products are and to whom. There are few data on the number of producers involved in any registered GI.[13] There are few data on the value of output, and often output values are given without any context. Thus, we may be told how many millions of PDO output is sold, but not the proportion of total agricultural output or agricultural and food-processing output. Indeed, such data are available only for France and Spain. But even here we do not get a good denominator for the French data—while GI products are 6.3 per cent of total French agricultural output, many GI products are processed and we do not know what percentage they are of total French output from agriculture and food processing. For Spain, this figure is just 1 per cent.[14]

While much of the discussion on GIs implies that most GI producers are small operators, it is clear that in some product lines very large producers play an important role. Rangnekar, for example, points out that in a case study of Tuscan extra virgin olive oil less than 2 per cent of certified production was by small producers (Rangnekar 2004: 5).

---

13 London Economics (2008: 107) provides data for total producers involved in all registered names for only six countries, and some of these data are partial. The *proportion* of all producers/processors involved in GI products is available only for France and Italy.

14 London Economics 2008: 107–9. Although more data are available in a separate European Commission commissioned report, this study too avoids giving relevant comparators for most statistics (AND-International 2012). The one useful comparison figure is that PDO/PGI agricultural products and foodstuffs represented about 2 per cent of the total value of extra-EU food exports in 2010.

Rationales for the GI intervention

The EU regulations, introduced in 1992 and amended in 2006 and 2012, show clearly that GIs are an important element of EU agricultural policy, with the additional stated aim of reducing consumer confusion. This second aim, the basis for using an IP mechanism, requires interrogation. It is based on economic theories about information asymmetries, developed in respect of consumer durables.[15] But most food and drink purchases are regularly repeated events, and so differ substantially from durable goods. The frequency of food purchases means that consumers quickly overcome any initial information asymmetry. This is rarely noted in the GI literature.[16]

This leaves the sole consumer information asymmetry argument for GIs as being that high-end agricultural products are credence goods—that despite purchase and use, the consumer may still be misled as to quality attributes. This argument applies to situations where the quality of a GI product does not noticeably vary between the GI region and non-GI regions. The core of the EU argument on GIs is therefore the *presumption* that consumers are confused, even if they are not—even if the taste experience is identical, consumers will be confused if their cheese is labelled 'brie-style cheese, product of Australia'.

Given the failure of consumer confusion justifications to stand up to scrutiny, are there producer arguments for the GI intervention? GIs are similar to trademarks, though their associated privileges are much stronger and they cannot be individually owned or traded. The producer argument for trademarks is that producers are protected from counterfeiter trading on their reputation. But the strong-form GI privilege prevents clear labelling that advises consumers clearly of the origin of the goods. Further, in the EU the registered GI name is protected well beyond the class of goods to which a similar trademark would apply. This might be justifiable if it increased net welfare; that is, if the gains to these producers and previously 'confused' consumers were greater than the losses to other producers and consumers who are not shopping for high-end food products. This is an empirical matter.

---

15   For an excellent and brief summary of this literature, see OECD (2000, Annex 1).

16   See, for example, Bramley, Biénabe & Kirsten (2009). An important exception is Teuber (2011), who also provides a sound analysis of the economic literature to date.

There is surprisingly little empirical literature on GIs. The literature on willingness to pay shows variable outcomes except for one issue: only a very small share of consumers are willing to pay a price premium for a higher-quality product (Bramley, Biénabe & Kirsten 2009). This finding is reflected in the outcome of the 2008 EU GI evaluation—retailers report that GI products have little impact on their profitability as they constitute a very low proportion of goods sold (London Economics 2008: 147–50). The even sparser empirical literature on the economic impact of GIs shows that the impact of GIs on rural development is variable and contingent, as is the overall economic impact (Callois 2004; Zago & Pick 2004; Bramley, Biénabe & Kirsten 2009; Grote 2009; Teuber 2011).

The above analysis suggests that agricultural goals remain the sole justification for GIs. But the policy is implemented in the form of an IP right, and in the best traditions of IP policy, the implementing processes are all formalities and procedural matters. There are no economic criteria brought to bear on key issues such as how regions are defined, what proportion of a production chain is designated, or how the proposed GI will impact on competitors. European GI policy trumps competition policy, without any questions asked.

Case law on GIs shows that there are few, if any, competition controls on the registration of a GI name. The Parma ham case raises doubts as to the processes in place for defining the length of the production chain covered by a registered GI (Evans & Blakeney 2006). The Melton Mowbray pork pie case raises doubts as to the processes in place for defining designated regions (Gangjee 2006). And the feta case shows that GIs are allowed to override existing trademark rights without any compensation mechanisms (Gangjee 2007).[17] As GIs are defined as 'industrial property' they are excluded from the application of the EU treaty articles that prohibit quantitative restrictions on exports. These articles are fundamental to the creation of a single competitive European market. Either GIs should be recognised as agricultural policy instruments and removed from this exemption, or procedures should be introduced to minimise anti-competitive elements in GI registration processes.

The EU's approach contrasts sharply with Australia's processes for certification marks. The Australian Competition and Consumer Commission (ACCC) is required to examine any proposed certification

---

17   These cases are discussed in Moir (2015b: 14–18).

mark 'to ensure [the proposed rules] are not to the detriment of the public, or likely to raise any concerns relating to competition, unconscionable conduct, unfair practices, product safety and/or product information'.[18] Only after an application has passed ACCC scrutiny can it be registered as an Australian certification mark. To date, only foreign organisations have used Australia's certified mark system to register geographical names, though there are two pending domestic applications, one for the Mornington Peninsula and one for Hinchinbrook shire.[19] Clearly, overseas GI producers are using the system. Equally clearly, there is as yet little demand from Australian producers.

EU GI goals and recent trade treaty outcomes

The analysis of the EU's GI demands is based on a close reading of the EU's new generation economic agreements with Canada, Central America, Columbia/Peru, Korea and Singapore. The EU's principal goals in GI negotiations with other countries are *sui generis* register-based systems, strong-form protection for all GIs, and administrative enforcement.

Register-based systems

Two of the EU's post-Global Europe treaties appear to require *sui generis*[20] register-based systems. These are with Central America and Singapore.[21] Three have clauses specifying systems that sound like *sui generis* register-based systems. But the legal language used in treaties can mislead.

---

18   www.accc.gov.au/business/applying-for-exemptions/certification-trade-marks.

19   As at the end of 2015 there were 474 registered certified marks in Australia, of which 116 were exclusively for agricultural products and a further 47 for both agricultural and non-agricultural classes of goods. An additional 41 certified marks for agricultural products were pending. Excluding the 21 registered marks for wines, only 19 marks were geographic marks registered (12 from Italy, two each from India, Jamaica and the USA, and one from the United Kingdom).

20   That is, a special form of protection regime outside the existing frameworks, or a regime especially tailored to meet a certain need.

21   Singapore has passed legislation that will come into force when the Treaty with the EU commences (www.wongpartnership.com/index.php/files/download/1259). At present the Intellectual Property Office of Singapore (IPOS) advises that GIs can either be protected as GIs or under the Trade Marks Act (www.ipos.gov.sg/AboutIP/TypesofIPWhatisIntellectualProperty/Whatisageographicalindication.aspx). This parallels the EU, with regulations governing both GIs and Community Trade Marks (CTMs). For a useful discussion of the relative merits of EU GIs or EU CTMs see Evans 2010.

From the treaty text it sounds like Korea agreed to such a system,[22] but the Korean Intellectual Property Office website clearly states that in Korea GIs are registered under the trademark system as collective marks.[23] Canada also retains its trademark-based system for GIs. The EU–Andean treaty does not directly touch on this issue; it is far shorter and less prescriptive than the other four treaties.

Associated with a register-based system is the requirement for transparent processes including opposition and appeal procedures. Other associated elements in the treaties are all very process-oriented, a characteristic of most IP regulations. As such, they are ideally suited to delivery of GIs through a trademark system, itself usually register based. The EU's Korean and Singaporean agreements have the largest number of EU-specified elements in the agreed GI procedures.

All five treaties include procedures for adding new GI names, and all list names that are to be recognised as GIs in the other jurisdiction.[24] These lists are subject to examination and opposition procedures in each country and there is a process for ensuring that names that have passed these processes are protected as GIs.[25] In all cases, the lists of names are very much longer for the EU than for the other party, and the EU lists have expanded. In the agreement with Colombia/Peru the EU listed 34 foods; in the EU–Korea agreement they listed 60 foods; in the EU–Singapore agreement they listed 82 foods; and in the 2014 Comprehensive Economic and Trade Agreement (CETA) the EU listed 173 foods. In contrast, Colombia/Peru listed only three foods and two non-foods. As yet, there is no information on GIs that Singapore and Canada might list. Korea appears to be one country that might use GIs as much as the EU—they listed 60 foods.

The 2014 implementation report on the EU–Korea agreement notes that the GI Working Group met for the first time in October 2012. The Working Group had discussed but not yet adopted rules of

---

22 Article 10.18.6, ec.europa.eu/trade/policy/countries-and-regions/countries/south-korea/.

23 'In the Republic of Korea, geographical indications have been protected as a collective mark under the Trademark Act (Act No. 7290) since July 1, 2005' (www.kipo.go.kr/kpo/user.tdf?a=user.english.html.HtmlApp&c=930002&catmenu=ek04_01_01, dated 20 February 2013 and accessed 22 February 2015).

24 Though the documents available as at December 2015 do not yet show GI name lists for Singapore or Canada.

25 In general, the treaties specify that opposition and examination procedures for listed GIs have already been completed or will be completed by the time the treaties come into force. As at the end of 2015, no GIs listed in Global Europe treaties for partner countries appear on the DOOR register.

procedure. Clearly, the priority for the Working Group was the new GIs that the EU had already proposed. The implementation report (European Commission 2014: 8) advises that:

> The EU emphasised the interest that EU Member States attach to GIs and the importance of increasing the list by as many GIs as necessary. Korea also announced the intention of proposing Korean GIs to the said Annex.[26]

Strong-form protection

A second EU priority is to gain strong-form protection for all GIs. Strong-form privileges lead to clawback of names that are generic in some parts of the world. The EU has achieved strong-form protection for many non-wine foodstuffs in the agreements with Korea, Central America, Singapore and Canada. In the cases of Colombia and Peru, the agreement allows weak-form GIs for wines and spirits, but leaves the door open for the adoption of strong-form protection, including for foodstuffs. It also extends GI protection beyond agricultural products. The EU–Andean agreement also covers misleading packaging, advertising or other practices. The use of flags and other images to denote a specific country or region is considered by the EU to undermine GI privileges.

Canada has agreed to allow coexistence of EU GIs with pre-existing Canadian trademarks. The EU claims this as a strong precedential victory, as it '"establishes for the first time in a common law" country like Canada a deviation from the principle "first in time first in right"' (European Union 2014: 14–15). Canada has, however, grandfathered certain GI names, providing for perpetual rights for existing users of the names feta, asiago, gorgonzola, fontina and munster. New producers will also be able to use these names, but with qualifiers.[27] Canada has also specified that any new GI names cannot be the same as existing trademarks, so the agreed coexistence is very limited in scope.

---

26 See trade.ec.europa.eu/doclib/docs/2014/march/tradoc_152239.PDF. As at January 2016, this was the latest available information about the implementation of agreed GI policy in the EU–Korea agreement.

27 The agreement also contains similar protections for the names of three meat products (Article 7.6).

These privileges need to be assessed side-by-side with the agreed safeguards. Like TRIPS, all five new generation EU treaties include important safeguards.[28] All provide that a GI will not be registered if it will cause confusion with an existing reputed or well-known mark, at least partially protecting trademark owners from appropriation. Existing trademarks may continue under all five treaties.

Some of the treaties allow continued trading using a geographical name if that has been past practice (Singapore, Canada). Some allow refusal of a GI if the name is customary.[29] Generally there is some form of prohibition on the use of plant variety or animal breed names—sometimes limited to where this will cause confusion (Korea), or to new GIs (Canada).[30] All allow a person to use their own name to trade as long as this will not cause consumer confusion.

Administrative enforcement

The third EU GI priority is administrative enforcement—this shifts enforcement costs from individual rights-holders to the overseas taxpayer. This appears to have been achieved in both the EU–Korea and EU–Canada agreements, but the EU has claimed neither as a precedent-setting win.[31] But as the benefit of a GI goes to the producer, the rationale for overseas taxpayers to pay enforcement costs is unclear. With a trademark the benefit accrues to the producer and enforcement is a responsibility of the producer. Why should enforcement costs for GIs be shifted to either domestic or overseas taxpayers?

The analysis paper accompanying the explanatory memorandum provided to the European Parliament for the 2012 revision of the EU's GI regulation considers a number of options for reform. The most important option— one that would ease trade negotiations—is that of using Community

---

28   The EU treaties with the Andean and Central American countries are more general than the other three treaties, with far fewer operational details specified, and fewer safeguards spelled out.

29   The EU–Central America treaty even allows continued use of customary names for wines and spirits.

30   Oddly, the EU–Singapore agreement states that a conflict with the name of a plant variety or animal breed will *not* prevent a GI being registered (Article 11.22.8). This may well be a typographical error as the EU regulations on GIs prohibit a GI 'where it conflicts with a name of a plant variety or an animal breed and is likely to mislead the consumer as to the true origin of the product' (Article 6.2, EU Regulation No. 1151/2012 and Article 3.2 in the 1992 and 2006 regulations).

31   The CETA wording is ambiguous and may simply allow GI owners to use administrative processes to resolve disputes rather than requiring official authorities to enforce GI names (Article 7.4).

Trade Marks (CTMs).[32] Important reasons given for dismissing this option include complexity (i.e. trademark registration would be needed in each country), cost (of trademark registration and enforcing such trademarks) and the lower degree of privilege. In respect of the latter, the paper notes that CTMs would allow competitors to use the registered name 'provided he [sic] uses them in accordance with honest practices in industrial or commercial matters' (European Commission 2010a: 33). Essentially, the lower degree of privilege would mean that potentially infringing practices would not actually infringe if consumers were not misled and the indication was used honestly. New World countries find this position hard to understand and hard to accept.

Evaluating the EU's GI demands

It was the EU who alone pushed for the inclusion of GIs in TRIPS. The EU remains committed to the extension of strong-form GI protection globally. In the Doha Round negotiations, the EU linked the agenda of yet stronger GI rights to developing country demands for fair sharing of genetic resources and protection of traditional knowledge, potentially extending GIs to non-agricultural products. This has created two blocks, divided both on the GI issue and on recognition of genetic resources. As at 2009, 111 countries had *sui generis* GI systems and 56 had trademark systems (Giovannucci et al. 2009: 14).

There are reports that GIs are a deal-breaker for the EU in relation to preferential economic agreements. Given that the multilateral trade negotiations are stalled, it is as yet impossible to say whether this is a deal-breaker globally. Certainly the post-2006 EU trade agreements all include GIs, though in some cases GI privileges do not move much beyond TRIPS.

To date, Australia has refused absolutely to consider any extension of strong-form GIs beyond wines and spirits. Unless Australia is able to bring together interested parties and be more open to other options on the GI issue, there is little point in commencing trade negotiations with the EU.

---

32 The system for EU-wide trademarks only came into operation in 1988, just four years before the first EU GI regulation was issued. In complete contrast to the GI system, a nation can object to a CTM being registered if it is a word that is generic in that country, and this prevents the CTM being registered.

The door to a more accommodating position has been opened by the recent report for the Rural Industries Research and Development Corporation (van Caenegem, Drahos & Cleary 2015). Further, the actual GI changes to Canadian policy consequent on CETA appear modest. It would seem possible, on this basis, that Australia might begin a domestic consultation and reform process to identify a GI strategy that both suits Australian interests and meets minimum EU demands. Such work could usefully incorporate an evaluation of the value of certification marks for GI policy purposes and explore why there is so little domestic demand for GIs for foodstuffs. Any GI strategy should learn from and avoid the worst pitfalls of EU GI policy. There should be clear economic criteria used in defining GIs, and a process, such as that in place for certification marks, to ensure anti-competitive effects are minimised. Consideration should be given to excluding GIs from the IP exception to competition laws.

Another missing element in EU GI policy is compensation for losers. Indeed, EU GI policy eliminates the absolute safeguards that are part of its CTM policy.[33] Should a new GI policy lead to trademark expropriation, there needs to be a clear procedure for providing sufficient compensation to create new marketing images. Ideally, this should be provided by the GI winners. For New World wine and spirit producers, such compensation took the form of increased access to EU markets.

In designing a GI system, Australia might be mindful:

- of the value of retaining weak-form GIs—these provide for consumer recognition of known products while allowing reasonable competition among producers. Canada has been able to protect important generic names such as feta in its negotiations with the EU, and Australia might develop a shortlist of generic names that are important in our markets;
- of the need to protect trademark rights or provide compensation where these rights have to be surrendered. The compensation should be from the winning party to the party that will have to begin anew on its marketing and market positioning;
- of the effectiveness of certified trademarks in providing appropriate protection for regional producers; and

---

33   Under the CTM policy any member state can object to a proposed registration, including on grounds that the name has become common or generic in their state, and the CTM registration will then fail.

- GIs being a government-enforced privilege that allows the users to extract a higher price from their consumers. These privileges come at a cost to consumers and to some producers. It is not reasonable, therefore, for enforcement action (and costs) to be shifted from the privilege-holders to taxpayers.

References

AND-International (2012), Value of production of agricultural products and foodstuffs, wines, aromatised wines and spirits protected by a geographical indication (GI), Commissioned by the European Commission (tender no. AGRI-2011–EVAL–04). Available at ec.europa. eu/agriculture/external-studies/2012/value-gi/final-report_en.pdf.

Bramley, Cerkia, Estelle Biénabe, & Johann Kirsten (2009), 'The economics of geographical indications: Towards a conceptual framework for geographical indication research in developing countries', in WIPO (eds), *The Economics of Intellectual Property: Suggestions for Further Research in Developing Countries and Economies in Transition* (World Intellectual Property Organization: Geneva), 109–49.

Calboli, Irene (2014), '*In territorio veritas*: Bringing geographical coherence into the definition of geographical indications of origin under TRIPs', *The WIPO Journal* 6(1): 57–67.

Callois, Jean-Marc (2004), *Can Quality Labels Trigger Rural Development? A Microeconomic Model with Co-operation for the Production of a Differentiated Agricultural Good*, Working Paper No. 2004/6 (Centre d'Economie et Sociologie appliquées à l'Agriculture et aux Espaces Ruraux: Dijon).

European Commission (2010a), *Impact Assessment on Geographical Indications: Accompanying Document to the Proposal for a Regulation of the European Parliament and of the Council on Agricultural Product Quality Schemes*, Commission Staff Working Paper (European Commission: Brussels). Available at ec.europa.eu/agriculture/sites/ agriculture/files/quality/policy/quality-package-2010/ia-gi_en.pdf.

European Commission (2010b), *Summary Impact Assessment on Geographical Indications*, Commission Staff Working Paper, SEC(2010) 1525 Final (European Commission: Brussels). Available at ec.europa.eu/agriculture/sites/agriculture/files/quality/policy/quality-package-2010/ia-gi-summary_en.pdf.

European Commission (2014), *Annual Report on the Implementation of the EU-Korea Free Trade Agreement*, COM(2014) 109 Final (European Commission: Brussels). Available at trade.ec.europa.eu/doclib/docs/2014/march/tradoc_152239.PDF.

European Union (2014), 'CETA—Summary of the final negotiating results'. Available at trade.ec.europa.eu/doclib/docs/2014/december/tradoc_152982.pdf, last accessed 5 August 2015.

Evans, G.E. & M. Blakeney (2006), 'The protection of geographical indications after Doha: Quo vadis?', *Journal of International Economic Law* 9(3): 575–614. doi.org/10.1093/jiel/jgl016.

Gangjee, Dev (2006), 'Melton Mowbray and the GI pie in the sky: Exploring cartographies of protection', *Intellectual Property Quarterly* 3: 291–309.

Gangjee, Dev (2007), 'Say cheese! A sharper image of generic use through the lens of Feta', *European Intellectual Property Review* 29(5): 172–79.

Geuze, Matthijs (2009), 'The provisions on geographical indications in the TRIPS Agreement', *Estey Centre Journal of International Law and Trade Policy* 10(1): 50–64.

Giovannucci, Daniele, Tim Josling, William Kerr, Bernard O'Connor, and May T. Yeung (2009), *Guide to Geographical Indications: Linking Products and Their Origins* (International Trade Centre: Geneva). Available at www.intracen.org/itc/market-info-tools/geographical-indications/.

Grote, Ulrike (2009), 'Environmental labeling, protected geographical indications, and the interests of developing countries', *Estey Centre Journal of International Law and Trade Policy* 10(1): 94–110.

London Economics (2008), Evaluation of the CAP policy on protected designations of origin (PDO) and protected geographical indications (PGI): Final report (London Economics: London). Available at ec.europa.eu/agriculture/eval/reports/pdopgi/report_en.pdf.

Moir, Hazel V. J. (2015a), European Trade Treaties: Key Intellectual Property Demands, *ANU Centre for European Studies Briefing Paper Series*, 6(4) (Canberra: ANU Centre for European Studies). Available at politicsir.cass.anu.edu.au/research/publications/european-trade-treaties-key-intellectual-property-demands-1.

Moir, Hazel V. J. (2015b), 'Geographic Indications: heritage or terroir?', Paper presented at 10th Annual Conference of the EPIP Association (European Policy for Intellectual Property), Parallel Session 4B— Geographical Indications and Regions, 2–3 September 2015, University of Glasgow. doi.org/10.2139/ssrn.2656136.

OECD (2000), *Appellations of Origin and Geographical Indications in OECD Member Countries: Economic and Legal Implications*, COM/AGR/APM/TD/WP(2000)15/FINAL (OECD: Paris). Available at www.oecd.org/officialdocuments/publicdisplaydocument pdf/?cote=COM/AGR/APM/TD/WP%282000%2915/FINAL& doclanguage=En.

Profeta, Adriano, Richard Balling, Volker Schoene, and Alexander Wirsig (2009), 'The protection of origins for agricultural products and foods in Europe: Status quo, problems and policy recommendations for the Green Book', *The Journal of World Intellectual Property* 12(6): 622–48. doi.org/10.1111/j.1747-1796.2009.00380.x.

Rangnekar, Dwijen (2004), *The Socio-Economics of Geographical Indications: A Review of Empirical Evidence from Europe*, UNCTAD-ICTSD Issue Paper No. 8 (International Centre for Trade and Sustainable Development and United Nations Conference on Trade and Development: Geneva). Available at www.ictsd.org/sites/default/files/research/2008/07/a.pdf.

Teuber, Ramona (2011), 'Protecting Geographical Indications: Lessons learned from the Economic Literature', paper presented at European Association of Agricultural Economists, 2011 International Congress, 30 August–2 September 2011, Zurich, Switzerland.

van Caenegem, William, Peter Drahos, and Jen Cleary (2015), *Provenance of Australian Food Products: Is There a Place for Geographical Indications?*, RIRDC No. 15/060 (Rural Industries Research and Development Corporation: Canberra). Available at rirdc.infoservices.com.au/downloads/15-060.

Zago, Angelo M. and Daniel H. Pick (2004), 'Labeling policies in food markets: Private incentives, public intervention, and welfare effects', *Journal of Agricultural and Resource Economics* 29(1): 150–65.

8

Gains for Trade in Services in an EU–Australia Free Trade Agreement: A European Perspective

Pascal Kerneis

The European Union (EU) and Australia are like-minded partners who share many common concerns in today's international trade environment, such as the initiatives to further liberalise the trade of goods and services and advance the Trade in Services Agreement (TiSA) that is currently under discussion. This chapter will discuss the common interests and then assess the potential content of an EU–Australia free trade agreement (FTA) that may benefit companies operating in the services sectors. It will analyse the traditional elements of market access related to the trade in services, and also the key concerns for services companies that seek to maximise their returns on the basis of a modern trade agreement, particularly where the agreement may cover issues of investment, public procurement and regulatory cooperation.

Services in the EU–Australia trade relationship

It is essential to demonstrate the importance of trade in services between the EU and Australia, in particular since, for too long, the bilateral trade discussions have been dominated in the political arena by the issues of agricultural trade, notably in the context of the World Trade Organization (WTO). Currently, Australia and the EU maintain close economic relations. In 2013, Australia ranked as the 15th-largest trade in goods partner of the EU, while the EU was Australia's third-largest trading partner after China and Japan. Total bilateral trade in goods that year amounted to €42.3 billion (Eurostat 2015). Traditionally, Australia's exports to the EU have been dominated by minerals (fuels and mining products) and agricultural products, while the EU's exports to Australia are predominantly manufactured goods. But services have become an important and growing part of the EU–Australia trade relationship. In 2013, total trade in commercial services amounted to €27.0 billion and represented 39 per cent of the total bilateral trade (Eurostat 2015). This is a significant increase from a share of 26 per cent in 2000, as Figure 1 shows, and demonstrates that the bilateral trade of services has increased faster than the trade of goods. It is also higher than the 20 per cent average share of trade in services in 2014 global trade (WTO 2015: Tables A4 and A5), and underlines that trade in services now plays an important role in this bilateral trade relationship.

The EU and Australia conduct their trade and economic relations under multilateral agreements to which both are signatories, such as the General Agreement on Tariffs and Trade (GATT) and the General Agreement on Trade in Services (GATS). Both also cooperated in the Doha Round of multilateral discussions on various issues that impact on bilateral trade, including services trade. The Doha Round has not yet been completed, but it has offered an opportunity to build consensus between the EU and Australia and to establish a foundation for further discussions about bilateral trade. In addition, the EU–Australia Partnership Framework of October 2008 has relevance for the EU–Australia trade relations. Although most of its clauses do not relate to issues of trade, the framework expresses a commitment to further cooperation including on trade issues. It is most explicit about reconfirming the bilateral mutual recognition agreement (MRA), which was revised a year later. Although the scope of this agreement is largely limited to mutual recognition of testing procedures that apply to certain products traded bilaterally, it leaves open opportunities to expand areas of mutual recognition in the future.

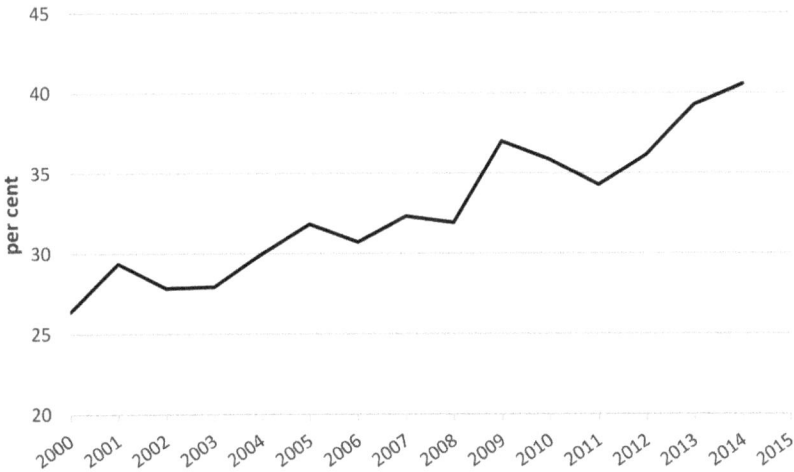

Figure 1. Share of services in the EU's total bilateral trade with Australia, 2000–13
Note: Total trade includes imports and exports.
Source: Calculated from Eurostat 2015.

The world economy is increasingly dependent on services. According to the WTO, international trade in services (excluding intra-EU trade) reached over US$3.7 trillion in 2014 (WTO 2015: Table 1.10). The value of international services trade has increased faster than the trade of goods during 2004–2014 (WTO 2015: Tables A4 and A5). Services provide essential components in all global supply chains and represent a growing share of the value added embodied in traded goods. Indeed, according to the WTO and the Organisation for Economic Co-operation and Development (OECD), global trade in services represents approximately one-quarter of global trade in terms of the value of final products, but nearly half of global trade in terms of the international trade in value added (TiVA) associated with these goods (OECD 2015).

This phenomenon is a consequence of the increasing internationalisation of supply chains, which not only involves semi-manufactured goods, but importantly also a wide range of services. In turn, this development is related to the rise of knowledge-based activities and the growing importance of intangible assets in all economies, together with the development of internet-based communications and applications, and the enhanced interplay between the services and the manufacturing and agricultural sectors. Major advances in computer networks, telecommunications, express delivery and air transportation have contributed this economic shift. These changes have provided the platform for raising countless small and large services companies from local establishments to international businesses. Together they are now creating millions of jobs worldwide.

The EU is by far the biggest exporter (€831 billion in 2015) and importer (€685 billion in 2015) of services in the world, with a significant positive trade balance of €146 billion (Eurostat 2017). The EU is also the world's biggest investor in services sectors, with nearly 60 per cent of its total outward foreign direct investment (FDI) directed at services sectors.[1]

Services components in the EU–Australia FTA: Building on TiSA

The EU–Australia FTA should be an ambitious and balanced, deep and comprehensive agreement. It should include provisions on all the key subjects: trade in goods and services, investment, intellectual property rights, public procurement, competition policy and dispute settlement. It should also contain provisions that allow for further consultation and cooperation with an eye to future regulatory reforms. Concerning the goods-related issues, the agreement should aim at removing tariffs with only few exceptions and should address non-tariff barriers and rules of origin issues. It should also look at possibilities to set up regulatory cooperation processes aiming at convergence of product standards and certification.

It will be important for the two negotiating parties to ensure that this FTA will deliver the best possible market openings for firms and establish rules that encourage firms to increase their bilateral activities. To that end, Australia will most likely look closely at the Comprehensive Economic and Trade Agreement (CETA), which the EU has negotiated with Canada in 2013, and which is currently the benchmark for FTAs with the EU. In turn, the EU will have a close look at the commitments Australia has made in its recent FTAs, including the content of the Australia–Korea

---

1   €3.5 trillion out of €6 trillion of extra-EU outward FDI stocks in 2014 (Eurostat 2017).

FTA, the Australia–Japan FTA and the China–Australia FTA, concluded in 2014, and the Trans-Pacific Partnership (TPP) in which Australia participates, concluded in October 2015. Despite the fact that the US decided to withdraw from TPP in January 2017, the text of this agreement remains a benchmark and an implementation of the agreement with the other 11 partners is still possible.

The rest of this chapter will address the possible content of an EU–Australia FTA as it applies to services companies. The chapter will discuss the market access pillar, including all modes of supply and access to the public procurement market, and then the regulatory cooperation and other rules that the agreement should include to be a really 'deep and comprehensive' FTA, as the EU prefers to label the 'new generation' or 'WTO-plus' FTAs it seeks to pursue.

To begin with, to have a real added value, the EU–Australia FTA should go beyond all aspects of the TiSA, which is currently still under negotiation. The fate of TiSA is uncertain after the cancellation of a TiSA Ministerial meeting on 9 November, one day after the US presidential elections. The ministerial was scheduled beginning of December 2016 to try to conclude the talks. However, parties agreed to keep all texts and offers as a starting point for any further resuming talks in due time. This chapter will therefore briefly discuss the TiSA and its components, before analysing in more detail the possible relevant elements of the bilateral agreement for services companies.

With the impasse in WTO negotiations in the Doha Round with respect to services, the idea of moving the trade agenda forward through a stand-alone agreement on trade in services was proposed in 2012. The process was an initiative of Australia and the United States of America (USA) and it was proposed to a group of countries that met in Geneva under the moniker the 'Really Good Friends of Services' (Vastine 2005). These countries took the initiative to craft the TiSA, which is currently being negotiated by 23 members of the WTO (or 50 countries in all, including all individual EU member countries).[2] Together, these countries account for approximately 70 per cent of world trade in services.

---

2   Australia, Canada, Chile, Taiwan, Colombia, Costa Rica, EU, Hong Kong, Iceland, Israel, Japan, Korea, Liechtenstein, Mauritius, Mexico, New Zealand, Norway, Pakistan, Panama, Peru, Switzerland, Turkey, USA.

Since April 2013, TiSA participants completed 21 negotiating rounds on the core text of the agreement. Relevant topics include domestic regulation, transparency, entry of business persons and sector-specific negotiations focusing on the new and enhanced trade rules for, *inter alia*, e-commerce and telecommunications, financial services, professional services, air and maritime transportation, information and communications technology (ICT) services and energy services. Regarding the market access pillar of the talks, participating countries have confirmed that they will use a 'hybrid approach', where commitments in the TiSA market access schedule will use a 'positive list' approach, meaning that only the services listed on the schedule are to be liberalised. In contrast, the national treatment commitments will be scheduled on a 'negative list' basis, which means that for any services where a party does not commit to apply full national treatment, a reservation must be listed (Broude & Moses 2016).

The countries participating in TiSA decided to start market access discussions by agreeing to table the highest level of commitment expressed by each party under its best (implemented) FTA at the date when negotiations started. However, the aim of TiSA is not to simply repackage existing commitments in completed FTAs, but to create genuine new opportunities through new market access commitments that go beyond current openness. For example, firms aim to provide the best customised service to their clients. An essential aspect of this commitment is 'talent mobility', the ability to move highly skilled services personnel rapidly to international locations where firms require their acumen (OECD 2008). The TiSA seeks to address this important issue of talent mobility to allow market access to service providers in a predictable and expedited way across all participating countries.

In almost every country the majority of the services sectors are subject to strict rules and regulations that govern their daily functioning, such as licensing and authorisation requirements, competition rules, product quality requirements and consumer protection. TiSA offers an opportunity to draft horizontal disciplinary provisions for the issues that are likely to become new challenges in the 21st century, such as cross-border data flows, forced localisation, and the conditions under which state-owned and state-sponsored enterprises compete in international commercial markets.

Going beyond TiSA: EU–Australia market access

Taking these elements into consideration and accepting that the EU–Australia FTA will want to go beyond the TiSA, what should be added? In short, to facilitate the bilateral trade of services further, the agreement should aim at facilitating cross-border trade in services and movement of people by removing remaining market access barriers of all kinds to the maximum degree possible. The question is, what degree is possible?

Many services are traded across borders as a consequence of service-providing firms investing in the establishment of a commercial presence in the form of a foreign subsidiary company. Ideally, the FTA should provide pre-establishment market access in all economic sectors, including in all services sectors. It should also offer post-establishment protection that sets clear protection for firms establishing foreign subsidiaries through FDI and puts into place a state-of-the-art investor–state dispute settlement (ISDS) mechanism (e.g. Bronkers 2015; Nottage 2015).

In addition, the FTA should also contain an intellectual property rights section that addresses the relevant issues related to copyright of software and patents of hardware used by services companies such as in ICT, energy, water and waste management, etc., as well as related to the transfer of data. The agreement should also ensure better mutual access to public procurement, including for services sectors in all public entities (Adlung & Mamdouh 2014: 203; Sheffler 2015). And the FTA should include chapters on rules, such as establishing a regulatory cooperation mechanism, provisions on competition and sustainable development, and a state-to-state dispute settlement body.

It must be remembered that the starting point of discussions about issues related to market access for services is the 1994 GATS, particularly Article XVI. An EU–Australia FTA would be a historical opportunity to substantially improve Australia's market access to the EU. Hence, the market access pillar in a bilateral FTA should be ambitious. If possible, it should correspond to a GATS + TiSA, or a GATS + TPP arrangement. To achieve this, the FTA should remove all caps on equity, although possibly with negotiated exceptions. It should also bind the practices that go beyond existing commitments (i.e. higher market access than in existing FTAs), and FTA negotiations should seriously consider removing existing barriers, so as to effectively create new market opportunities for service providers from both sides.

As in CETA, the FTA should include so-called 'standstill' and 'ratchet' clauses (Adlung & Mamdouh 2014: 200–1) to ensure that parties to the agreement will not revert to trade legislation and regulation that was in place at the time of the signing of the agreement, unless provided for in the agreement. This would warrant the spreading of trade liberalisation on a non-discriminatory basis after a party to the agreement has unilaterally decided to open up the market. The FTA should be particularly ambitious in the sectors of professional services, telecommunication services, postal and express services, and financial services that are often left behind in such negotiations.

The scheduling of market access and national treatment commitments should follow the negative list approach. A schedule of commitments undertaken under the negative list approach would simply provide a much better visibility for a company, clear indications of what it cannot do, and hence which sectors are open for investment and trade (Hufbauer et al. 2012: 5–7, 35–37). This would therefore be the preferred choice of the EU services industry.

In this approach, each country compiles a list of restrictions on the existing measures (also called Annex I) and another list of restrictions on future and sensitive measures (Annex II). Furthermore, most of the recent trade agreements that have used the negative list approach list the restrictions in financial services in a separate annex (Annex III), with the restrictions on existing measures in financial services in a Section A, and the restrictions on future measures in a Section B. Everything that is not listed is considered open and unrestricted. The listed restrictions are called 'non-conforming measures', as they do not conform to the norm of being liberalised.

The standstill and ratchet clauses, that prevent the signatories from implementing protectionist measures and that bind any measures implemented by the signatories that goes beyond what was agreed on in the agreement, are tools that ensure spreading of trade liberalisation on a non-discriminatory basis, once a party has unilaterally decided to open up the market. They fully respect the democratic control, and allow avoiding the necessity to renegotiate out-dated agreements.

There, the participation of all administrative levels of the signatories would be a *sine qua non* condition to the use of the negative list. Since this list is much more exhaustive than the positive list, it requires a clearer view of what can or cannot be done at Australian sub-federal level and at EU member state level. Not involving the signatories at sub-federal levels would result in a great lack of transparency and could lead to situations in which local entities could refuse to comply with the text of the agreement (Kukucha 2015).

Going beyond TiSA in all modes of EU–Australia services trade

A major issue with services trade is that services are heterogeneous and intangible. It is therefore relevant that the EU–Australia FTA ensures that the parties will take substantial commitments that apply to all possible modes in which services are supplied. GATS identifies four modes of international services trade (UNStats 2010: 3–5).

Firstly, a mode of delivery in which neither the supplier nor the client moves across borders, but stay in their respective countries. The EU and Australia will have to make particular significant efforts in taking new commitments in this type of cross-border trade of services. This mode includes shipping or other transport services. It also includes a growing range of services that are traded through electronic transmission; not only the e-commerce of goods, but also financial services and architectural services, etc. There is a huge undiscovered potential to increase the cross-border trade of such services through ICT advances. An EU–Australia FTA would be a real opportunity to go beyond what has been done so far in identifying and addressing the issues in this services delivery mode.

The commitments related to this category may also include transactions that require the consumer to move to the country of the supplier, which is the second mode of delivery identified under GATS. It typically includes tourism, travel, education and, increasingly, health services. Arguably, there are very few remaining barriers in this mode of supply, but the FTA will be an opportunity to identify those and resolve ways to remove them.

The third mode of delivery involves the establishment by the service company of a commercial presence in another country through FDI. This is a preferred route for services companies to undertake international activities. Companies using this delivery mode generally need to establish a physical presence in another country in order to be able to transact with clients on a face-to-face basis. Contrary to the production of goods, the services are often produced at the same time that they are delivered to the consumer. It is crucial, therefore, for many services companies to have direct contact with their customers. A wholly owned or joint-venture subsidiary, or possibly a branch that is controlled by headquarters, generally serves this purpose.

The FTA will have to ensure that the companies that would wish to use this mode of service delivery are able to establish a subsidiary in any legal form that they see fit for themselves, and also that firms are able to own and control their foreign establishments, which would involve the removal of all equity caps. A particular aspect of this mode of service delivery is that after access to the market is granted, the activity of the subsidiary company will, in the vast majority of cases, be accounted for in the GDP of the host country, rather than the host country's data on international services trade. The only data that are accounted for in international trade under this service delivery mode are the eventual profits that are repatriated to the parent firm in the home country. The initial inflow of capital to create a greenfield establishment or to acquire or merge into an existing local firm is calculated as an inflow of FDI. Nevertheless, the guarantee of market access needs to be provided for in international trade agreements.

With the 2007 Lisbon Treaty, the EU members granted new supranational competences to the EU in the area of FDI, starting in 2009 (Meunier 2014). Hence, FDI issues can now formally be negotiated with the EU in the context of FTAs. Nevertheless, there is limited precedent for negotiation partners in this respect. Pre-market access FDI by services companies was actually already part of the EU's competence through its responsibility for trade policy. And even before the Lisbon Treaty came into force, the EU had negotiated pre-market access commitments for FDI in non-services sectors. Particularly, the 2008 EU–CARIFORUM Economic Partnership Agreement included such commitments. However, it does not cover the protection of investments, post-market access. The FTAs that the EU negotiated before the Lisbon Treaty—such as those with South Korea, Columbia, Peru and six Central America nations—do not include an investment protection chapter at all. In other words, should companies from such countries encounter a problem of market access in the EU, the only way for them to seek redress is to hope that the government of their country of origin is willing to spark up the state-to-state dispute settlement specified in the relevant FTA.

On the other hand, the EU member states have now granted—through new or revised mandates—negotiating power to the EU on foreign investment protection in the context of the concluded agreements with Canada and Singapore, and for the ongoing negotiations with the Association of Southeast Asian Nations (ASEAN) countries (Vietnam, Malaysia, Philippines, Thailand), with India, and with USA and Japan. Consequently, there is little doubt that the EU–Australia FTA will include an investment protection chapter, covering pre-market access commitments as well as post-establishment protection.

In addition, before the Lisbon Treaty, FDI protection was the competence of the member states of the EU. The current EU member states themselves have concluded over 1,400 bilateral investment treaties (BITs) of high-level protection since the end of the 1950s (UNCTAD 2015). Australia has signed 21 BITs, including five with relatively new EU member states (Czech Republic, Hungary, Lithuania, Poland and Romania). Investment is about trust. Investment protection, including the right to defend it through a neutral dispute settlement, provides that trust. Most of these existing 1,400 BITs include an ISDS mechanism. There is a clear positive correlation between the volume of investment and the presence of an FTA and a BIT, and to a lesser extent of an ISDS mechanism (Berger et al. 2013). Investors take a decision to invest knowing that, should there be a problem with their investment, there is a means of redress. Hence, BITs and ISDS are an integral part of the trust that investors require in making investment decisions.

The competences between the EU and its member states in terms of FDI and BITs are still fluid (Burgstaller 2011). Nevertheless, it will be vital that discussions about the EU–Australia FTA include high-level investment protection with a neutral, binding and efficient ISDS mechanism. This mechanism is likely to include some reforms, notably new transparency obligations. The question of ISDS is of great sensitivity within the EU (Burgstaller 2014), and possibly Australia as well, and further public debate may have the advantage of making the process more accountable to the public. This may need to be taken into consideration in the process towards an FTA.

The fourth mode for supplying a service involves the temporary movement of natural persons associated with a services company from one country to another. It includes both the independent services suppliers and the employees of foreign services suppliers. Provisions facilitating the issue of the mobility of the services suppliers should have a key priority in the EU–Australia FTA. 'Talent mobility', or the mobility of highly skilled business personnel, is a key component of the daily activities of services companies (OECD 2008). Commitments to facilitate mobility and expedite business visas and work permits are a matter of high importance to internationally active service providers. The FTA should cover temporary movement only, rather than permanent migration.

Migration policy is not a full competence of the EU, and decisions for granting visas and work permits are taken at the member state level. However, some progress has been made within the EU among some countries with the establishment of the so-called Schengen Area in 1995, which now covers 26 European countries (including non-EU members, such as Switzerland). As a consequence of this agreement, movement of residents across these countries is now entirely free, although recent terror and refugee-related events are imposing challenges on the Schengen Area. However, this freedom does not apply to third countries and negotiations of GATS Mode Four commitments (movement of natural persons) are a first step to facilitate greater legal access for business travellers. The commitments taken by the EU under this service delivery mode are divided into the following four sub-sections: (i) movement of business visitors; (ii) movement of intra-corporate transferees/employees; (iii) movement of a services supplier to a client in the host country under the terms of a contract between two companies (contract service supplier); and (iv) movement of an independent services supplier in contract with a company in the host country.

Firstly, in terms of intra-company transferees across borders, the EU's 2014 Intra-Corporate Transferees Directive should be of great interest to Australia. Together with several directives that aim to simplify procedures, and also the so-called 2009 Blue-Card Directive, the 2014 Directive—despite imperfections (Schmitz 2015)—should offer new opportunities for an Australian services firm to dispatch its personnel to supply services across different EU member countries before returning home.

The conditions allowing for an intra-corporate transferee should be that the natural person must have worked within the company (juridical person) for at least one year, and that they are only transferred temporarily in the context of the provision of a service through a commercial presence in the territory. Entry and stay in the EU should be limited to a maximum of three years for managers and specialists (with some longer periods in some EU countries) and of one year for trainees. Intra-corporate transferees should not be submitted to any economic needs tests, limits or quotas.

Secondly, the conditions allowing for contract service suppliers into the EU must be that the person is employed by a company (juridical person) that has no commercial presence in the EU; that the company has obtained a service contract for a maximum period of 12 months from a final consumer; that the person has worked for the company for at least one year before the contract; and that the person possesses a university degree or the required technical and professional qualifications, and has at least three years of professional experience in the sector. Where the degree or qualification has been obtained in a third country, an EU member state may evaluate whether this is equivalent to a university degree required in that member state.

Replicating GATS, the EU has allowed professional service suppliers from several partner countries to be contracted for transactions on a bilateral basis.

These 'contract service suppliers' are restricted to legal services, accounting and bookkeeping, taxation advisory services, architectural services, urban planning, engineering services, integrated engineering services, computer and related services, research and development services, advertising, management consulting services, services related to management services, technical testing and analysis services, related and technical consulting services, maintenance and repair of equipment in after sales of after-lease services contracts, translation services, construction services, site investigation work, higher education services, environmental services, travel agencies and tour operator services, entertainment services, and services related to the sale of equipment or to the assignment of a patent.

Of course, these sectors are the result of bilateral negotiations, and might either be extended or restricted, depending on the reciprocity that will be granted by the partner country to EU service providers. Commitments might also be subject to the application of a numerical ceiling (i.e. a minimum quota, but without a fixed cap) that will be determined during the negotiations.

Going beyond TiSA: EU–Australia public procurement

The FTA should also provide comprehensive market access to public procurement of services, with low thresholds and substantive coverage of all public institutions and entities, committing the partners to remove any discrimination in the tender process by any EU or Australian firms. It is of crucial importance to increase access for services companies to all public entities that use public procurement processes. This is obviously true for construction and construction-related professional services, such as architectural and engineering services, and urban planning. But on a daily basis all public administrations and entities also purchase telecommunications and ICT services, insurance and banking services, transport and logistic services, cleaning and catering services, legal and accounting services, and so on.

The FTA negotiations could generate considerable gains in public procurement, given that Australia is only an observer of the international Agreement on Government Procurement (GPA), not a signatory. It is currently negotiating its accession to the GPA, and it is not clear when this process will come to a conclusion. It must be emphasised, however, that this accession should not be seen as the end of the road for Australian FTA negotiators, because their EU counterparts are likely to insist on commitments beyond the GPA from Australia.

Australia is a federal state composed of sub-federal entities. Although this is likely to be a 'balancing act' (Sheffler 2015), negotiators should ensure that all the provisions apply not only at the federal level, but also to the sub-federal levels (states and territories).

The EU public procurement directives have, over the years, opened up the public procurement markets across EU member states, and have established transparency and process rules that opened up public procurement in the EU. The EU is the GPA party that has the most significant package of commitments, but it has also kept some domains exclusively reserved to EU member states or to partners of recent FTAs who agreed to open their markets beyond the GPA. This has been the case for Canada (Kukucha 2015), and it could therefore also be the case for Australia.

For example, the EU has not just opened up 'government' procurement only, but has opened up 'public' procurement more generally. This includes all public entities that are using procurement processes for their daily operations—from provinces, counties and municipalities to public schools, universities and hospitals. This is clearly an issue that will be put forward in the EU–Australia negotiations. Some aspects may then already be covered by Australia's GPA commitments. Nevertheless, the added value of the FTA could therefore be the reduction of the thresholds at which companies from either trade partner will be allowed to participate in tender processes of public entities in general.

As a minimum commitment, the EU will likely require Australia to allow upfront that all European companies already established in Australia and hence incorporated as an Australian enterprise should be treated as domestic companies and granted an automatic right to participate in tender calls of all Australian public entities. This is a proposal that the EU has also carried into the ongoing TiSA negotiations.

Going beyond TiSA: Regulatory disciplinary arrangements and other rules

To be effectively a deep and comprehensive FTA that embraces all new elements of 21st-century trade deals, the EU–Australia FTA would have to go beyond the traditional market access commitments. For example, beyond the traditional commitments on public procurement, as mentioned. But to become an agreement that sets a really new benchmark for others to consider, the EU–Australia FTA will also have to deal with beyond-the-border issues. Here we will not discuss the provisions that are likely to tackle labour and environmental rules in the sustainable development chapter of the FTA, although labour provisions will also have an impact on services companies, which are together by far the biggest employers in the EU and in Australia. Instead, we will analyse the obligations that both parties will have in relation to discrepancies in domestic regulation, as well as other 'horizontal' rules such as cross-border data flows.

The FTA should include a strong horizontal chapter with disciplinary provisions for domestic regulation. This chapter should establish obligations that go beyond the rules that could be adopted in the context of the WTO's post-Bali 2014 work programme, or in the TiSA agreement, which will essentially establish basic rules for better transparency in licensing and qualification procedures. Such a chapter of the FTA should be divided into two sections: one on regulatory coherence and one on regulatory cooperation. A concrete example might be envisaged in the area of mutual recognition of qualifications of some professional services (Kerneis & Prentice 2011).

Principles such as regulatory transparency, prior consultation with stakeholders before adoption of new or revised rules, impartiality and due process with regard to licensing and qualification requirements and procedures, and a right of appeal are already normal practice in Australian and EU jurisdictions and are part of most of their respective recent bilateral trade agreements. These regulatory principles and practices should be applied systematically in the FTA at all levels of the market regulation, to help limit the degrees of regulatory divergence in the future.

The relevant chapter should therefore include an impact assessment mechanism. Both the EU and Australia already use this classical 'better governance' principle at home (Dunlop & Radaelli 2015; Kupiec 2015). Before adopting a new regulation or revising an existing legislation, the relevant regulatory body must conduct an impact assessment study of the new proposed rules to evaluate their potential impact on the targeted market, on the economy in general, on labour and the environment, and on the public budget.

In 2014 the EU started a process to revise its own rules so as to make them more efficient, suggesting that impact assessments should be made not only at the beginning of the drafting process, but also at the end of the legislative process, since the proposal might have changed in the meantime. It is likely that the EU will propose similar processes for inclusion in the EU–Australia FTA to establish the potential and actual impact of regulatory activities on bilateral trade. The purpose will be to establish a mechanism for information exchange between regulating agencies in sectors in order to increase transparency and inform possible changes to achieve better regulatory coherence. When implemented, the process should, for instance, provide full transparency about the licensing requirements and procedures, particularly the objectives of the regulator, obligation proportionate to the goal, least burdensome administrative costs as possible, short and predefined delays, right of appeal, etc.

Closer regulatory cooperation could be important to progressively achieve a more integrated international marketplace as well as to ensure that both trade partners together promote the development of international regulations applicable to all economic sectors. Changes towards greater regulatory coherence is a necessary first step, but the ultimate goal will be the reduction of unnecessary costs associated with regulatory differences by promoting greater compatibility through equivalence, mutual recognition or other agreed means. The outcome would be avoiding the cost of double licensing, double certification, double qualification procedures, etc.

Apart from accommodating the principles in the FTA, implementation would require sector-specific regulators of both trade partners to meet with their counterparts and exchange views on the respective objectives and methods of regulation. This may facilitate in some instances the identification of procedures that instil mutual trust and provide a basis for the authorisation of equivalence or the mutual recognition of the authorisation process of the trade partner.

To allow such a result, the horizontal regulatory cooperation chapter in the EU–Australia FTA could establish a mechanism whereby the regulators would agree to meet and exchange. The regulators will remain independent. They will not be subject to any obligations as a result. It may be appropriate for such a chapter not to be subjected to the dispute settlement system in the FTA, but to impose an obligation of cooperation on the regulators in case an issue of mutual interest is identified. The regulators could establish an annual or pluri-annual program, report on the progress of their discussions, and provide explanatory notes. In this way, the chapter will establish a living process that would put into place a regulatory cooperation mechanism on a long-term basis with the aim of achieving regulatory compatibility.

The FTA could also include sector-specific disciplinary provisions that could be included either in the sector-specific chapters of the FTA, such as telecommunication services or financial services, or in sector-specific annexes attached to the horizontal regulatory cooperation chapter.

All specificities should indeed be taken into consideration; the regulators themselves are better positioned to set up specific arrangements as they would see fit for their own sector.

One example where regulatory cooperation could lead to concrete results is in the domain of professional services (Kerneis & Prentice 2011). Even full market access and national treatment commitments in the FTA in all areas of professional services—including in allowing temporary movement of professionals in regulated professions, such as architects, lawyers, engineers, accountants and auditors—will not result in substantial increases in bilateral trade if service providers are forced to re-qualify before being able to provide services across borders.

The EU–Australia FTA, through regulatory cooperation provisions, could put in place a mechanism encouraging and enabling the regulators of these sectors to achieve—when there is a mutual demand from the professional bodies—mutual recognition agreements (MRAs) in professional qualifications in an EU–Australia FTA. They could, for instance, follow the example set in the EU–Canada CETA. Research shows that mutual recognition in the 2005 Services Directive enhanced services trade in the EU (Nordås 2016). A similar effect may be possible in the EU–Australia context. While the EU Treaty gives full competence to EU institutions on all external aspects of the internal market, including on professional qualifications, the EU still needs to find a way to reconcile its authorities in the areas of professional services (shared by the DG GROW, relevant member state ministries, and professional bodies), and of the international trade (shared by the DG TRADE, the Trade Policy Committee comprising member state trade representatives, and the European Parliament).[3]

For many years, the private sector in the EU was expected to work on the details of mutual recognition in professional services via 'profession to profession' agreements, which would then be examined by the relevant regulatory institutions of two trading partners, before becoming an annex to a binding international treaty. But this was not that easy, and some MRAs finalised by private sector organisations in the areas of architecture services were never implemented due to the lack of coordination across all involved parties.

---

3   DG GROW is the Directorate-General for Internal Market, Industry, Entrepreneurship and Small and Medium-sized Enterprises of the European Commission; DG TRADE is the Directorate-General for Trade of the European Commission.

With the framework agreement that is part of CETA, the European Commission and Canada have found a way forward. It describes the modalities of how MRAs on sector-specific professional qualifications— once concluded by the private sector together with the 'licensing bodies'— will finally be transformed into the binding international treaty, i.e. CETA (Sosnow, Kirby & Stephenson 2014: 255). All the competent authorities in the member states and the provinces have been involved in reaching this solution.

Thus, the framework agreement is an enabling tool containing guidelines for the services sectors that ensure legal security to the agreement, if— and only if—the professional services sectors want to conclude an MRA. Even though CETA is not yet in force, the associations of architects have already started to work on an MRA. This model reveals quality and efficiency and it could be followed in the EU–Australia negotiations. It is, however, important to emphasise that such a model can only be relevant if all administrative levels of the signatories—that is to say the EU member states and the Australian states and territories—are involved.

Finally, the FTA should include other disciplinary provisions that are of cross-sectoral nature, but that will have a direct impact on the services companies. These rules should reflect what is already under consideration in other trade agreements, such as the TPP or the TTIP, as well as possibly the TiSA, since they should contribute to establishing international standards.

Although cross-border commercial data flows are a very sensitive subject in the EU, they are the real backbone of the digital economy, and important to sustaining growth of output and employment in all sectors of the economy, including small and medium-size enterprises (Meltzer 2015). The EU–Australia FTA will have to include rules on cross-border data flows. The commitments taken on this issue should be applied across all services sectors, including financial services. Any exceptions to these provisions would have to be limited to legitimate public policy objectives and only in full compliance with the provisions of GATS covering data privacy (GATS Article XIV). With the objective of enhancing trust of users and certainty of companies, and thus trade in goods and services, it is essential that firms comply with data protection and security rules in force in the country of residence of the data subjects.

Nevertheless, the FTA should seek to ensure that cross-border data flows are not limited by a requirement to establish a local presence; with only few mutually agreed and well-justified exceptions. The parties should allow cross-border data flows without the requirement of locally based servers. The obligation to use local infrastructure or to establish a local presence should not be required as a condition for supplying data services. Preferential treatment to national suppliers should be prohibited in the use of local infrastructure, national spectrum, or orbital resources. Finally, the EU and Australia should ensure that local infrastructure used to convey signals on electronic communications networks is made available to services suppliers under fully non-discriminatory terms and conditions.

Lastly, the agreement should look at stating specific rules to ensure that the competition legislation also applies to state-owned and state-sponsored enterprises that compete in commercial markets. These rules could be part of the provisions in the competition chapter of the agreement. Consideration could be given to the EU regime on state aid. It imposes obligations of transparency on state-owned companies in EU member countries. It also ensures that the companies have transparent accounting rules, and it prohibits any cross-subsidisation transfers between different departments of a state-owned firm.

Conclusion

Services are an important and growing part of bilateral EU–Australia trade flows; they now account for close to 40 per cent of total trade flows between Australia and the EU, significantly higher than the 1990s, and higher also than the 20 per cent share of services trade in global trade flows. Against this background, both the EU and Australia can be expected to commence FTA negotiations with high ambitions on both market access and regulatory cooperation. The starting point for FTA negotiations on services would have four elements: (a) the 1994 GATS, supplemented by the current TiSA negotiations under WTO auspices in which both the EU and Australia are active participants; (b) the plurilateral GPA on government procurement within the WTO, which Australia is currently negotiating access to; (c) the EU–Canada CETA, which is currently considered the trade liberalisation benchmark for an FTA with the EU; and (d) the Trans-Pacific Partnership (TPP), which was signed in Auckland in February 2016 and to which Australia is a party.

An ambitious FTA outcome on services between Australia and the EU would go beyond TiSA by providing pre-establishment access for investment capital in all sectors without restriction, and post-establishment investment protection through an ISDS mechanism. An ambitious EU–Australia FTA should also go beyond the GPA and CETA by opening up access to public procurement tenders and contracts issued by sub-federal and regional governments and by removing all equity caps in inwards investment.

Strong regulatory cooperation powers and the pursuit of greater regulatory coherence through mutual recognition, and the recognition of differing certification requirements of equivalent intent in relation to services, should also be an important feature of an EU–Australia FTA. MRAs on professional qualifications of, for example, architects, lawyers, engineers, accountants and auditors could be a significant trade-creating outcome of such cooperation. The recent EU–Canada CETA has broken new ground in this field.

Finally, an ambitious FTA between the EU and Australia should be one that encompasses two key issues. First, market access and national treatment commitments are to be taken on the basis of a negative listing, rather than a positive listing. Such an approach provides for all services sectors to be liberalised other than those reserved to an 'exceptions' list. A negative-listing approach to commitments provides for greater transparency and is more trade creating. Second, liberalisation commitments should be taken on all the modes through which international services are traded internationally, i.e. cross-border trade in services, commercial presence abroad through FDI, and the movement of natural persons.

References

Adlung, Rudolf & Hamid Mamdouh (2014), 'How to design trade agreements in services: Top down or bottom-up?', *Journal of World Trade* 48(2): 191–218.

Berger, Axel, Matthias Busse, Peter Nunnenkamp & Martin Roy (2013), 'Do trade and investment agreements lead to more FDI? Accounting for key provisions inside the black box', *International Economics and Economic Policy* 10(2): 247–75. doi.org/10.1007/s10368-012-0207-6.

Bronckers, Marco (2015), 'Is Investor–State Dispute Settlement (ISDS) superior to litigation before domestic courts? An EU view on bilateral trade agreements', *Journal of International Economic Law* 18(3): 655–77. doi.org/10.1093/jiel/jgv035.

Broude, Tomer & Shai Moses (2016), 'The behavioral dynamics of positive and negative listing in services trade liberalization: A look at the Trade in Services Agreement (TiSA) negotiations', in Pierre Sauvé & Martin Roy (eds), *Research Handbook on Trade in Services* (Edward Elgar: London), 385–411.

Burgstaller, Markus (2011), 'The future of bilateral investment treaties of EU Member States', in Marc Bungenberg, Joern Griebel & Steffen Hindelang (eds), *International Investment Law and EU Law* (Springer: Berlin), 55–77. doi.org/10.1007/978-3-642-14855-2_4.

Burgstaller, Markus (2014), 'Dispute settlement in EU international investment agreements with third states: Three salient problems', *Journal of World Investment & Trade* 15(3–4): 551–69. doi.org/10.1163/22119000-01504010.

Dunlop, Claire A. & Claudio M. Radaelli (2015), 'Impact assessment in the European Union: Lessons from a research project', *European Journal of Risk Regulation* 6(1): 27–34.

Eurostat (2015), Eurostat online database. Available at ec.europa.eu/eurostat/data/database.

Hufbauer, Gary Clyde, J. Bradford Jensen & Sherry Stephenson with Julia Muir & Martin Vieiro. (2012), *Framework for the International Services Agreement*, Policy Brief No. PB12–10 (Peterson Institute for International Economics: Washington, DC).

Kerneis, Pascal & Joshua Prentice (2011), 'The European Union as a market for professional services', *Australian Journal of International Affairs* 65(4): 436–53. doi.org/10.1080/10357718.2011.585224.

Kukucha, Christopher J. (2015), 'Federalism matters: Evaluating the impact of sub-federal governments in Canadian and American foreign trade policy', *Canadian Foreign Policy Journal* 21(3): 224–37. doi.org/10.1080/11926422.2015.1074926.

Kupiec, Tomasz (2015), 'Regulatory Impact Analysis practice in New Zealand in the light of models of evaluation use', *Management and Business Administration* 23(2): 109–28.

Meltzer, Joshua Paul (2015), 'The internet, cross-border data flows and international trade', *Asia & the Pacific Policy Studies* 2(1): 90–102. doi.org/10.1002/app5.60.

Meunier, Sophie (2014), *Integration by Stealth: How the European Union Gained Competence over Foreign Direct Investment*, EUI Working Paper No. RSCAS 2014/66 (Robert Schuman Centre for Advanced Studies, European University Institute: Florence), December.

Nordås, Hildegunn Kyvik (2016), 'Does mutual recognition of qualifications stimulate services trade? The case of the European Union', *Applied Economics* 48(20): 1852–65.

Nottage, Luke (2015), 'The evolution of foreign investment regulation, treaties and investor-state arbitration in Australia', *New Zealand Business Law Quarterly* 21(3): 266–76. doi.org/10.2139/ssrn.2685941.

OECD (Organisation of Economic Cooperation and Development) (2008), *The Global Competition for Talent: Mobility of the Highly Skilled* (OECD: Paris).

OECD (2015), Trade in Value Added (TiVA)—October 2015 database. Available at stats.oecd.org/.

Schmitz, Jan (2015), 'The temporary movement of natural persons in the context of trade in services: EU Trade Policy under Mode 4 (WTO/ GATS)', in Marion Panizzon, Gottfried Zürcher & Elisa Fornalé (eds), *The Palgrave Handbook of International Labour Migration: Law and Policy Perspectives* (Palgrave Macmillan: New York), 382–402. doi.org/10.1057/9781137352217_16.

Sheffler, Scott (2015), 'A balancing act: State participation in Free Trade Agreements with 'sub-central' procurement obligations', *Public Contract Law Journal* 44(4): 713–47.

Sosnow, Clifford, Peter Kirby & Sean Stephenson (2014), 'The Canada– European Comprehensive Free Trade Agreement and the mining sector: Key issues and opportunities', *Global Trade and Customs Journal* 9(6): 253–59.

UNCTAD (2015), International Investor Agreement database (November). Available at investmentpolicyhub.unctad.org/IIA.

UNStats (2010), *Manual on Statistics of International Trade in Services 2010 (MSITS 2010)* (United Nations Statistics Division: New York).

Vastine, J. Robert (2005), 'Services negotiations in the Doha Round: Promise and reality', *Global Economy Journal* 5(4): 1–22. doi.org/ 10.2202/1524-5861.1146.

WTO (World Trade Organization) (2015), *International Trade Statistics 2015* (World Trade Organization: Geneva). Available at www.wto.org/ english/res_e/statis_e/its2015_e/its15_world_trade_dev_e.htm.

9

'Mutual Evaluation': A New Policy Tool for Dealing with 'Behind the Borders' Barriers

Anne McNaughton and Jacqueline Lo

Introduction

Continued economic integration increasingly reveals measures behind borders that may or may not be non-tariff barriers. These measures may be the result of differing policy imperatives or lack of regulatory equivalence. The principle of mutual recognition, first created by the Court of Justice of the European Union, was a response to dealing with such measures. In some instances, the measures under challenge were held incompatible with EU law; in other instances, although incompatible with EU law, the measures were permitted under one of the accepted derogations under the treaty or as a result of EU case law. The principle was quickly taken up in EU legislation, becoming a centrepiece for the European Commission's approach to continued economic integration in the EU.

However, as economic integration proceeded, the measures challenged as 'behind the borders' barriers to trade were increasingly associated with areas in which the member states retained significant legislative competence and around which there were greater national sensitivities. This was highlighted in the controversy around the promulgation of the 2006 Services Directive. The original draft directive proposed that service providers be regulated only in accordance with their country of origin (the so-called country of origin principle set out in Article 16 of that document) without any intervention or veto from the host state. This was met with great resistance with many in the 'older' member states fearful they would be inundated by service providers who were governed by unsatisfactory regulatory requirements in their country of origin. Such fears, however unrealistic or unreasonable, almost caused the proposed Directive to founder. The version of the Directive that finally entered into force in 2006 contained a milder version of the concept of mutual recognition—what has been described elsewhere as a form of 'managed mutual recognition' (Nicolaïdis 2001).

What lay at the heart of this resistance to the application of the country of origin principle (mutual recognition in its strongest form) was a lack of trust between member states; a lack of trust that the regulatory framework, particularly in the newer member states, was sufficiently rigorous to ensure that consumer interests in host states would be at least as well protected as they were by the host state regulatory environment. There was and is no empirical evidence to suggest that the concerns were well-founded, nor that the Directive in its final form would increase or reduce transaction costs. The Directive was an example of politics being the art of the possible. What it also introduced, however, was a novel policy tool for dealing with this lack of trust: the process of mutual evaluation. That process and its relationship with the principle of mutual recognition is the focus of this chapter.

Origins of the concept of mutual recognition in the EU

Mutual recognition was expressly referred to in the original European Economic Community Treaty (EECT) in the title on the free movement of persons and services. Article 57 of the EECT required the member states to adopt directives 'for the mutual recognition of diplomas, certificates and other evidence of formal qualifications'. However, the treaty was silent on mutual recognition in relation to the production and marketing of goods. It was not until the 1970s that the concept of mutual recognition was developed and applied in that context and, then, it was as a result of the jurisprudence of the European Court of Justice. The first relevant decision concerned the importation of Scotch whisky from France to Germany.[1] This decision was a preliminary ruling of the court on the interpretation of Community (now EU) law. Before dealing with the decisions themselves, it is therefore necessary to speak briefly about this aspect of the court's jurisdiction.

In the Treaty of Rome, the member states had committed themselves to creating a common market for the purpose, among other things, of enhancing the welfare and standard of living of their citizens. The treaty provided for the member states to develop Community measures to that end. However, at the time, the voting procedure for such measures required unanimity. This—combined with a period of political paralysis in the late 1960s as a result of France's resistance to measures it perceived to be harmful to its national interest[2]—resulted in a failure on the part of the member states to act to bring about the common market. In the face of the member states' inaction, the European Court of Justice, in effect, took the lead in pushing forward the integrative process to which the member states had committed themselves in the Treaty of Rome.

In 1962, no doubt concerned that the member states (and their Community institutions) could not be relied upon alone to drive that process, the court had established a doctrine of Community law: the doctrine of direct effect. According to this doctrine, if certain criteria were satisfied, a person or economic agent of a member state could rely directly before their own national courts on provisions of Community law to protect themselves against domestic laws of their state that were incompatible with the Community measure. In effect, the European Court of Justice empowered member states' nationals to hold their own governments to account for failing to comply with the latter's treaty obligations. Member states, for their part, could have avoided such actions if they had given effect to their obligations under the Treaty of Rome in the time frame they had stipulated in the treaty. This is the context of the two decisions that are the foundation of the principle of mutual recognition in the EU: *Dassonville,* and the more famous 'mutual recognition' decision of *Cassis.*[3]

---

1   *Procureur du Roi v. Dassonville* (C 8/74) (1974) ECR 837.
2   Leading to the 'Luxembourg Compromise', a political compromise in which the six member states agreed that a qualified majority vote would not be used on any issue on which a member state felt that important (national) interests were at stake. Although this formally did not amount to a veto by a member state, practically that was the result.
3   *REWE-Zentral AG v. Bundesmonopolverwaltung für Branntwein* (C-120/78) (1979) ECR 649 ('*Cassis*').

Dassonville

In 1970 Belgian wine merchants sought to import into Belgium whisky that had been imported legally into France from Scotland. France did not require a certificate of origin for such imports whereas Belgium did. This meant that the merchants were unable to bring the Scotch whisky across the border from France into Belgium. In order to resolve this issue, the merchants made their own certificates of origin, which they affixed to the whisky being imported. The forgeries were discovered and the merchants prosecuted under Belgian law. In their defence, they argued in effect that the Belgian requirement for a certificate of origin on goods already in circulation within the Community was incompatible with Belgium's obligations to avoid maintaining measures having an effect equivalent to a quantitative restriction. In making its ruling, the court stated [7]:

> All trading rules enacted by Member States which are capable of hindering, directly or indirectly, actually or potentially, intra-Community trade are to be considered as measures having an effect equivalent to quantitative restrictions.

Cassis

It was in the context of this broad definition of what is now Article 34 of the Treaty on the Functioning of the European Union (TFEU) (ex Article 30 EECT) that the court later ruled in the better-known decision of *Cassis de Dijon*. In that case, a German company, REWE-Zentral AG, sought authorisation from the German Federal Monopoly for Spirits to import certain spirits into Germany from France, including a liqueur, Cassis de Dijon. This liqueur had an alcohol volume content of 15–20 per cent. German law at the time, however, stipulated that only spirits with an alcohol volume content of 32 per cent could be marketed in Germany. On this basis, the Germany Federal Monopoly for Spirits refused to grant the authorisation requested. The company appealed this decision and a question was referred to the European Court of Justice on the interpretation of the term 'measure having equivalent effect [to a quantitative restriction]' (an MEQR). In effect, the court was asked to rule on whether the interpretation of that term meant that a national measure setting a minimum alcohol content that was above the content of traditional spirit products of other member states would amount to an MEQR. In answering this question, the court made two significant statements in that judgment relevant to the development of the concept of mutual recognition. At [10] it noted:

> In the absence of common rules relating to the production and marketing of alcohol … it is for the Member States to regulate all matters relating to the production and marketing of alcohol and alcoholic beverages on their own territory. Obstacles to movement within the Community resulting from disparities between the national laws relating to the marketing of the products in question must be **accepted in so far as those provisions may be recognized as being necessary in order to satisfy mandatory requirements relating in particular to the effectiveness of fiscal supervision, the protection of public health, the fairness of commercial transactions and the defence of the consumer.** [emphasis added]

The statement from the judgment more usually quoted is in [16]:

> There is … no valid reason why, provided that they have been lawfully produced and marketed in one of the Member States, alcoholic beverages should not be introduced into any other Member State …

This statement is the basis of the mutual recognition concept although the court did not label it as such. In fact, the court has been reluctant to 'unambiguously' embrace the concept (Janssens 2013: 12). This reticence on the part of the court has resulted in a variety of alternative terms being used to refer to the concept including the principle of equivalence and the principle of home states control (Janssens 2013: 12). The statement from [10] of the judgment is also relevant here for two reasons.

First, the court acknowledged the broad legislative discretion left to the member states to legislate *where the Community institutions had failed to act.* Second, it created an inexhaustive list of grounds (the so-called mandatory requirements) that would justify member states derogating from the application of the mutual recognition approach it subsequently introduces. At [10] the court is acknowledging that, *in the absence of common rules,* an absence of regulatory equivalence in the common market may be justified. These 'mandatory requirements' are distinct from the 'derogation power' contained in Article 36 TFEU (also ex Article 36 EECT) and only apply to indistinctly applicable measures (i.e. those that apply equally to domestic and imported goods but in fact impose a heavier burden on imports).

A rich and complex case law has developed since these decisions, generating considerable academic comment including discussion about the limits of the meaning of 'measure having equivalent effect', and the relationship with the case law on the derogations and mandatory requirements. Such developments also gave rise to a directive on mutual recognition (European Union 2006a; subsequently repealed); a regulation (European Union 2008) and non-binding guidelines developed by the European Commission.[4]

Evolution of the concept of mutual recognition

In its strongest form, the concept of mutual recognition requires the jurisdiction of an importing or host state to accept the regulatory determination of the exporting or 'home' state. Bhagwati and Hudec (1997: 91) define it as requiring jurisdictions to accept:

> [f]or domestic purposes certain regulatory determinations of other jurisdictions even though those determinations and the criteria on which they are based are not harmonized.

The mutual recognition concept now also appears in its strongest form in the TFEU in Title V (Area of Freedom, Security and Justice) in relation to the recognition of criminal judgments and civil judgments and extrajudicial rulings (e.g. arbitrations) (Arts 70, 81 and 82 TFEU). However, the principle is hardly ever given effect in that form.[5] Far more frequently, it is given effect as 'managed mutual recognition', a term coined by Kalypso Nicolaïdis.[6] She defines this as a form of regulatory cooperation motivated primarily by trade liberalisation concerns (Nicolaïdis 2001: 107):

> The 'managed' character of mutual recognition entails the reintroduction of regulatory imperatives 'through the back door', as it were, in the process of trade liberalisation. The management of recognition is the trick that regulators have found to satisfy their political masters and trade colleagues while at the same time minimising the effects of recognition in terms of regulatory competition. The conditions and caveats attached to

---

4   Found at ec.europa.eu/growth/single-market/goods/free-movement-sectors/mutual-recognition/index_en.htm.
5   A notable exception is the Trans-Tasman Single Economic Market (TTSEM). See further, Leslie & Elijah (2015).
6   See, for example, Nicolaïdis (1997).

recognition are meant to ensure against such competition by transforming mutual recognition into a sophisticated form of regulatory co-operation. In short, the 'management' of recognition can be thought of as the contribution of regulators to the process of recognition.

The extent to which 'mutual recognition' is 'managed' varies depending on the nature of the regulatory regime to be recognised. The attributes of mutual recognition that give it a 'managed' character for services have been summarised (Nicolaïdis 2001: 107). They consist of prior conditions for equivalence between national systems; automaticity and regulatory scope; and scope of market access. 'Prior conditions for equivalence' involves the relevant parties establishing equivalence of some sort between their national regulatory systems (Nicolaïdis 2001: 107). 'Equivalence' is defined as meaning that the parties are agreed on what are the acceptable differences between their systems and that their respective systems have reached such equivalence either through convergence or by agreement to respect supranational regulations (Nicolaïdis 2001).

'Automaticity' refers to automatic recognition of the beneficiaries of mutual recognition: the automatic right of economic agents—a service provider, for example—of one member state being able to access the host state market without first having to satisfy some initial requirement. Such a requirement might be as simple as providing evidence that the service provider is duly authorised in its home state to provide the service in question. The greater the number of requirements, the less automatic the recognition, the less one can speak of 'horizontal delegation' (Nicolaïdis 2001: 107). Regulatory scope refers to the scope of regulation that will be recognised; the narrower the scope, the less 'automatic' the recognition. A host state might recognise the licensing regulation of a home state for particular service providers, but may retain considerable residual regulatory jurisdiction to determine where, when and how such licensed service providers may operate in the host state's market. Related to this last point is the third criterion for 'managed' mutual recognition, the scope of market access. For this criterion, it is necessary to ask what kind of market access is granted as a result of mutual recognition and on what terms (Nicolaïdis 2001: 108).

In its strongest form, mutual recognition results in regulatory harmonisation in the field in question. The work on the 'management' of mutual recognition reveals the reluctance of states, for a variety of reasons, to undertake the regulatory reforms that result in such harmonisation.

The risk of too much 'management' of mutual recognition is that the result can be that nothing is in fact recognised mutually in any substantive way. There are many reasons why states are reluctant to pursue mutual recognition in its strongest form: resistance from domestic agencies fearing a loss of authority; concerns within a market that domestic operators will be forced out of the market by operators from other states; and fear among consumers that operators from other states will not be regulated as rigorously as those from the home state. Most of these concerns can be allayed if trust and confidence in the home state's regulatory practice can be fostered and promoted. One of the most effective ways of achieving this is to share information about differing practices and to engage in dialogue around similarities and differences of approach. The new policy tool of mutual evaluation is directed to this end.

The concept of mutual evaluation as established in the EU Services Directive

The process of mutual evaluation was first introduced by the European Commission in the EU Services Directive in 2006. It is set out in Article 39 of that Directive under the heading 'Mutual Evaluation'. The procedure involves member states reporting to the Commission essentially on three matters: the measures they have retained in their systems with which service providers from other member states must comply in order to be able to provide services and/or establish themselves in the host member state; the justification for these measures, including demonstrating that they have complied with the essential criteria of non-discrimination, necessity and proportionality; and the measures they have abolished in relation to the delivery of cross-border services and the right of establishment.

The next steps in the process are fascinating and potentially contain the strength of this process. Having received the reports from the member states concerning all the measures they have maintained, together with the reasons and justifications for them, the Commission then circulates these to the member states for their observations. Essentially, the member states comment on each other's restrictions and compliance measures and forward those comments to the Commission, which collates them and forwards them to a committee established under the Directive (Article 40) to assist the Commission. The committee may make observations and the Commission then presents a summary report to the European Parliament and the European Council in light of the observations of the member states and of the committee. Where appropriate, the Commission's summary report will also be accompanied by proposals for additional initiatives (Article 39[4]).

The mutual evaluation process was an evidence-based 'peer review' exercise following a methodology established by the Commission across 30 states, including the European Free Trade Association states of Iceland, Liechtenstein and Norway. The Commission reported on the outcomes of the process in 2011 (European Commission 2011a). The strength of this procedure is, by putting in place a structured dialogue between member states, the process has created transparency around the implementation of the Directive itself and helped in identifying and promoting good regulatory practice (European Commission 2011a: 6). A detailed consideration of the process and the methodology adopted by the Commission must wait for another occasion. The relevance to the present discussion is the Commission's findings concerning development of a practice of engaging in dialogue and the resulting benefits of transparency of process and promotion of goods regulatory practice. These are the aspects the Commission sought to strengthen in its 2013 amendment to the Professional Qualifications Directive (European Union 2013).

The concept of mutual evaluation as set out in the Professional Qualifications Directive

The concept of *mutual evaluation,* developed by the European Commission, was first introduced in the EU Services Directive discussed above. The same process was included in the Professional Qualifications Directive of 2005 (amended in 2013). However, the process was varied slightly in the latter instrument, ostensibly due to the different legal bases of the two directives.

The Professional Qualifications Directive was first enacted in 2005 (European Union 2005). The aim of the Directive is to facilitate mobility of professionals within the EU by defining a set of rules allowing professionals qualified in one member state to exercise their profession in another member state. The Directive consolidates a system of mutual recognition based on 15 directives. It provides for automatic recognition for a limited number of professions based on harmonised minimum training requirements (sectoral professions), a general system for the recognition of evidence of training and automatic recognition of professional experience. In 2011, the Commission evaluated the Directive against the criteria of effectiveness, efficiency, relevance, consistency and acceptability (European Commission 2011b: 5). The Commission involved a wide array of stakeholders in the assessment, resulting in revisions to the amendment being made by directive in 2013. The mutual evaluation process was incorporated into the Professional Qualifications Directive by the amending directive.[7]

The Recitals in the Professional Qualifications Directive specifically refer to the 'positive experience' with the mutual evaluation process in the Services Directive. Curiously, however, the Professional Qualifications Directive has a similar but not identical evaluation process and it is not referred to as 'mutual evaluation'. At [35] of the Recitals and Article 59, the concept of 'transparency' rather than 'evaluation' is highlighted.

This 'similar' evaluation system was included in the Professional Qualifications Directive to 'contribute to more transparency in the professional services market' (Recital [35]). The original version of Article 59 was replaced by a provision with the heading 'Transparency'. This is an interesting choice of title for the section, given that it was simply called 'Mutual Evaluation' in the Services Directive. It is explained in the Directive's preamble (at [35]) on the basis that such a system would contribute to more transparency in the professional services market.

Casting the mutual evaluation process in the Professional Qualifications Directive as a means of enhancing transparency might well be explained by the fact that whereas the free movement of services is a fundamental freedom established by the primary law of the treaty, the recognition of professional qualifications is not. This distinction is significant for the following reason: the Services Directive is a secondary measure of EU law intended to give effect to primary obligations under the treaty, i.e. the freedom to provide (and to receive) services within the internal market; and the right of establishment (Article 49, TFEU: Establishment; Article 56, TFEU: Services). The treaty prohibits restrictions on the freedom of establishment of nationals of a member state in the territory of another member state (Article 49, TFEU). This prohibition also applies to

---

7   Directive 2013/55/EU of the European Parliament and of the Council of 20 November 2013 amending Directive 2005/36/EC on the recognition of professional qualifications and Regulation (EU) no. 1024/2012 on administrative cooperation through the Internal Market Information System ('the IMI Regulation') [2013] OJ L354/132.

restrictions on the setting up of agencies, branches or subsidiaries by nationals of one member state in the territory of any other member state. The Article defines 'freedom of establishment' to include the right to take up and pursue activities as self-employed persons and to set up and manage undertakings under the same conditions as a member state's own nationals.

The Services Directive is anchored in the fundamental freedoms of services and establishment. Since the 1970s, the treaty provisions establishing these freedoms have been directly effective in the EU legal system. This means that citizens have rights under EU law corresponding to the obligations imposed on the member states in those treaty provisions. More significantly, from the perspective of the member state, it means that the member states cannot legislate inconsistently with their obligations under EU law. In the context of services, this means that member states may not introduce measures that could constitute a restriction on the freedom of establishment (Article 49) or the provision of services (Article 56). Now, in both treaty provisions, the obligation is qualified by the phrase, 'Within the framework of the provisions set out below …'. The Services Directive is a measure that has been introduced within that framework and it is one of the more recent pieces of secondary legislation in the field of services. As a matter of EU law, when the EU institutions begin to legislate in a particular field, the member states lose their legislative competence in that field, to the extent that the EU measure covers it. Practically speaking, what this means is that, in respect of services, the member states retain little unilateral legislative competence in the field of services. It was in this context that the Services Directive was developed. The political compromise in the Services Directive was, on the one hand, to preserve to member states the right to establish or maintain authorisation schemes for the establishment in their state of service providers, provided such schemes met criteria of EU law of non-discrimination, necessity (overriding reason relating to the public interest) and proportionality. On the other hand, member states are required under the Directive to report to the Commission on their authorisation schemes (under Article 9[2]), the criteria they require to be evaluated (under Article 15[5]) and the restrictions they maintain on multidisciplinary activities (under Article 25[3]). The Commission is required under Article 39 to circulate these reports to all member states for their comment and to consult interested parties on those reports.

Similarly, restrictions on the freedom to provide services within the EU are also prohibited in respect of nationals of member states who are established in a member state other than that of the person for whom the services are intended. The rights of establishment and freedom to provide services are subject to the qualifications in Articles 51–54. In these provisions, activities that may, even occasionally, be connected with the exercise of official authority of a member state are exempt (Article 51); national measures providing for special treatment for foreign nationals on the grounds of public policy, public security or public health prevail over the right of establishment and freedom to provide services (Article 52); activities of self-employed persons are subject to measures of EU law concerning the mutual recognition of qualifications and the coordination of member states' laws concerning taking up and pursuing activities as self-employed persons (Article 53); and legal entities are to be treated in the same way as natural persons in respect of the right of establishment and freedom to provide services (Article 54).

Professional qualifications, on the other hand, do not benefit from any primary obligation on the part of the member states for cross-border recognition.

The Professional Qualifications Directive is justified under what are now Articles 46, 53(1) and 62, TFEU. Article 46 authorises the European Parliament and the Council to issue directives or make regulations setting out the measures required to bring about freedom of movement for workers. Article 53 requires the European Parliament and Council to issue directives and make regulations for the mutual recognition of diplomas, certificates and other evidence of formal qualifications and for the coordination of the provisions laid down by law, regulation or administrative action in member states concerning the taking-up and pursuit of activities as self-employed persons. Article 62 stipulates that the provisions of Articles 51–54 shall apply to the freedom to provide services. In other words, the Professional Qualifications Directive is an ancillary measure intended to facilitate the realisation of the fundamental freedoms of services and establishment. This would seem to have implications for the way in which the mutual evaluation concept can be implemented in this context.

The evaluation process that has been incorporated into the Professional Qualifications Directive differs from that in the Services Directive in one significant aspect: whereas in the Services Directive, member states are required to report to the Commission on both those measures they have dismantled and those measures they have retained (including demonstrating that such measures satisfy the essential criteria of non-discrimination, necessity and proportionality), under the Professional Qualifications Directive, states are only required to report on those measures they have dismantled. There is no requirement for states to report on the measures they have retained and the justification for doing so. The reason for this difference in reporting requirements may be explained by the fact that, as explained above, the balance of legislative competence (although shared) is weighted more heavily in the sphere of the member states in the case of professional qualifications and in the sphere of the EU institutions in the case of services.

However, if that is the explanation, it is difficult to understand why this distinction was not made from the beginning. A review of the Commission's draft proposal for the amendments to the Professional Qualifications Directive reveals that it was not until the very last stage of the legislative process that the text was amended, apparently without explanation, to require that only one, rather than both reports, be circulated among the member states. The text that was accepted by the European Parliament seemed to require both the report on the measures that had been retained as well as that on those measures that had been abolished, to be submitted to the Commission for subsequent circulation among the other member states.[8]

The final text on which the Council voted, however, only required the report setting out the measures that had been dismantled to be submitted.[9] It may be that the change was simply a textual correction to remove a perceived ambiguity in the language (after all, without comparing the same provision across all the official language versions of the instrument,

---

8   European Commission 2011c: 50, Article 59(6): 'The Commission shall forward *the reports* to the other Member States which shall submit their observations within six months. Within the same period, the Commission shall consult interested parties, including the professions concerned' (emphasis added).

9   European Union 2011: 145, Article 59(7): 'The Commission shall *forward the reports referred to in paragraph 6* to the other Member States which shall submit their observations within six months. Within the same period of six months, the Commission shall consult interested parties, including the professions concerned' (emphasis added). The reports in paragraph 6 deal only with requirements that have been removed or made less stringent.

it is impossible to say whether the change only occurred in the English-language version). It is unclear why the mutual evaluation process set out in the Services Directive was not simply replicated in its entirety in the amendments to the Professional Qualifications Directive. However, it is still an improvement on what was in place prior to those amendments. It is also encouraging that the mutual evaluation principle, more broadly, appears to have been accepted as a useful and effective policy tool in the market integration process.

Structuring dialogue through mutual evaluation

Mutual recognition, whether managed or not, concerns the acceptance of the 'other' as being as trustworthy as one's 'own' system. Mutual evaluation, however, applies to the stage before that: where the parties are establishing their prior conditions for equivalence. It is argued here that mutual evaluation is not a part of 'managed' mutual recognition, it is the precursor to it. It is part of the process of convergence that results in one of the preconditions for 'managed' mutual recognition noted by Nicolaïdis and discussed earlier—that of 'prior conditions for equivalence'. 'Managed mutual recognition' is set out in Chapters III–VI of the Services Directive. The mutual evaluation process is set out in Chapter VII, 'Convergence Programme'. Mutual evaluation is a 'trust-building' tool, it enables a conversation between the negotiating parties that may lead to greater convergence but certainly to greater trust over time simply by virtue of the transparency it inculcates in the process. Under the mutual evaluation procedure in the Services Directive, states are required to report on the measures they have dismantled and on those they have retained, giving reasons both for why they have retained them and explaining how they satisfy the proportionality, non-discrimination and necessity criteria.

The process itself, as set down in the Services Directive, is one that negotiating parties could always undertake, similar to the '*ex post guarantees*' to which Nicolaïdis refers (2001: 108); that is, guarantees between the parties after the treaty—in which the mutual recognition process is set out—has been adopted. However, the advantage of formalising this process, as has been done in the Services Directive, is that it imposes a discipline on the contracting states to undertake the process. Strictly speaking, as a matter of EU law, failure by a member state to comply with its obligations to report and to provide observations as stipulated in Article 39 of the Services Directive puts it in breach of EU law and can result in the state being the subject of infringement proceedings brought by the European Commission before the Court of Justice of the European Union. Such proceedings seldom run their course because the member state, working with the Commission, will do what is required to meet its obligations. The threat, and the initiation of infringement proceedings, however, assist the state in prioritising such obligations in a way that would not happen in the absence of such sanctions.

The same discipline could also be achieved in an international (as distinct from a supranational) agreement if the parties included provisions establishing a joint committee that would have responsibility for ensuring such reporting obligations were met.

Conclusion

As the discussion in this chapter has demonstrated, the principle of mutual evaluation has great potential as a policy tool for trade negotiators in the current and future negotiating environment. Barriers to trade— perceived or real—will be, for the foreseeable future, increasingly located behind borders, embedded in domestic policy settings. Understandably, in this context, even managed mutual recognition is difficult to achieve. The extent to which negotiating parties have reciprocal trust and confidence in their respective regulatory systems is varied and fragmented even where such parties are homogenous. This becomes even further accentuated where the regulatory, political and social cultures are heterogenous, as is the case, for example, among many of the states currently negotiating the Trade in Services Agreement (TiSA).

Mutual evaluation offers negotiators an effective tool to progress cross-cultural dialogues with a view to developing mutual trust and confidence in differing governance and regulatory structures, where there is significant equivalence of intent. The majority of World Trade Organization (WTO) members continue to confirm their commitment, publicly at least, to a multilateral trading regime under the auspices of the WTO rather than the network of plurilateral and bilateral trade and investment agreements that have flourished in the last two decades.

If we accept, at face value, the commitment of governments across the world to trade liberalisation as a means of improving the standard of living of their citizens, and that this is best done in a multilateral trading context (both arguable propositions when one considers how states behave), we must conclude that those governments are willing to take the steps necessary to remove barriers to trade as they appear. We must also conclude that those governments accept that the removal of such barriers must necessarily result in greater regulatory convergence—there are limits to which different regulatory structures can deliver equivalent outcomes, after all. However, for the reasons set out in this chapter, the further behind the borders such trade barriers are, the greater the difficulty in addressing them. This difficulty is undoubtedly one of the contributing factors to the lack of progress on such trade negotiations through the WTO. This inertia has spawned the plethora of regional and bilateral free trade agreements (FTAs) that have been and are being negotiated at present.

If mutual evaluation is incorporated into the preferential agreements and FTAs currently being proposed or negotiated (e.g. EU–Australia FTA, EU–New Zealand FTA, Transatlantic Trade and Investment Partnership, EU–India FTA, EU–Japan FTA), there is a real chance of progress in liberalising trade in the more contentious areas behind borders. In the case of agreements that have been finalised, whether or not they have entered into force, contracting states can still choose to apply the principle of mutual evaluation informally in their dealings with each other.

The strength of mutual evaluation as a policy tool is that it can foster mutual trust and confidence between the negotiating parties in their respective regulatory systems, even if, initially, there is considerable divergence between those systems. As Figure 1 shows, mutual evaluation is an effective tool to prepare the preconditions identified by Nicolaïdis for establishing managed mutual recognition between systems.

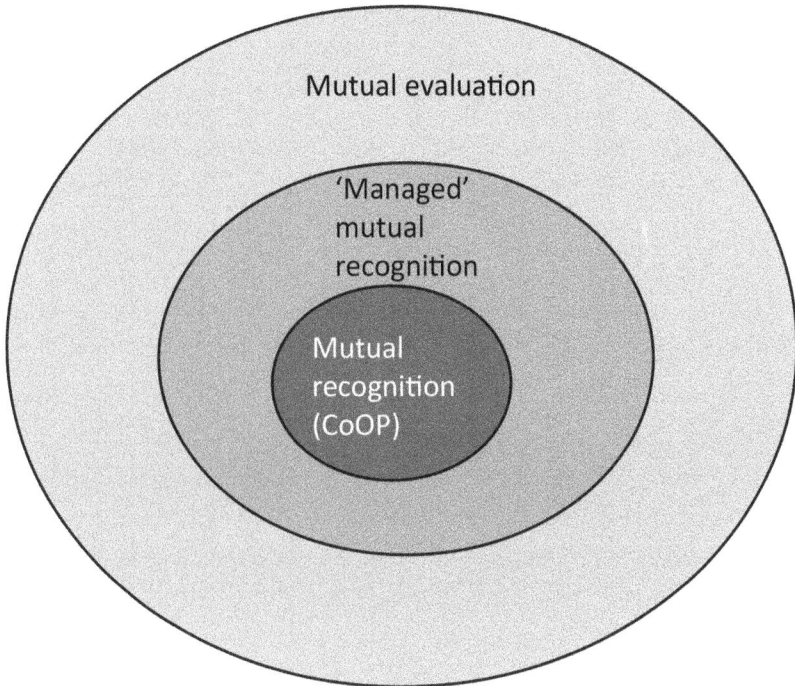

Figure 1. Mutual evaluation as a precursor to mutual recognition
Source: Author.

References

Bhagwati, Jagdish N, & Robert E. Hudec (eds) (1997), *Fair Trade and Harmonization: Prerequisites for Free Trade?* Vol. 1: *Economic Analysis*, (MIT Press: Cambridge, MA).

European Commission (2011a), *Communication from the Commission to the European Parliament, the Council, the European Economic and Social Committee and the Committee of the Regions: Towards a better functioning Single Market for services – building on the results of the mutual evaluation process of the Services Directive*, COM(2011) 20 Final (European Commission: Brussels), 27 January.

European Commission (2011b), *Evaluation of the Professional Qualifications Directive (Directive 2005/36/EC)* (European Commission: Brussels), 5 July.

European Commission (2011c), *Proposal for a Directive of the European Parliament and of the Council amending Directive 2005/36/EC on the recognition of professional qualifications and Regulation on administrative cooperation through the Internal Market Information System*, COM(2011) 883 Final (European Commission: Brussels), 19 December.

European Union (2005), 'Directive 2005/36/EC of the European Parliament and of the Council of 7 September 2005 on the recognition of professional qualifications', *Official Journal of the European Union* 48, L 255: 22–142.

European Union (2006a), 'Commission Directive 70/50/EEC of 22 December 1969 based on the provisions of Article 33(7), on the abolition of measures which have an effect equivalent to quantitative restrictions on imports and are not covered by other provisions adopted in pursuance of the EEC Treaty 19.1.1970', *Official Journal of the European Union* I-1970(1): 17–19 (originally [1970] OJ L 13: 29–31).

European Union (2006b), 'Directive 2006/123/EC of the European Parliament and of the Council of 12 December 2006 on Services in the Internal Market', *Official Journal of the European Union* 49, L 376: 36–68.

European Union (2008), 'Regulation (EC) No. 764/2008 of the European Parliament and of the Council of 9 July 2008 laying down procedures relating to the application of certain national technical rules to products lawfully marketed in another Member State and repealing Decision No. 3052/95/EC', *Official Journal of the European Union* 51, L 218: 21–29.

European Union (2011), 'Position of the European Parliament adopted at first reading on 9 October 2013 with a view to the adoption of Directive 2013/.../EU...amending Directive 2005/36/EC on the recognition of professional qualifications...', EP-PE_TC1-COD(2011)0435 (European Parliament: Brussels), 9 October.

European Union (2013), 'Directive 2013/55/EU of the European Parliament and of the Council of 20 November 2013 amending Directive 2005/36/EEC on the recognition of professional qualifications and Regulation (EU) No. 1024/2012 on administrative cooperation through the Internal Market Information System ("the IMI Regulation")', *Official Journal of the European Union* 56, L 354: 132–70.

Janssens, Christine (2013), *The Principal of Mutual Recognition in EU Law* (Oxford University Press: Oxford). doi.org/10.1093/acprof:oso/9780199673032.001.0001.

Leslie, John & Annmarie Elijah (2015), 'From one single market to another: European integration, Australasian ambivalence and construction of the Trans-Tasman Single Economic Market', in Annika Björkdahl, Natalia Chaban, John Leslie & Annick Masselot (eds), *Importing EU Norms: Conceptual Framework and Empirical Findings* (Springer International Publishing: Switzerland), 79–96. doi.org/10.1007/978-3-319-13740-7_6.

Nicolaïdis, Kalypso (1997), 'Managed mutual recognition: The new approach to the liberalization of professional standards'. Available at users.ox.ac.uk/~ssfc0041/managemr.htm.

Nicolaïdis, Kalypso (2001), 'Harmonisation and recognition: What have we learned? Some preliminary reflections', in OECD (ed.), *Trade and Regulatory Reform: Insights from Country Experience* (OECD Publications: Paris).

Procureur du Roi v. Dassonville [*Dassonville*] (C-8/74) [1974] ECR 837.

Rewe-Zentral AG v. Bundesmonopolverwaltung für Branntwein [*Cassis de Dijon*] (C-120/78) [1979] ECR 650.

Section 3

10

Bringing Australia and the EU Closer: Is an FTA a Solution?

Paul Gretton

Introduction

At a time when the prospects for finalising the Doha Round of trade negotiations is bleak, it is timely to consider what kind of trade policy agenda governments should be pursuing. One possible approach is the continuation of strategies based on the negotiation of preferences through bilateral and regional deals. Another approach would be to refocus attention on trade liberalisation based on the most favoured nation (MFN) and national treatment principles of the international trading system, supported by domestic reform. Such an approach would be directed at enabling economies to adapt to the increasingly integrated global trading environment and to reach their productive potential. Bringing the like-minded trade-oriented economies of the European Union (EU) and Australia together provides the opportunity to eliminate remaining impediments to trade and investment between the regions according to MFN/national treatment principles. It also affords an opportunity to consider mutually beneficial behind-the-border reforms.

Industry consultations towards securing improved economic cooperation will indicate some business priorities—ones that are properly focused on overcoming sticking points in international commerce and providing market access to business.

The perspectives on what a trade agenda and trading environment may deliver, though, will vary. Individual companies could ask: 'What is in it for my business?' The wider community should ask: 'Will an agreement provide community-wide benefits?' The answer to these questions is not necessarily the same for all. But the subtext for all scenarios is to consider: 'Are benefits the greatest available?' 'Will an arrangement impede future commercial and policy options?'

This leads to the need to consider appropriate architectures and trade liberalisation strategies. It appears to this writer that there are no 'free trade' agreements. Yes, there are binding agreements between countries and groups of countries that exchange preferences, and the formation of such arrangements has clearly gained momentum with the stalling of the Doha Round. But such arrangements:

- encourage holding back worthwhile domestic reforms to maintain 'negotiating coin' for the next negotiation;
- involve diversion of highly skilled resources in tit-for-tat negotiations;
- lead to new regulations in the form of rules of origin and preferences impeding efficient decision-making in merchandise and services trade, and investment; and
- favour businesses directly advantaged by negotiated preferences.

This is at the cost of other domestic businesses that may be more productive and internationally competitive, and at the expense of those countries and their businesses that are excluded from the particular agreement in question.

There is also an emerging tendency to include in preferential trade agreements provisions that depart from the national treatment principle to afford procedural rights to foreign companies not available to local enterprises through investor–state dispute settlement (ISDS) or impose more stringent intellectual property (IP) provisions that benefit IP holders while raising the cost of IP use to the rest of the community.

In short, bringing the Australian and EU economies closer together in a mutually beneficial way depends on ongoing domestic economic reforms that are genuinely trade liberalising. What could the elements be?

Trade and competitiveness — where do impediments bite?

While the trade strategies will have a major impact on potential benefits and what is realisable, the footprint of activities brought within the negotiations will also be important. One broad way of looking at this issue is to look at what is traded across borders and what is 'behind the border' or, put another way, the value added in trade.

Global trade statistics show that trade relations between economies are dominated by merchandise trade, mainly in manufactures (Figure 1). Further analysis now becoming available based on input–output modelling shows that behind-the-border services are key to realising the potential of economies. Assessments of how the productivity of domestic service provision can be improved would be a good starting point for improving the overall competitiveness of an economy. However, trade barriers in the form of tariffs, rules of origin and non-tariff barriers (NTBs) will not only raise the cost of imports to domestic industry and consumers, but also impede realisation of the productive potential of services.

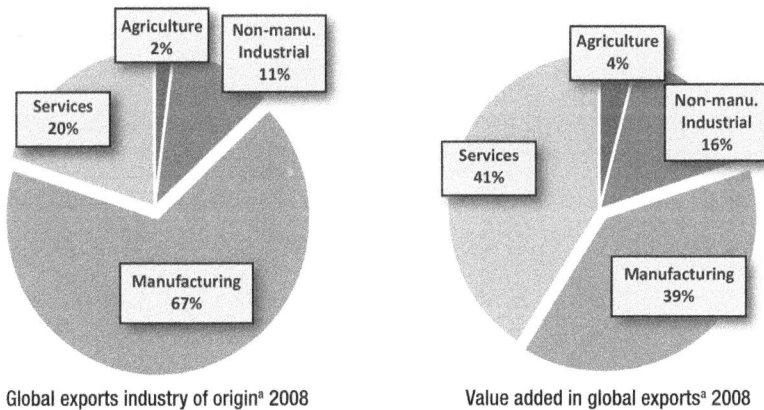

Global exports industry of origin[a] 2008

Value added in global exports[a] 2008

Figure 1. While trade relations are dominated by merchandise trade, behind-the-border services productivity is key to competitiveness

a) Agriculture includes forestry, hunting, and fishing. Non-manufacturing industrial production includes mining and quarrying, electricity/gas/water supply, and construction. Manufacturing is the remainder of industrial production

Source: Johnson 2014.

World trade and production are also increasingly structured around 'global value chains'. A value chain identifies the full range of activities that firms undertake to bring a product or a service from its conception to its end use.

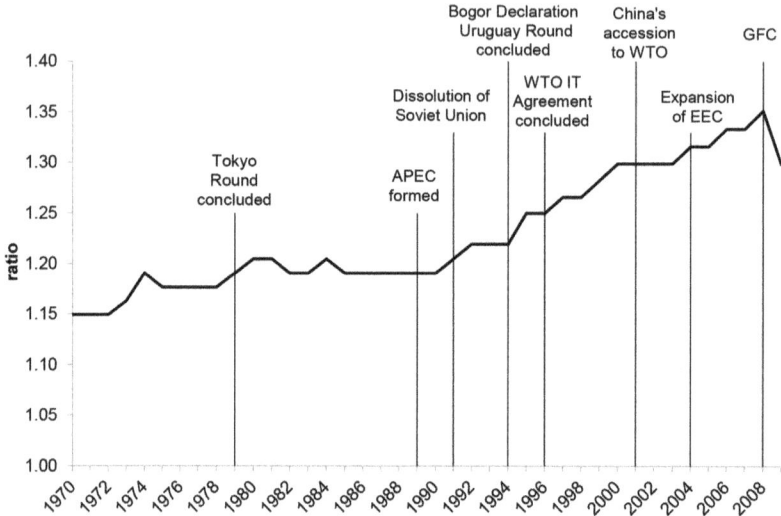

Figure 2. The ratio of the global gross value of exports to the value added in exports has increased, 1970 to 2009[a]

APEC, Asia-Pacific Economic Cooperation; EEC, European Economic Community; GFC, global financial crisis; IT, Information Technology; WTO, World Trade Organization

a) The original estimates of Johnson and Noguera were expressed in terms of value added exports to gross exports (the VAX ratio), the inverse of the ratio reported in this figure.

Sources: Based on Johnson & Noguera 2012; Productivity Commission 2015a.

As production processes have increasingly been dispersed across countries to take advantage of lower-cost production opportunities and the level of inter-industry trade has increased, the gross value of exports to the value added generated has increased. Over the period 1970 to around 2009, available estimates indicate exports per unit of value added increased from 1.15 to 1.33—that is, by around 15 per cent (Figure 2).[1] Most of this increase occurred after 1990, coinciding with major trade liberalisations—including those associated with the formation of the

---

1   'Gross exports per unit of value added' is the inverse of what is commonly known in the empirical trade literature as the ratio of 'value added exports' (VAX) to gross exports (Johnson & Noguera 2012). Aggregate value added exports is less than gross exports because of the existence of intermediate stages of production within and across countries.

Asia-Pacific Economic Cooperation (APEC) in 1989 and the Bogor Declaration of 1994, China's accession to the World Trade Organization (WTO) in 2001, the expansion of the EU to include former Soviet bloc economies, and the emergence and uptake of advanced information and communication technologies. With the contraction of global trade associated with the 2008 global financial crisis, global exports per unit of value added, however, declined.

The increase in the ratio of gross exports to value added between 1970 and 2009, and particularly after 1990, predominantly reflects structural changes within the global manufacturing sector (Figure 3). In particular, while exports of final manufactures grew, the number of stages (or slicing up) of the stock of final manufactures increased faster. As a result, the value of exports of manufactures relative to the value added embodied in those exports has risen over 30 per cent—mainly since 1990. In contrast, exports of agriculture and services per unit of value added has slightly declined—as the value of exports of agriculture and services have grown slower than the use of those products as inputs into the increasingly fragmented manufacturing sector and into final consumption.

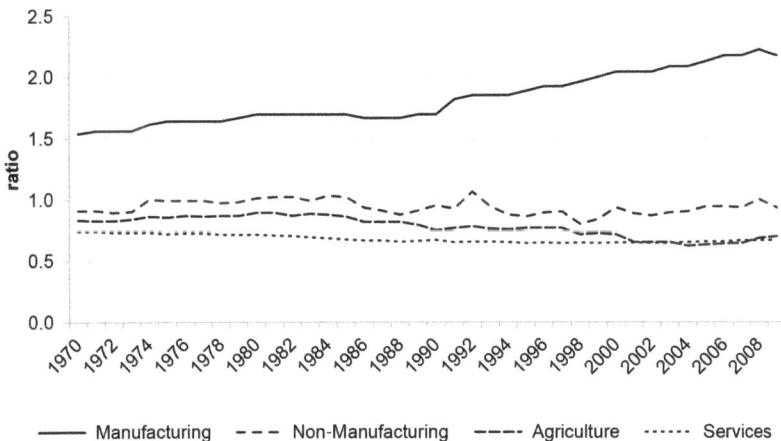

Figure 3. Changes in global exports per unit value added by sector, 1970 to 2009[a]

a) Non-manufacturing includes oil and gas, iron ore and other mining.

Source: Based on Johnson & Noguera 2012.

A key impediment to liberalising merchandise trade—remaining tariffs and rules of origin

Average tariffs are low in EU economies and Australia for primary products and manufactures, both in absolute terms and relative to other economies (Figure 4, left-hand panel) while average tariffs at a global level have been on the decline (Figure 4, right-hand panel).

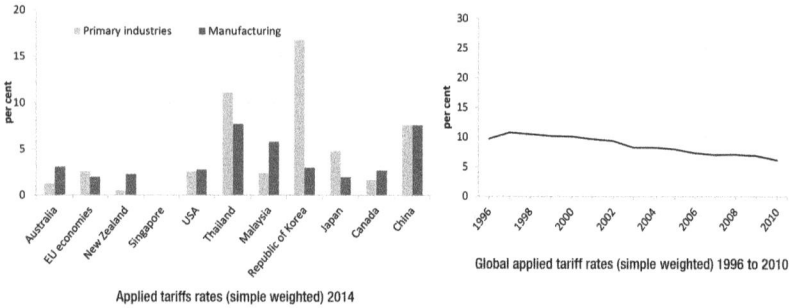

Applied tariffs rates (simple weighted) 2014

Global applied tariff rates (simple weighted) 1996 to 2010

Figure 4. Customs tariffs remain
Source: World Bank 2016b.

Despite the fact that import tariffs are at historically low levels and suggestions that tariff protection is less important than was historically the case, the formation of modern preferential bilateral and regional trade agreements has been accompanied by the negotiation of complex product-specific rules of origin to establish eligibility for trade preferences under an agreement. The requirement for product and agreement-specific origin rules suggests that remaining tariffs do bite and that the tariff preference is material. Tariff preferences extend tariff assistance to qualifying firms in partner economies otherwise reserved for local firms (Productivity Commission 2004a). Although difficult to quantify, trade preferences and origin rules have a number of effects that impede economic efficiency and lower productivity. They can:

- divert trade in final goods from lower-cost suppliers of competing products;
- lead some firms to adopt a more costly input mix and higher cost structure in order to obtain preferential access for finished products; and
- induce changes in the location of investment between members of a preferential agreement and between members and non-members (Productivity Commission 2004b).

They also add to the risk of doing business arising from the potential for delay in documentation and clearance and failure to meet origin requirements.

With the increasing number of preferential trade agreements, there are now many countries that have separate, differently specified rules of origin with different trading partners. This has led to a complex system of 'criss-crossing' trade preferences where products entering a particular country enjoy access on widely varying terms depending on their origin, leading to a 'spaghetti/noodle bowl' across agreements or 'hub and spoke' effect between one (large) economy and trading partners linked to it by bilateral agreements.

Preferential trade agreements contain a range of approaches for conferring origin that businesses must consider when sourcing inputs to attain concessional tariff rates for merchandise trade commonly centred around change of tariff classification, specified process or regional value content tests. Some products, typically agricultural or mining, can also be prescribed as being 'wholly obtained' or 'produced entirely locally'.

These approaches (or tests) are variously applied individually or in combination to determine origin. In the case of agreements entered into by Australia to date, the application of the approaches varies between products within agreements and, for individual products, between agreements—for example, from a single three-tiered rule in the agreement with Singapore based on a regional value content approach to more than 5,200 individual rules in the agreement with Korea based on product-specific rules for each Harmonized System (HS) item (Table 1).

Table 1. Count of listed rules of origin by trade agreement

Number of rules listed in agreements	
New Zealand	2813
Singapore	1
Thailand	2907
USA	980
Chile	2803
ASEAN	3102
Malaysia	2677
Korea	5205
Japan	2171
China	1784

Source: Productivity Commission 2015b; Author estimates.

In addition to differences in the number of origin rules listed in schedules, there is also a diversity of approaches used for conferring origin. The most common rule is the change in tariff classification (CTC) test, but there is considerable variation in how CTC rules are combined with other rules (Figure 5, left-hand panel) and how they are applied across agreements (Figure 5, right-hand panel).

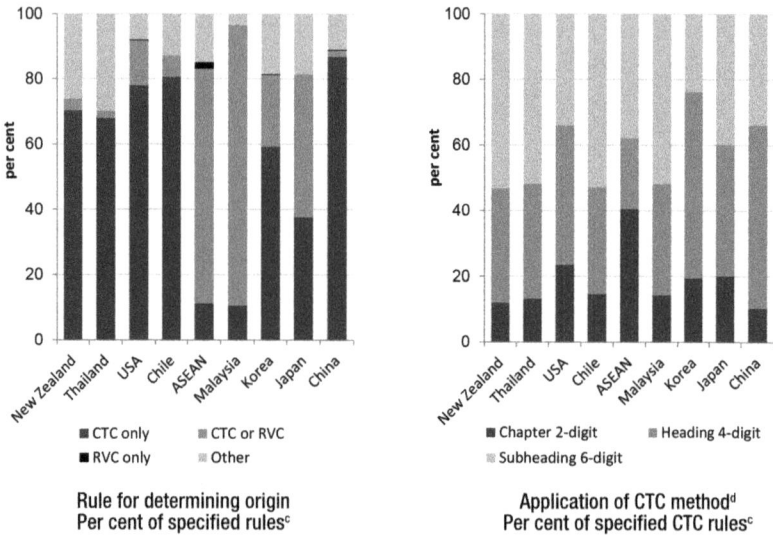

Rule for determining origin
Per cent of specified rules[c]

Application of CTC method[d]
Per cent of specified CTC rules[c]

Figure 5. Methods used to determine origin of merchandise trade in Australian preferential trade agreements[a,b,c,d]

a) CTC refers to a change in tariff classification test. RVC refers to a regional or qualifying value content rule. 'Other' includes combined CTC and RVC rules, CTC rules with exceptions and specified process tests requiring particular production methods to be applied; b) The agreement with Singapore is not included as it applies a single three-tiered test of origin; c) Individual rules can be expressed at the 4-digit heading level, 6-digit subheading level or groupings of tariff line items; d) When the Australia–New Zealand Closer Economic Relations (CER) agreement entered into force in 1983, an RVC rule with a simple technical test was the main rule applied. The rules reported replaced that rule and have been in force since 1 January 2007.

Source: Productivity Commission 2015b; Author estimates.

The different rules and rule structures across agreements mean that a firm trading with multiple countries faces greater complexity and compliance costs through the need to interpret, and comply with, different rules of origin. Although difficult to quantify, it has been estimated that the economic cost associated with these requirements could be as high as 25 per cent of the value of goods traded within the Association of Southeast Asian Nations (ASEAN) (APEC 2009, with reference to Manchin & Pelkmans-Balaoing 2007). At this level, it would be more cost-effective to pay the tariff than seek the tariff concession for many products. In a recent assessment of the potential impacts of a trans-Pacific partnership by the World Bank, it was conjectured that rules of origin could lead to the replacement of 40 per cent of imported inputs, on average, with higher-cost inputs from agreement partners, as members diverted trade to take advantage of preferential tariffs under such an agreement (World Bank 2016a). These estimates illustrate the additional drag on productive efficiency introduced by preferential rules of origin.

In an attempt to move away from the ever-increasing complexity of rules of origin schedules in trade agreements, the Australian Productivity Commission has recommended on a number of occasions that, for locally sourced products, the rules be 'waived' between agreement partners when tariff rates in partner countries are similar or low—that is, when the risk of trans-shipment of non-partner exports is low (Productivity Commission 2004b, 2010). Given the low average tariff rates in both the EU and Australia and the distance separating the two areas (and attendant relatively high transport costs), this recommendation would have particular applicability in any agreement involving the exchange of tariff preferences between Australia and the EU.

Rules of origin apply to services and investment too

While the existence of rules of origin in goods trade is well known, their application (and associated consequences) in services trade and investment has received much less attention. Rather than defining the physical origin of the service or investment (the focus in goods trade), trade agreements have generally sought to delineate ownership or control and through this the origin of a service supplier or investor (Fink & Nikomborirak 2007). The effect is to deny foreign (non-party) owned or controlled companies access to the provisions negotiated in trade agreements, although, as with rules of origin on merchandise trade, the expression of the rules differs between agreements.

For example, the Australia–United States of America (USA) bilateral agreement (in force since 2005) has adopted a services and investment origin rule denying benefits 'if the service supplier is an enterprise owned or controlled by persons a non-Party or of the denying Party that has no substantial business activities in the territory of the other Party' (Articles 10.11 and 10.12). The Thailand–Australia Agreement (also in force since 2005) stipulates that a service supplier or investor must not be owned or controlled by persons of a non-party (Articles 804 and 905).

The recent economic partnership agreement between Australia and Japan (in force since 2015) is more specific about the level of ownership, stipulating that an enterprise may be denied the benefits of the agreement if it is more than 50 per cent owned by a non-party or has a majority of its directors appointed by a non-party that has no substantial business activities in the area of the other party (Articles 9.14 and 9.17). On the other hand, the Australia–New Zealand Closer Economic Relations Agreement (ANZCERTA) (which entered into force in 1983) requires that a service or investment must not be *indirectly* provided by a person of neither member state (Articles 14 and 18).

This variability across agreements adds to the complexity and uncertainty facing foreign-owned or controlled service suppliers and investors with Australian operations seeking to utilise negotiated access commitments. The discretionary nature and vagueness of the services and investment rules of origin leave a number of questions concerning the actual or potential impact of the rules of origin on services trade and investment activity. For example:

> 'To what extent would the provisions chill (or influence) commercial activity that may otherwise have occurred?' and 'Under what circumstance would the partner government invoke the provisions and in such an event, how would terms such as 'enterprise', 'ownership and control' and 'substantial business undertaking' be interpreted in the context of the transaction in question?'

An issue is whether there is merit in seeking to confine liberalising measures for services and investment on the basis of ownership and control of the entities involved, or whether MFN/national treatment principles should be applied more widely.

What about services?

The coverage of modern bilateral and regional trade agreements is typically inclusive of chapters on services. This can be justified by the growth in services trade and the movement of natural persons for work and pleasure, and also on the grounds of the importance of services in supporting merchandise trade—the services value added component of trade. In looking at the services aspect of the implications of Australian bilateral and regional trade agreements up to 2010, the Productivity Commission found in a number of areas that the main impediments to effective competition by Australian service providers in partners' services markets appeared to be related to regulatory and institutional issues that lie outside the scope of agreements (Productivity Commission 2010a).

An earlier survey of offshore investment by 201 of Australia's largest firms indicated that the commercial imperative of getting closer to the customer is the main driver of offshore investment (Productivity Commission 2002). The survey also indicated that government influences were of secondary importance with tax being the most significant, ahead of labour market policies, foreign tariff arrangements, mergers and environmental regulation, and access to capital.

An issue for services trade liberalisation is whether in fact negotiated bilateral or regional preferential market access arrangements are the most effective way towards services trade liberalisation.

Looking within for economic reform potential

While remaining tariffs are still a defining feature of international merchandise trade and the trading relationship between economies given economies' resource endowments and proximity to global trading partners, the domestic institutional and regulatory environment will be a determining feature of economies' cost competitiveness and preparedness to trade in both goods and services. As with customs tariffs, governments can directly address possibilities to improve economic competitiveness and thereby raise economic output and incomes.

The importance of the domestic operating environment to the trading potential of agreement partners highlights the role of domestic reform in adding to commercial opportunities and contributing to the potential for trade and investment between economies. One approach is to identify and assess at the national level NTBs to international trade in goods and services, and investment to:

- identify regulatory and other impediments to efficient investment and the conduct of commerce, and reform potential;
- assess the potential direct impacts of possible reforms on economic variables such as productivity, costs and prices of local industry, participation of the workforce in employment, and the mobility of labour across industries and regions; and

- assess the economy-wide impacts of possible changes and the timescale over which benefits may accrue and adjustment costs be incurred (Figure 6).

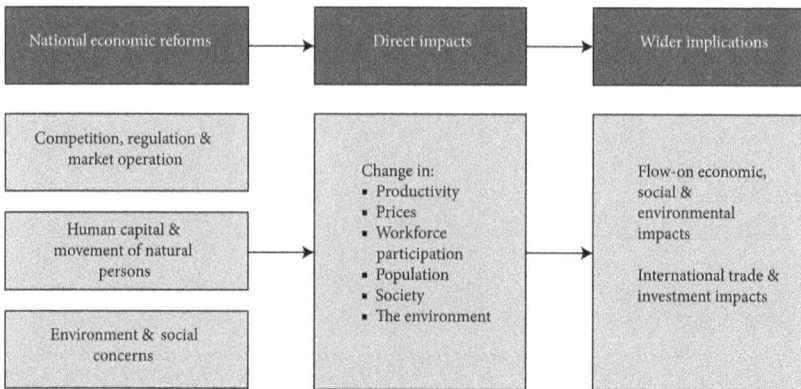

Figure 6. Identifying and assessing the impacts of reform potential
Source: Based on Productivity Commission 2010b.

Such a framework has been developed and recently applied in the Australian context to assess the impacts of economic reforms in Australia (Productivity Commission 2010a, 2012). A similar framework was previously applied to assess the economic benefits of national competition policy reforms in Australia and an agenda for national reform (Productivity Commission 2005, 2006; Gretton 2013).

In relation to the 2012 study, the Productivity Commission was asked to assess the economic impacts of 17 business regulatory reforms underway. The reforms spanned a diverse range of activities and industries—some related to individual areas of domestic economic activity such as health workforce, wine labelling, construction and rail safety, while others operated more broadly, such as trade measurement, consumer law and occupational health and safety. A distinguishing feature of each of these reform areas required cooperation between Australian state and territory governments (which have jurisdiction over many of the matters considered) and the Australian Government, which has national responsibility for economic management.

Among other things, the policies include trade-related measures to improve the mobility of labour between jurisdictions with reference to the health workforce, and measures to facilitate trade with reference to trade measurement. In relation to the health workforce, until recently, registration of health professionals in Australia occurred on a state-by-state and profession-by-profession basis, with an array of government bodies and specific legislation. While accreditation was mainly undertaken on a national basis, there were still over 20 different bodies, with considerable differences in approaches across professions. Some were established in cooperation with peak professional associations, while others had explicit statutory functions or had responsibilities delegated from registering authorities. In order to improve the mobility of health labour across jurisdictions in Australia, the Commonwealth, state and territory governments implemented a new, nationally consistent system of registration and accreditation of health professionals intended to reduce the administrative burden, improve labour mobility, and increase the consistency and quality of training.

In consultation with regulators and industry participants, it was assessed that the changes would generate cost savings of around A$160 million per year, with some associated one-off adjusted costs (with around A$20 million being incurred by government and A$24 million by practitioners). Implementation was undertaken over a relatively short period and depended on broad-based and sustained commitment of both governments and the sector. It was conjectured that a more gradual approach to that adopted could have jeopardised the development.

The second area relates to trade measurement. While this reform was assessed as affording modest benefits in financial terms (a national cost reduction for business of around A$5 million per year), it draws attention to the myriad often small steps that can be taken by government to help facilitate trade. In this case, matters relating to the millions of consumer and business transactions in which the price paid is dependent on measures of quantity and/or quality (or product 'grade'). The use and verification of product measures in Australia is governed by trade measurement regulation. Despite the earlier changes, inconsistencies in approaches remained and a further change was made to centralise the approach within the Australian Government with the intention of achieving greater consistency and lowering administrative and business costs.

Across all areas, while any estimates of impacts are subject to a margin of error, it was assessed that full implementation of the reforms could lower business costs in *gross* terms by a value approaching A$3.6 billion (2010–11 Australian dollars). After account is taken of additional compliance costs to business the reforms together could raise gross domestic product (GDP) by around 0.4 per cent (or around A$6 billion in 2010–11 Australian dollars). On the basis of implementation plans and possible adjustment lags, it was assessed that around 60 per cent of the total economy-wide effects would be felt by 2020 with some short-run national adjustment costs (Figure 7).

This study illustrates a workable approach to assessing and quantifying the impacts of economic reforms which differ in nature and economic footprint.

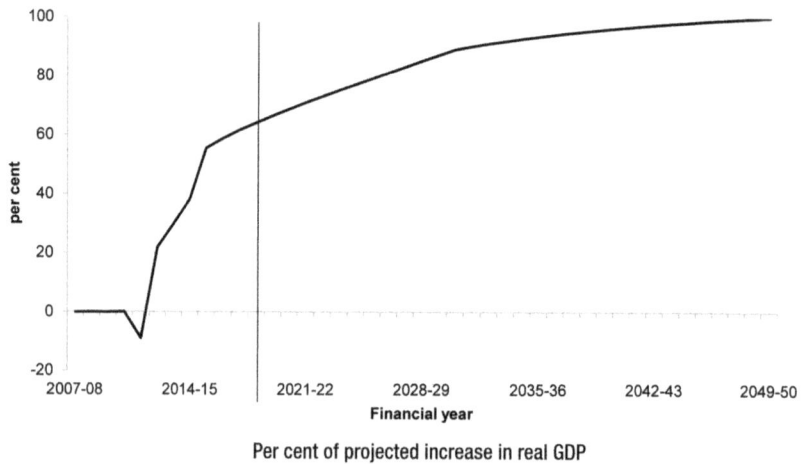

Per cent of projected increase in real GDP

Figure 7. Timescale over which the estimated longer-run impacts of selected regulatory reforms are estimated to occur, 2007–08 to 2049–50
Source: Productivity Commission 2012.

Mutual recognition agreements

Mutual recognition agreements provide means of fostering integration between like-minded economies. Typically, they are formed separately from bilateral and regional trade agreements. For example, in the 1990s, governments in Australia and New Zealand agreed that they would mutually recognise compliance with each other's laws for the *sale of goods* and the *registration of occupations*.

The agreements adopt a negative list approach under which all goods and occupations are covered other than where exemptions are specified to restrict the coverage of the laws (such as to protect public health or safety) or to quarantine the coverage of the laws (such as on how goods are to be sold or in relation to sovereign rights).

The schemes are inherently decentralised, with administration and compliance largely delegated to individual regulators in each jurisdiction. There are also a number of central bodies—including an administrative appeals tribunal, a trans-Tasman occupations tribunal, ministerial councils and central government departments—that provide oversight and coordination roles, and a cross-jurisdictional review forum that enables jurisdictions to collectively oversee the schemes and coordinate actions.

Under the terms of the mutual recognition schemes, the agreements are required to be reviewed every five years, with reviews having occurred in 2003, 2009 and 2015 (Productivity Commission 2003, 2009 and 2015c, respectively). The latest review found that the schemes are well established as a means of making it easier to do business across borders. However, it was found that the value of the schemes risks being slowly eroded due to regulators not always implementing mutual recognition as required, weak oversight, and an increase in the number of goods and related laws permanently kept outside the scope of the schemes. There are also specific concerns being found with the operation of mutual recognition of occupations that have the potential to weaken the community's and regulators' trust in the schemes and undermine their legitimacy. Proximate influences identified include licensing in the least stringent jurisdiction in order to obtain registration through mutual recognition in a jurisdiction with more stringent regulation (termed shopping and hopping); continuing professional development requirements; background checking; and determinations of occupational equivalence. There is scope to improve governance arrangements and administration of the Australian and New Zealand system to enhance effectiveness and regulatory trustfulness.

An issue is to what extent can mutual recognition of goods and occupations under the Australia–New Zealand systems be meaningfully integrated with the EU system. A further issue is whether any integration could be extended according to a negative list approach or would it be more practicable to adopt a positive list approach? Importantly, would any move towards mutual recognition between systems generate a new set of administrative and origin requirements that could add to cost and erode in-principle advantages and cost effectiveness?

Some areas of concern with preferential trade agreements

Intellectual property provisions

The protection of intellectual property (IP) rights has become a mainstream feature of trade agreements at the bilateral, regional and multilateral level. While the WTO Trade-Related Aspects of Intellectual Property Rights (TRIPS) Agreement set (high) minimum standards for the scope, length of term, administration and enforcement of IP rights, some preferential agreements (including those to which Australia is a participant) have provided, or are seeking to provide, more stringent protections.

For individual countries, the impact of these provisions will depend directly on whether they are net exporters or importers of different forms of IP material. The ultimate impact of the provisions will depend on how they affect the level and growth in economic activity of national economies, partner economies and the broader global economy. For Australia, doubts have been raised about whether recent internationally negotiated IP provisions are likely to deliver benefits. In particular, the extension of the terms of patent protection from 16 to 20 years under TRIPS and the extension of copyright protection from the life of the author plus 50 years to plus 70 years under the Australia–United States trade agreement (AUSFTA) have been assessed as imposing net economic costs (Gruen, Bruce & Prior 1996 and SCFTAAUSA 2004, respectively).

The relevance of trade-related IP issues for Australia has gained even greater prominence because of the potential for increased stringency in IP provisions in future agreements without commensurate economic benefits. The introduction of longer terms of IP protection (including patents, trademarks and copyright), lower hurdles for qualifying for IP rights, a greater role for government in enforcement and substantially increased penalty provisions, all could impose additional net costs on consumers and industry. To the extent that the return to IP holders awarded by more stringent IP laws outweighs the benefits to the broader economy, the provision would also impose net economic costs, lowering trading and growth potential across the bloc. If more stringent IP provisions negotiated in preferential agreements are projected into plurilateral and multilateral agreements, any costs could be even higher.

Given the capacity of IP systems to influence creative activity, trade and commerce and the complex legal and management systems established to manage IP law, the desirability of an overarching framework review of Australia's IP system was suggested (Productivity Commission 2013). The Australian Government's Competition Policy Review (Competition Policy Review 2015) later recommended that such a review be conducted by an independent body. Among other things, it recommended that the review cover the incorporation of IP provisions in international trade agreements.

The government then asked the Productivity Commission to undertake a public inquiry into Australia's intellectual property system. The Commission was asked to consider the current balance between access to ideas and products, and incentives to innovate and create, and to make recommendations to improve the wellbeing of the Australian community. In its final report, amongst other things, the Commission recognised that poorly designed IP rights can impose costs irrespective of whether a country is a net exporter or importer of IP (Productivity Commission 2016). This would occur when an IP system is weighted in favour of rights holders to the detriment of consumers and intermediate users. The Commission found that international agreements often contain prescriptive obligations that significantly constrain Australia's domestic policy arrangements. It suggested the need to improve the evidence base and analysis to inform international engagement, together with more transparent policy development.

An issue is to what extent can engagement between Australia and the EU with its diversity of member states, improve the evidence base and analysis of the impact of IP on the wellbeing of communities? A further issue is to what extent can such engagement provide leadership in the formulation of multilateral IP standards that better contribute to trade and commerce and improved community wellbeing?

Investor–state dispute settlement

Some trade agreements and investment treaties entered into by the Australian Government contain provisions for settling disputes between an investor of one party to the agreement and the government of the other party—termed ISDS provisions. Under the provisions, dispute settlement options can include third-party arbitration. For example, the ISDS provisions in the bilateral investment treaty between Australia and Hong Kong were used by Philip Morris Asia to initiate third-party arbitration in relation to Australia's tobacco plain packaging laws (Productivity Commission 2014, 2015a).

There has been a growing number of ISDS cases in recent years, rising to at least 70 new claims in 2015 from around 50 in the immediately preceding years (Figure 8). While claims have historically been initiated against developing and transitional states, recent years have witnessed an increase in the number of cases against more developed economies (around 40 per cent of the total for 2014 and 2015 were accounted for by claims on EU/OECD member states). A broad range of government measures have been challenged in recent years, including changes related to investment incentive schemes, concessional arrangements, cancellation or alleged breaches of contracts, revocation or denial of licenses and alleged direct or de facto expropriation (in part, the issue motivating Philip Morris Asia's claim against the Australian Government).

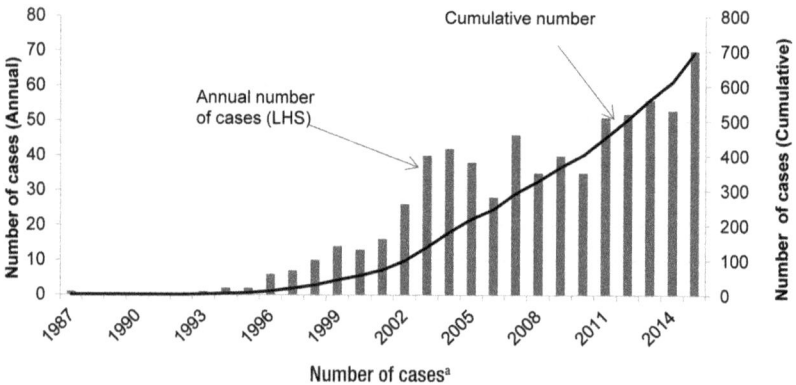

Figure 8. Known ISDS cases: 1987 to 2014

LHS, left-hand side; RHS, right-hand side. a) The total number of treaty-based investor–state disputes published on the UNCTAD Investment Policy Hub web page is 696 at April 2015. This estimate is adopted in the cumulative tally charted. The number of cases reported for 2014 and 2015 is based on a count of cases on the UNCTAD webpage at April 2015.

Source: UNCTAD 2016.

While information on the amount of compensation sought by applicant investors is not available for all reported cases, the United Nations Conference on Trade and Development (UNCTAD) has reported claims ranging from less than US$1 million (five cases) in 2015 to US$1 billion or more (80 cases) in that year (UNCTAD 2016). Information on awards by tribunals is available for 112 cases. Of these, 27 were for US$500 million or more. The largest group of awards totalled around US$50 billion and related to a series of claims on the Russian Federation for actions by respondents against the Yukos Oil Company.

The inclusion of ISDS provisions in Australia's preferential trade agreements and investment treaties has become an increasingly contentious issue with concerns centering around the growth in the number of ISDS cases brought internationally; extension of substantive appeal rights available to foreigners but not available to domestic firms; risk of inhibiting regulatory change assessed to be in the communities' best interest (regulatory chill); effectiveness of safeguards and carve-outs; and lack of transparency and inadequate parliamentary scrutiny of ISDS (and other) provisions (SFADTLC 2014). There have also been concerns for the potential for the authority of domestic courts to be undermined by ISDS arbitration (French 2014).

Public consultations were organised by the European Commission in response to public debate about investment protection and ISDS in the proposed EU–USA trade agreement known as the Transatlantic Trade and Investment Partnership (TTIP). The consultations indicted that there was scope for improvement in agreement provisions including in relation to the protection of the right to regulate; the establishment and functioning of arbitral tribunals; the relationship between domestic judicial systems and ISDS; and the review of ISDS decisions through an appellate mechanism (European Commission 2015a). The European Commission subsequently proposed a new Investor Court System to replace existing ISDS provisions in trade negotiations including in the TTIP (European Commission 2015b). The proposal, amongst other things, includes an appellate body, precise definition of conditions under which investors can make a case and preservation of governments right to regulate.

In a parallel development, Germany, after indicating that it would not ratify the recently signed EU–Canada agreement (known as the Comprehensive Economic and Trade Agreement, CETA), which contains ISDS clauses, was reported to have subsequently withdrawn from that position (ICTSD 2014a , 2014b). A joint press announcement by European

Commissioner for Trade and Canada's Minister of International Trade indicated that a legal review of the CETA text had been completed and that the investment chapter had been revised to 'strengthen the provisions on governments' right to regulate; move to a permanent, transparent and institutionalised dispute-settlement tribunal; revise the process for the selection of tribunal members, who will adjudicate investor claims; set out more detailed commitments on ethics for all tribunal members; and agree to an appeal system' (Freeland & Malmstrom 2016). The intention to pursue a multilateral investment tribunal was also announced.

Australia has included ISDS clauses in six of its bilateral trade agreements: Singapore (2003), Thailand (2005), Chile (2009), ASEAN and New Zealand (2010), Korea (2014) and China (2015). Recent agreements include safeguards to protect the government's ability to regulate in the national interest. Australia also has ISDS provisions in its 21 traditional Investment Protection and Promotion Agreements (IPPAs) signed over the last three decades.[2] An examination of foreign investment trends with Australia's main foreign investment partners suggests that ISDS provisions are unlikely to have been relevant considerations in the investment decisions of Australian firms investing abroad or foreign firms investing in Australia (Productivity Commission 2015a).

Given the persistent and unresolved debate surrounding foreign investment protection and ISDS and the emergence of substantive protections and appellate processes to address concerns, a relevant question to be considered is: 'What impact have existing ISDS provisions (or their absence) had on investment flows and do those impacts deem ISDS provisions worthwhile from a national perspective?' A further question is: 'Whether the evolution of ISDS provisions in recent trade agreements is likely to afford benefits in the national interest that warrant giving foreign corporations procedural rights (or investment guarantees) not available to resident investors?'

In its report on bilateral and regional trade agreements (Productivity Commission 2010b: 271), the Productivity Commission concluded there was an absence of an identifiable underlying economic problem on market failure grounds necessitating the inclusion of ISDS provisions in bilateral and regional trade agreements.

---

2   There are agreements are with Argentina, China, Czech Republic, Egypt, Hong Kong, Hungary, India, Indonesia, Laos, Lithuania, Mexico, Pakistan, Papua New Guinea, Peru, Philippines, Poland, Romania, Sri Lanka, Turkey, Uruguay and Vietnam.

Key messages from the Productivity Commission's 2010 study into trade agreements

After considering the evidence received from business and government and quantitative modelling, the Productivity Commission in 2010 not surprisingly concluded that unilateral and MFN (that is non-discriminatory) reforms are likely to offer the greatest benefits to Australia. This conclusion could reasonably be applied to other economies and federations of economies including the EU.

It also concluded that the likely economic benefits of preferential agreements are 'oversold', expectations are too high, and improvements are needed to the independence, transparency and timing of assessments of trade agreements, particularly when including issues that are traditionally domestic policy or that can add to costs.

The complexity of bilateral and regional trade agreements, the potential for provisions to impose net costs on the community and the availability of alternative reform options present a compelling case for analysis in advance of negotiations to answer the question, 'What are the most beneficial liberalisation measures available?', and of the agreement text at the conclusion of negotiations to answer the question, 'How well does the negotiated text compare to the benchmark?' Current processes, however, tend to be aspirational and fail to adequately assess the potential impacts and broader liberalisation alternatives. They also do not systematically quantify the costs and benefits against what otherwise may occur (the counterfactual), fail to consider the opportunity costs of pursuing preferential arrangements compared to non-discriminatory and other reform options, tend to ignore the extent to which agreements actually liberalise existing markets and are silent on the need for post-agreement evaluations of actual impacts.[3]

---

3   This is not to suggest that such analyses would be an easy undertaking. There are many practical difficulties involved in quantifying the impacts of agreements due to the variable quality and completeness of international services trade and investment statistics and the inherent difficulty in quantifying services and investment trade barriers compared to tariff measures. Nevertheless, given the potential for preferential agreements to impose net costs, these difficulties should not be used as a justification to avoid greater scrutiny, including through the quantification of potential impacts.

Although there could be debate as to the most appropriate methodology for quantifying and assessing the scale and scope of the impacts of a bilateral or regional trade agreement, one point of reference is an economy-wide methodology for assessing the impacts and benefits of national economic reforms (Box 1). Such a methodology would identify the scope for change, the likely direct effects and economy-wide effects in a series of steps beginning with the identification of intended incremental changes and concluding with an overall assessment, including scope for improvement (Figure 9). The methodology could be applied in an *ex ante* analysis of the potential impacts of an agreement and in an *ex post* analysis of an agreement text.

Under the methodology, *ex ante* evaluation would enable mutually beneficial unilateral reforms to be identified and considered as trade liberalisation alternatives. One of the most obvious options would be consideration of the removal of remaining customs tariffs on an MFN basis rather than the granting of tariff preferences supported by yet another regimen of rules of origin. Similarly, possible extensions to market access and the application of national treatment of service providers and investors could be considered on a non-preferential basis to maximise domestic benefits to negotiating partners and avoid the efficiency costs of trade diversion. The scope for and relative merits of appropriate mutual recognition arrangements could also be assessed as a means of overcoming impediments to trade and investment that cannot be overcome simply by negotiating market access.

A comprehensive *ex post* evaluation of a negotiated text would include a consideration of the likely incremental effects of an agreement over what would have occurred in its absence and alternatives, and an analysis of the prospective impacts of the negotiated text against the potential identified in the *ex ante* evaluation. It would cover the likely direct effects on trade and investment after taking account of all incremental changes, including how the take-up of any negotiated preferences would be influenced by rules of origin and other NTBs, carve-outs (sectors or activities where the agreement's commitments are quarantined) and negotiation and ongoing administration (and legal) costs. Economy-wide impacts to participating economies would be canvassed, taking account of the direct effects on barriers to trade and investment, and resource constraints in sectors gaining market access and the economy more broadly (such as labour market constraints). The prospect of inhibiting regulatory change (regulatory chill) through new treaty obligations would also be considered as would the contingent liabilities created by the agreement. Finally, the opportunity costs of the agreement in terms of delaying unilateral liberalisation for the sake of maintaining negotiating coin would be again evaluated.

Box 1. Possible evaluation framework for trade agreements

A comprehensive and rigorous analysis of an agreement would:

- provide information on the potential national economic impacts of the full agreement, including estimates of the economy-wide and distributional effects of change and the time paths over which benefits are likely to accrue and costs be incurred;
- assess, where practicable, the impact of the agreement to assist participating economies achieving their productivity and trade potential and the opportunities for improvement, considering remaining customs tariffs and other barriers to trade and investment, carve-outs and phasing, as well as the nature of merchandise trade, services trade, direct and portfolio investments, IP and the movement of natural persons between agreement partners and between the partners and other economies;
- assess the scope for the agreement to evolve over time to further assist participating economies achieving their productivity and trade potential, including through review provisions and built-in agendas; and
- assess the scope and appropriateness of the agreement to act as a model or template for other agreements to encourage effective, adaptable and accountable approaches to improve economic wellbeing.

At a more detailed level, the analysis would (for each chapter of the agreement):

- identify the current institutional settings and changes from those settings, including phasing arrangements;
- list the eligibility requirements (including rules of origin for goods, services and investment) for the receipt of preferences under the agreement;
- report on who or what could be potentially directly affected by the agreement, and levels and trends in bilateral trade and investment;
- identify the nature of potential direct benefits and costs of full implementation of the text of an agreement and impediments, if any, to the take-up of preferences;
- quantify, where practicable, the potential benefits and costs and the timescale over which they are likely to occur;
- identify and quantify, where practicable, transition costs compared to 'business as usual' that are likely to be incurred achieving preferences under the agreement;
- assess any potentially adverse impacts of an agreement, including inhibiting regulatory change (regulatory chill); and
- assess the opportunity cost of an agreement, including holding back domestic reform to maintain negotiating coin.

Sources: Based on Productivity Commission 2015: Box 4.5; Productivity Commission 2010a, 2010b.

Comprehensive evaluation	Some potential evaluation indicators
Identify intended incremental changes to existing policy settings & regulation	Requirements for new or revised legislation affecting bilateral trade & investment & movement of people
Identify scale of activities affected	Trade & investment & local activity subject to provisions People affected
Estimate likely direct effects	Import price changes Take-up preferences Productivity effects Movement of people
Identify/estimate timescale, & compliance & administrative costs	Phasing arrangements Trade negotiation costs RoO & market access tests and costs
Project likely economy-wide impacts	Quantitative modelling of trade, investment productivity & population effects
Assess potential risks	Regulatory chill (arising from treaty obligations) Contingent liabilities (such as from ISDS)
Detail opportunity costs of delayed reform	Quantify loss of benefits from foregoing unilateral tariff reductions & services reform
Identify alternatives for reform	Assess and compare gains from pursuing unilateral and multilateral alternatives
Provide overall assessment and scope for improvement	Measure of net benefit from agreement

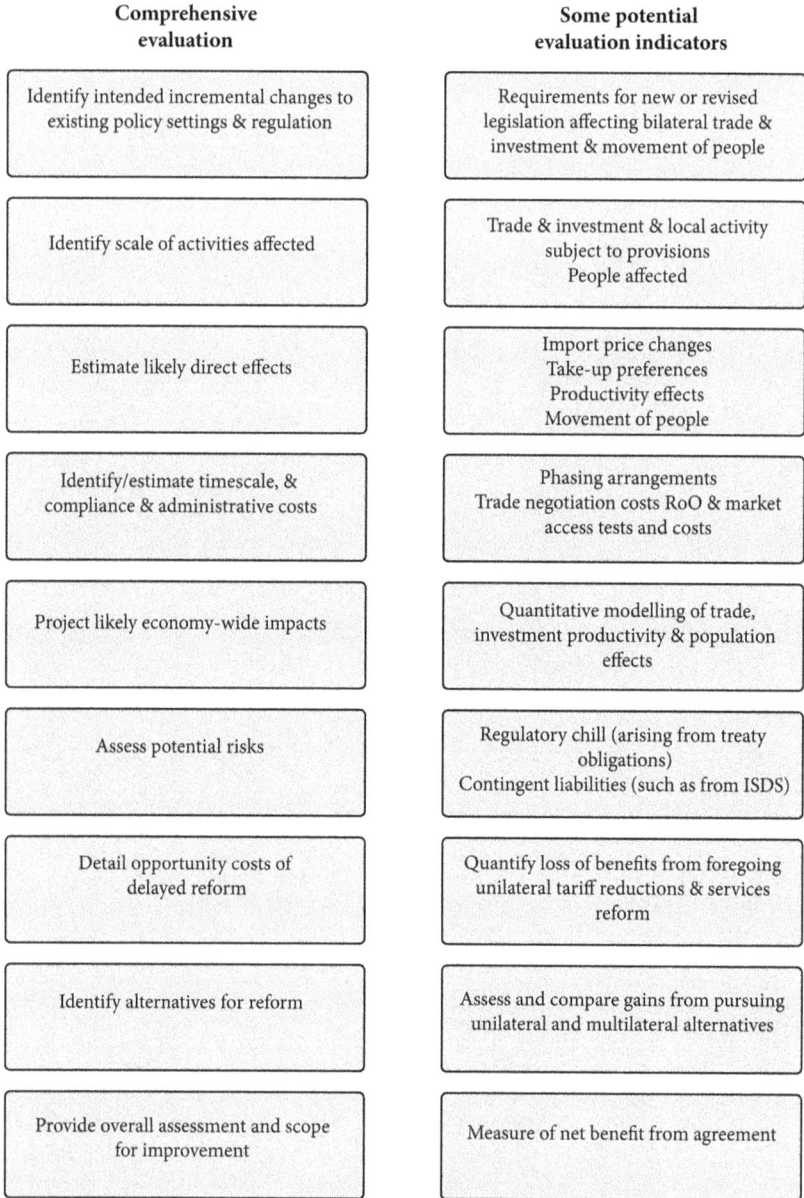

Figure 9. Stages of a comprehensive evaluation and possible evaluation indicators

Source: Based on Productivity Commission 2015: Figure 4.3.

Bringing the EU and Australia closer together

Bringing the EU and Australia closer together is naturally supported by similarly high regulatory standards and stages of economic development. There is also a similar intent of academic and trade qualifications and ways of working despite geographic separation. These common elements naturally bring the economies of the EU and Australia closer together. But there are impediments, including traditional trade barriers; protectionist sentiment in professional bodies and ways of working; local regulatory requirements relating to service provision; technology moving ahead of regulations—just think what can be done with information and communications technology compared to a decade ago; and geographic and time zone differences, which still matter. There are also differences in language and cultural norms. There are workarounds for business (such as foreign direct investment, movement of natural persons and business partnerships), but these may not be optimal, warranting attention to the barriers to trade and investment. (The workarounds also do not cover the need for governments to cooperate on matters of taxation and other protocols.)

So, what might be brought up internationally that will lead to worthwhile domestic reform and provide a bridge to bring Australia and the EU closer? On the merchandise trade side, remaining tariffs and rules of origin seem obvious candidates. Other candidates may be identified around product standards, packaging and labelling and the movement of merchandise through border security. And, while it is often said that tariffs are low and have little protective value, if this is the case, 'why are governments persisting with tariff regimes?' And, more puzzling, with low tariffs, 'why the insistence on complex rules of origin in bilateral and regional agreements?'

On the services side, mutual recognition of qualifications and affiliations would seem to be a strong candidate for early attention. But this raises the potentially sensitive question of how to allow for differences in professional, regulatory and other standards, and allow for criminal and other checking. The pacing of regulation with technology, which gives recognition to the reality of the latest advances, is another matter that would seem to require ongoing vigilance, and that would lend itself to close cooperation between like-minded economies. Questions in this regard include 'Is enough already being done and what more could reasonably be done to deliver community-wide benefits?'

But, in all these developments, in bringing Australia and the EU closer, can there be compelling reasons to sidestep the MFN and national treatment principles? In conclusion, one final question: 'What would it take to make EU–Australian cooperation truly trendsetting in the application of these principles and to compensate for lack of progress in Doha?'

References

APEC (Asia Pacific Economic Cooperation) (2009), 'APEC elements for simplifying customs documents and procedures relating to rules of origin', Appendix 3, in Committee on Trade and Investment, *Annual Report to Ministers* (APEC: Singapore).

Competition Policy Review (2015), *Competition Policy Review Final Report* (Professor Ian Harper, Chairman) (Commonwealth of Australia: Canberra).

European Commisson (2015a), *Online Public Consultation on Investment Protection and Investor-to-State Dispute Settlement (ISDS) in the Transatlantic Trade and Investment Partnership Agreement (TTIP)*, Commission Staff Working Document, SWD(2015) 3 Final (European Commission: Brussels), January.

European Commisson (2015b), 'Commission proposes new Investment Court System for TTIP and other EU trade and investment negotiations', Press release, Brussels, September.

Fink, Carsten & Deunden Nikomborirak (2007), *Rules of Origin in Services: A Case Study of Five ASEAN Countries*, Policy Research Paper No. 4130 (World Bank: Washington, DC), February.

Freeland, Chrystia & Cecilia Malmström (2016), 'Joint Statement by European Commissioner for Trade and Canada's Minister of International Trade on Canada–EU trade agreement', 29 February.

French, Robert (2014), 'Trade Law and the Australia Courts', Speech to Law Council of Australia, International Trade Law Symposium, 18 September, National Portrait Gallery, Canberra.

Gretton, Paul (2013), 'National economic reform in a federal system: The case study of Australian National Competition Policy and related reforms', in Stephen Howes and M. Govinda Rao (eds), *Federal Reform Strategies, Lessons from Australia and Asia* (Oxford University Press: New Delhi). doi.org/10.1093/acprof:oso/9780198092001.003.0002.

Gruen, Nicholas, Bruce, Ian & Prior, Gerard (1996), *Extending Patent Life: Is It in Australia's Economic Interest?*, Staff Information Paper (Industry Commission: Canberra).

ICTSD (International Centre for Trade and Sustainable Development) (2014a), 'Germany Changes Tack on ISDS in EU-Canada Trade Deal', Media release, 4 December. Available at www.ictsd.org/bridges-news/bridges/news/germany-changes-tack-on-isds-in-eu-canada-trade-deal, last accessed 25 April 2016.

ICTSD (2014b), 'EU, Canada sign trade deal as Germany raises ISDS questions', Media release, 2 October. Available at www.ictsd.org/bridges-news/biores/news/eu-canada-sign-trade-deal-as-germany-raises-isds-questions, last accessed 25 April 2016.

Johnson, Robert C. (2014), 'Five facts about value-added exports and implications for macroeconomics and trade research', *Journal of Economic Perspectives* 28(2): 119–42. doi.org/10.1257/jep.28.2.119.

Johnson, Robert C. & Noguera, Guillermo (2012), *Fragmentation and Trade in Value Added over Four Decades*, NBER Working Paper No. 18186 (National Bureau of Economic Research: Cambridge).

Manchin, Miriam & Annette O. Pelkmans-Balaoing (2007), *Rules of Origin and the Web of East Asian Free Trade Agreements*, Policy Research Working Paper No. 4273 (World Bank: Washington, DC), July.

Productivity Commission (2002), *Offshore Investment by Australian Firms: Survey Evidence*, Commission Research Paper (AusInfo: Canberra).

Productivity Commission (2003), *Evaluation of the Mutual Recognition Schemes*, Research Report (Productivity Commission: Canberra).

Productivity Commission (2004a), 'Industry assistance in Australia and New Zealand under the CER Agreement', Supplement to Productivity Commission Research Report, *Rules of Origin under the Australia–New Zealand Closer Economic Relations Trade Agreement* (Productivity Commission: Canberra), June.

Productivity Commission (2004b), *Rules of Origin under the Australia–New Zealand Closer Economic Relations Trade Agreement*, Research Report (Productivity Commission: Canberra).

Productivity Commission (2005), *Review of National Competition Policy*, Inquiry Report No. 33 (Productivity Commission: Canberra).

Productivity Commission (2006), *Potential Benefits of the National Reform Agenda*, Research Report (Productivity Commission: Canberra).

Productivity Commission (2009), *Review of Mutual Recognition Schemes*, Research Report (Productivity Commission: Canberra).

Productivity Commission (2010a), *Bilateral and Regional Trade Agreements*, Research Report (Productivity Commission: Canberra).

Productivity Commission (2010b), *Impacts and Benefits of COAG Reforms: Reporting Framework*, Research Report (Productivity Commission: Canberra).

Productivity Commission (2012), *Impacts of COAG Reforms: Business Regulation and VET*, Research Report (Productivity Commission: Canberra).

Productivity Commission (2013), *Trade & Assistance Review 2011–12*, Annual Report Series (Productivity Commission: Canberra).

Productivity Commission (2014), *Trade & Assistance Review 2012–13*, Annual Report Series (Productivity Commission: Canberra).

Productivity Commission (2015a), *Trade & Assistance Review 2013–14*, Annual Report Series (Productivity Commission: Canberra).

Productivity Commission (2015b), *Trade & Assistance Review 2013–14*, Methodological Annex (Productivity Commission: Melbourne).

Productivity Commission (2015c), *Mutual Recognition Schemes*, Research Report (Productivity Commission: Melbourne).

Productivity Commission (2016), *Intellectual Property Arrangements*, Final Report (Productivity Commission: Canberra).

SCFTAAUSA (Select Committee on the Free Trade Agreement between Australia and the United States of America) (2004), Final Report, August.

SFADTLC (Senate Foreign Affairs, Defence and Trade Legislation Committee) (2014), *Trade and Foreign Investment (Protecting the Public Interest) Bill 2014*, Final Report (Commonwealth of Australia: Canberra), August.

UNCTAD (United Nations Conference on Trade and Development) (2016), 'Investment Policy Hub, Investment Disputes Navigator'. Available at investmentpolicyhub.unctad.org/ISDS?status=1000, last accessed 20 April 2016.

World Bank (2016a), 'Topical Issue, Potential Macroeconomic Implications of the Trans-Pacific Partnership', in *Global Economic Prospects, January 2016: Spillovers amid Weak Growth* (World Bank: Washington, DC), 219–36.

World Bank (2016b), 'World Development Indicators: Table 6.6, Tariff Barriers'. Available at wdi.worldbank.org/table/6.6, last accessed 17 May 2016.

11

EU and Australia: Europe's Challenges and Policy Options for Future Trade

Roderick Abbott and Hosuk Lee-Makiyama

Introduction

At this point, Europe's trade relationships with the Asia-Pacific region have entered a period of constant activity following a general reorientation of its policy priorities since the 'Global Europe' strategy. The 2006 statement of future trade policy recognised the shift in economic growth patterns towards Asia and aimed to establish closer links with the region.

By 2015, the European Union (EU) had already concluded its first 'next-generation' free trade agreement (FTA) with Korea, in force since mid-2011, followed by Singapore, the Andean Community and Canada. There are a number of bilateral negotiations ongoing with other countries, including Japan, India and Malaysia. The Transatlantic Trade and Investment Partnership (TTIP) was launched in mid-2013 and its fate remains unclear.

Meanwhile, on the Asia-Pacific stage, one major and important development has been the Trans-Pacific Partnership (TPP) negotiations. The talks included Australia, Brunei, Canada, Chile, Japan, Malaysia, Mexico, New Zealand, Peru, Singapore, the United States of America

(USA) and Vietnam.[1] Other influential actors in the region, including South Korea, the Philippines, Taiwan, Thailand (and even China), have formally or informally shown their interest in joining the negotiations or acceding to the agreement (Bauer et al. 2014).

The TPP negotiations were a response to a rapid progression that marks the Asia-Pacific region as the emerging global economic centre: intra-regional trade this region has more than tripled since 2000 (Bauer et al. 2014). The region has undergone a process of profound change marked by the extraordinary rise of China and growing intra-regional industrial linkages, especially strong in East and Southeast Asia. This has resulted in a staggering increase of the intra-regional trade and investment, with China increasingly gaining weight at the expense of other trading partners outside of the region, mainly the EU and the USA.

The EU has reacted only recently to these developments with the launch of trade negotiations with Japan and the USA. However, Australia and New Zealand are not yet in negotiations with the EU, a trade policy blind spot that is yet to be addressed. The markets of Australia and New Zealand taken together are considerable in terms of gross domestic product (GDP). EU trade with these two countries is underdeveloped, and roughly equivalent to EU trade with Singapore or the United Arab Emirates.

Meanwhile, Australia is increasingly more embedded in its own hemisphere. Australia had already made its own 'pivot to Asia', an inevitable trend given its geographical location and the structure of its economy. In preparation for the TPP, Australia has concluded an FTA with Japan. Outside the TPP context, Australia has also concluded an FTA with Korea (2014) and, more recently, one with China (2015).

In assessing the impact of these developments, it becomes clear that both sides of the EU–Australia relationship are organising their trade affairs in a wider global context. If Asia is considered the hub of the wheel, Australia and the EU are two spokes to the region that complement each other; but this does not exclude a strut between the two, which would reinforce both—namely, through an Australia–EU FTA. Such an

---

1   In January 2017, President Donald Trump withdrew the USA from the TPP negotiations. This was part of a broader move away from trade agreements. However, in May 2017 the remaining 11 members of the TPP announced they would continue to pursue the agreement, the negotiating text of which remains that released on 26 January 2016.

agreement might not be of central significance in the region, but might play a supporting role in areas of more specific interest to both parties and offer them complementary advantages to the wider agreements already in place.

Europe's challenges in the Asia-Pacific region

Europe and the creation of the single market is proof that geography is a central theme. Geographic proximity was, and still is, a powerful and growing force in the way economies integrate with the world. Natural trading trends in the region are pointing towards more intra-regional trade, with or without policy-induced liberalisation through FTAs. Europe is already competing against the Asian economies, which are, naturally, integrating and consolidating their supply chains in the region and with the USA. In goods trade, almost half of US exports are already destined for countries that are participating in the TPP negotiations, while the equivalent EU number is closer to 30 per cent—even with exports to the USA included.[2] The picture is especially worrisome for EU exporters of agricultural products (Messerlin 2012).

This is why Europe's challenge is to minimise the degree of policy restrictions in its trade with the Asia-Pacific region—even in the absence of competing liberalisation from the TPP. In the absence of full-scale multilateralism, this liberalisation needs to take place as coherently as possible within the region.

The combined effect of natural and policy-induced market integration will change the competitive relationship between European and local firms already present in the Asia-Pacific region. Any delay in engaging with TPP members could be too costly: the TPP will be the first competing trade agreement that is large enough to cause measurable negative impact. The estimates by Kawasaki (2011) demonstrate that the EU's aggregate income (in terms of purchasing power) falls by 0.1 per cent as a result of the trade diversion created by the TPP. While Europe has negotiated bilaterally with some TPP countries, it has no strategy equivalent to the TPP, which could address tariffs and regulatory divergences with the economies in the

---

2   Calculations based on UN Comtrade (2013).

Asia-Pacific region. This is why Europe is likely to address the Oceania blind spot by negotiating FTAs with Australia and New Zealand, using its own template.

In sum, these FTAs with the TPP signatories are primarily not about additional market access—but are to maintain the current baseline and defend existing market shares. By doing so, Europe maintains its current utilisation rates in manufacturing, employment and profitability in services and its agenda-setting powers in world trade.

It is worth mentioning that the EU faces other competing geometries besides the TPP. The Association of South-East Asian Nations (ASEAN) is on a trajectory towards transforming itself into a common economic area. The Regional Comprehensive Economic Partnership (RCEP) aims to create a region-wide free trade area by merging ASEAN's existing FTAs (including China, India, Japan and Australia/New Zealand) and the proposed trilateral China–Japan–Korea FTA, although the future of this one is uncertain due to recent geopolitical tensions.

The RCEP is built on existing (and relatively weak) old-style tariff-centric FTAs, while the TPP could achieve market access and regulatory disciplines on new trade issues that are 'World Trade Organization-plus' ('WTO-plus'). In contrast, the TPP is the agenda-setting pillar in the region, not the EU FTAs. TPP membership has now reached 37.5 per cent of global GDP, or 60 per cent of world trade, and other potentially standard-setting FTAs (including TTIP and RCEP) will follow the TPP in terms of timing (Bauer et al. 2014).

Australia in Europe's map over the Asia-Pacific region

The EU trade strategy is, by default, multilateral, while its bilateral FTAs were not necessarily commercially motivated and instead aimed at specific goals and problems in its neighbourhood around the Mediterranean and the pre-accession countries in Eastern Europe. Almost 10 years after the Global Europe strategy, the plan to trial FTAs in the Asia-Pacific region, starting with Korea, still holds. This is an operation of economy of scale—to conclude a large number of FTAs in the region based on a European model text. By and large, this strategy was sustained until the opening of the TTIP that pivoted political attention back to the Atlantic.

Interestingly, any ventures that have boldly gone beyond that objective— for instance, when the EU attempted to negotiate with economies that are yet to sign FTAs with the USA—have either failed or been subject to delays. These include the failed regional deal with ASEAN, India and Mercosur.

Europe already negotiates bilaterally with some TPP countries and has already concluded a few agreements, some quite recently. Yet it has no strategy equivalent to the TPP that builds a larger framework in the Asia-Pacific region and addresses future trade issues. This European lack of initiative is merely an expression of the absence of a much broader vision and a 'grand map' in Europe on what trade relations with the Asia-Pacific region should evolve into.

On the European map of FTAs, it has already signed agreements with three TPP members: Mexico, Chile and Peru. Singapore and Canada Comprehensive Economic and Trade Agreement (CETA) negotiations have been concluded but await ratification. Moreover, the EU is already in negotiations with the USA, Japan, Malaysia and Vietnam, leaving only three TPP alliance economies (Australia, New Zealand and Brunei) to be negotiated with.

Both Australia and New Zealand have favourable business climates and consistently ranked high in terms of ease of doing business in the past decade, and Australia in particular has trade that is expanding quite rapidly by the standards of a mature Organisation for Economic Co-operation and Development (OECD) economy. However, their trade with Europe is lower than economies of similar economic size—Australia has a smaller share of EU trade than Canada, while New Zealand falls behind Peru and Vietnam (Eurostat 2013).

There are a number of arguments for Europe to open up negotiations with Australia. Firstly, Australia maintains tangible trade barriers with an average tariff near 9 per cent, which is relatively high for a developed economy (WTO 2013). This suggests there is a plain mercantilist case and an export-driven rationale for liberalising trade between the EU and Australia. Exports, or the prospects of export-led growth, are rarely the biggest gains of FTAs compared to consumer gains and the long-term impact of increased dynamic competition, leading to more competitive economies. However, Europe—suffering from overcapacities and anaemic growth at home—often acts on such mercantilist instincts.

Table 1. Economic performance of TPP signatories

Country	Average applied tariff, MFN	Ease of doing business rank, 2000–14 average	Real growth in trade (%) 2000–14 average	Services barriers STRI (1–100), 2000–14, average	Share of EU trade (%), 2013
TPP signatories with EU FTAs					
Singapore	0.63	1.0	7.9	22.7	1.4
Canada	3.88	8.0	1.2	51.1	1.7
Peru	8.92	58.0	8.3	24.6	0.3
Mexico	14.17	49.0	4.6	35.8	1.3
Chile	6.62	41.7	7.1	9.5	0.5
TPP signatories with ongoing EU FTA negotiations					
USA	2.96	3.7	3.1	65.2	14.2
Japan	6.76	13.3	2.7	48.8	3.2
Malaysia	4.26	23.0	5.3	25.4	1.0
Vietnam	18.2	90.3	17.2	30.1	0.8
TPP signatories without EU FTA negotiations					
Australia	8.88	9.3	5.9	58.9	1.2
New Zealand	4.02	2.0	3.9	52.2	0.2
Brunei	5.15	91.0	2.2	4.4	0.0

MFN, most favoured nation; STRI, Services Trade Restrictiveness Index

Sources: UN Comtrade 2013; World Bank 2014a, 2014b; OECD STRI 2014; Eurostat 2013.

Secondly, the competition Europe faces on the Australian market from similar, high value-adding economies is evident. Looking at Australian consumption and import penetration, Europe is outcompeted in each of its key export sectors: on the transport equipment sector, which includes railway equipment, the market share of the USA is five times larger; and on passenger cars and motor vehicles, Japanese exports hold more than half of the Australian market and outcompetes Europe by 50 to 1. The USA leads on other key EU export interests such as machinery and chemicals and, interestingly, Europe only enjoys a sizeable lead on food, beverage and agriculture, areas that are traditionally sensitive for Europe.

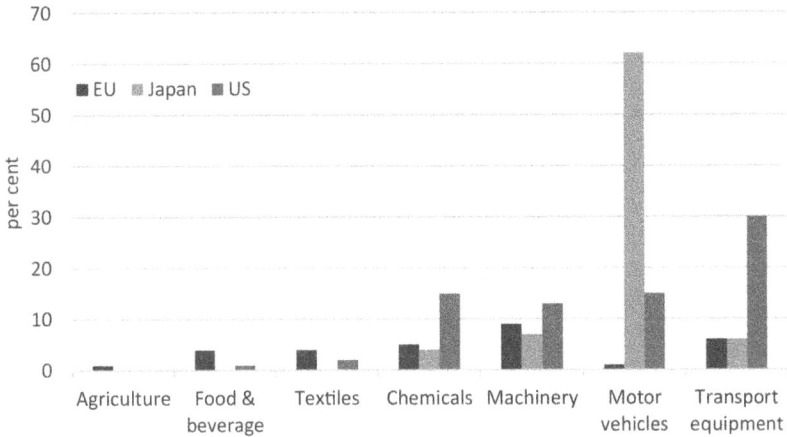

Figure 1. Import penetration, Australia in select sectors
Sources: OECD STAN 2013; UN Comtrade 2013.

Europe's sensitivities

Minerals and natural resources such as coal, gold and copper account for one-third of Australia's exports to the EU, which is consistent with Australia's trade with the world. However, agricultural products account for an additional 21 per cent. This is dominated by beef, wine and seeds, while other basic staples in Australia's agricultural trade such as wheat, cotton and barley are missing (UN Comtrade 2013).

Table 2. EU imports from Australia, top 20 categories

Top 20 EU import products from Australia	% of EU imports from Australia
Coal	23.0
Rape or colza seeds	9.4
Gold	6.3
Wine	4.7
Unwrought lead	3.7
Copper ores and concentrates	3.3
Zinc ores and concentrates	3.2
Diamonds	2.4
Wool, not carded or combed	2.3
Unwrought nickel	2.3
Lead ores and concentrates	2.0

Top 20 EU import products from Australia	% of EU imports from Australia
Silver	1.9
Medicaments	1.8
Orthopaedic appliances	1.8
Meat of bovine animals	1.5
Other nuts, fresh or dried	0.9
Radioactive chemical elements	0.9
Titanium ores and concentrates	0.9
Meat of sheep or goats	0.9
Niobium, tantalum, vanadium, etc.	0.8

Source: UN Comtrade 2013.

Agriculture is a central determinant of trade policy for both the EU and Australia. Whereas Europe maintains its common agricultural policy (CAP), which consumes 40 per cent of its budget, Australia has some of the most efficient agricultural producers in the world, including items that are among the most sensitive for Europe, especially regarding crops. Currently, the level of agricultural support (in terms of gross farm receipts, i.e. revenues) is 10 times higher in the EU than in Australia.

However, given the fiscal position of the EU, it is evident that CAP is being forced to reform. With a 13 per cent cut in subsidies approved in the 2013 multiannual financial framework, it is evident that the EU will orient itself towards export-driven agriculture, especially in sectors where the EU has comparative advantages, such as processed agricultural products, wine, pork or dairy (European Commission 2013a, 2013b).

Given the EU is facing unilateral reform in agriculture, the bargaining chips of agricultural tariffs and tariff rate quotas will quickly pass their due dates. Europe's choice on CAP is either to put agriculture up for negotiation now or lose them as bargaining chips in FTAs through inevitable unilateral reforms. But with 2.5 per cent of GDP coming from agriculture (compared to 1.4 per cent in the USA or 1.7 per cent in France) (FAOSTAT 2012), and more than half (52.8 per cent) of its territory being arable land (World Bank 2013), Australia has also the capacity to scale up its production if given the opportunity. OECD and Food and Agriculture Organization of the United Nations (OECD-FAO) projections show that it is likely to do so in the coming 10 years (OECD-FAO 2014).

Regulatory divergences

Australia and New Zealand may be smaller players internationally. However, they are like-minded polities with extensive mutual recognition agreements (MRAs) signed in 1999 covering telecom equipment, electronics, pharmaceutical products, medical devices, machinery and pressure equipment.

Australia and New Zealand are also signatories of the United Nations Economic Commission for Europe (UNECE) agreement of 1958 that sets common automobile standards, championed by the EU to become global standards. The centrality of these standards in recent EU trade negotiations (including Korea, Japan and TTIP) is evident. But it is worth noting the USA (which follows its own competing regional standard—the federal motor vehicle safety standards) is outperforming the European car industry on the Australian market despite the commonality of standards between the EU and Australia.

Where New Zealand has concluded a series of comprehensive sanitary and phytosanitary agreements and achieved data privacy adequacy with the EU, Australia also has a wines agreement in place that protects some European geographic indications.

TPP countries have a divergent view on geographic indications going back to the Doha Round, when the EU tabled a proposal to secure geographic indication protection through the Agreement on Trade-Related Aspects of Intellectual Property Rights (TRIPS) that would create *prima facie* assumptions for their legal protection among WTO members, while Australia endorsed a voluntary system.

In conclusion, the manner that regulatory divergences are addressed plays an increasingly important role in market integration. Current FTAs dedicate a fair amount of negotiation time and political capital (or finger-pointing in case of failure) on sanitary and phytosanitary issues, technical barriers to trade and sector annexes on non-tariff measures. Especially for the EU, these annexes are a necessity to advance key export interests such as the pharmaceutical, chemical or automobile sectors.

Australia and New Zealand already enjoy the level of regulatory cooperation that the EU generally achieves through its FTAs.

This is particularly true for the recognition of conformity assessment bodies that allow parties to maintain their own standards while avoiding duplicate testing. This supplements the approach where the EU seeks outright adaptation of its own regulations or standards, as the case of UNECE car safety regulations or FTA provisions on e-commerce that are directly transposed from internal EU directives. Previous generation FTAs, modelled on the EU–Korea FTA, addressed regulatory divergences through positive integration of EU internal rules. Whereas the EU single market is built on mutual recognition, the EU does not seek (or achieve) similar comprehensive mutual recognition or functional equivalence through its external agreements (Kenyon & Hussey 2011).

Europe's current difficulties in the TTIP and EU–Japan FTA negotiations show that any notion of 'shared values', 'like-mindedness', common heritages or geopolitical interests is no match against old mercantilist interests that awaken in every FTA negotiation. However, the pre-existing state of regulatory cooperation with Australia and New Zealand provides a starting point that did not exist with other counterparts before negotiations began.

Wider regional perspectives

Australia is also tied to New Zealand through the Closer Economic Relations (CER) trade agreement, which is the most comprehensive FTA between two OECD countries and the only cross-border market integration that incorporates elements that comes close to the European single market. The CER even incorporates elements that go beyond the European single market, with full liberalisation of services on a negative list basis. The full mutual recognition (provided through the Trans-Tasman Mutual Recognition Arrangement, TTMRA) also covers professional qualifications, and individuals registered to practise an occupation in each jurisdiction are entitled to practise an equivalent occupation in the other, without the need for further testing or examination.

The CER and its construct offer an interesting alternative approach to the EU FTAs. Unlike the single market, the CER achieves market integration through decentralisation and avoids institution building and supra-national harmonisation of standards and regulations. Instead, the CER is built on mutual recognition using existing judicial systems of its signatories, presenting a model that may be more suitable to bilateral FTAs than Europe's own internal integration.

Moreover, the common economic area created by the EU, Australia and New Zealand would have an economic output the size of the ASEAN or North American FTA (NAFTA), but where the socioeconomic disparities (such as income and wages) would not exceed the already existing differences within Europe (Eurostate 2014; WTO 2013).[3] A three-party negotiation of EU–CER is not unlikely, whether it takes place through two separate FTAs that is later consolidated into a common and singular framework in the following phase, or whether the parties decide to conduct a TPP-style negotiation based on bilateral negotiation on market access overarched by common rules and annexes.

Australia and New Zealand are also tied through their joint FTA with ASEAN (AZEAN–Australia–New Zealand Free Trade Agreement, AANZFTA)—the most ambitious FTA concluded by the ASEAN bloc. This phased out 96 per cent of the tariffs, introduced simplified rules of origin, trade facilitation and sanitary and phytosanitary agreements. The AANZFTA is unusual as it liberalises services significantly, notably in educational, financial and telecommunication services, and provides transparency and national treatment, limiting anti-competitive practices (Vitalis 2015). The multiparty FTA also contains horizontal commitments on domestic regulation, facilitation of business movement, and investment rules (with investor–state dispute settlement, ISDS), electronic commerce, intellectual property and competition policy. The agreement achieves some level of recognition of equivalence through a 'comply or explain' approach that is applied horizontally to all regulatory divergences.

Australia's successful venture of integrating with Southeast Asia should be seen in the light of Europe's own failed attempt to negotiate a region-to-region FTA with ASEAN. The completion of FTAs between the EU and both Australia and New Zealand could open up options that are not available to European trade policy today, including region-to-region integration with either the CER, or CER and ASEAN, or eventually both.

---

3   Eurostat 2014; World Bank, World Development Index 2013.

Europe's policy options

The lack of rapid response and comprehensiveness in addressing the competition from the TPP could be costly for the EU. Nonetheless, whether it is due to agricultural sensitivities or negotiation fatigue, EU trade policy could choose to remain passive on remaining countries in the Asia-Pacific region that it has not opened up negotiations with. The EU and Australia are already part of a few plurilateral negotiations in the trading system, including the Trade in Services Agreement (TiSA) and the Environmental Goods Agreement that could, at least in theory, provide some WTO-plus commitments. Both are also parties to some WTO plurilaterals (Information Technology Agreement and General Agreement on Trade in Services (GATS) additional protocols on services) but not all of them: Australia is yet to accede to the Agreement on Government Procurement (signed by New Zealand in 2015) or the plurilateral agreement on pharmaceuticals.

Such non-action would have short-term negative effects coming from trade diversion. Over the long term, further negative effects could be expected because of the impact of the TPP on non-participating countries.

As TPP and other intra-regional agreements are likely to incorporate at least some form of trade or regulatory standards, European exports will certainly face some new compliance costs, further increasing the productivity gap between the EU and the USA. TPP disciplines on corporate governance, investment, competition and state-owned enterprises could substantially transform the business environment of the signatories, and lead to higher returns, while the returns on the European home markets will remain relatively low.

This raises two issues. The first concerns the timing because, as the earlier discussion on CAP suggested, Europe's negotiation leverage against Australia would deteriorate with successive unilateral reforms. Moreover, a conclusion of the TPP could turn Europe into rule-takers rather than rule-makers, and leave it unable to advance its own priorities (for example, on issues like automobile standards, geographic indications or public procurement) in the world's most expansive economic region.

The second question is closely linked to the first, and concerns sequencing—that is, the order with which trade negotiations will take place and concessions will be given. When an economy seeks regulatory convergence, it will seek to harmonise its rules with the largest potential market first, as it would give them the best chance to reap the reciprocal benefits. This is the pattern followed by many Asian economies (e.g. Korea, Japan, Singapore) that opened up negotiations with the USA first, and went subsequently into smaller negotiations where they gave away concessions they had already made in the first deal to others. The threat of trade diversion is often a leverage that is used to open up negotiations with reluctant partners.

As the world's largest trading bloc, sequencing tends to come out reverse logic. The EU tends to start with the smaller (and thereby less threatening) and more flexible counterpart first (Lee-Makiyama 2015). This would allow Brussels to receive a better first offer in terms of both market access and excluding its sensitive products. The strategy was deployed against Korea/Japan, and to some extent also CETA/TTIP.

As Australia's GDP is eight times larger than New Zealand's, Europe's sequencing strategy could be its default strategy towards Oceania. While the market potential of Australia is larger in terms of GDP, and Australia's exports into the EU are three times larger than New Zealand's, less of its trade is currently exempt from duties. Australia's agricultural exports are far more diversified, with considerable quantities of products where EU subsidy reforms are still pending.

Conclusions

EU trade policy is shaped by the long-term economic developments where the world economy pivots towards the Asia-Pacific region, at the same time as the relative importance of Europe's domestic markets are declining. In order to counter the aggregate income drop expected from the TPP, the EU has very few policy options except to negotiate bilaterals with all TPP countries to advance its own FTA template. Following this logic, FTA negotiations with Australia and New Zealand may be just a matter of time.

Europe's offensive export interests tend to be in highly regulated sectors where technical standards play a major role for market access. Achieving regulatory compatibility and avoiding regulatory compliance costs matters for export competitiveness, especially in sectors like automobiles, machinery, pharmaceuticals, medical devices and chemicals—and EU firms are already underperforming vis-à-vis their TPP competitors on these sectors in Australia. If the TPP succeeds in setting new regulatory standards, EU exports will inevitably face additional compliance costs where their TPP competitors do not. On agriculture, European exports could even be locked out from the TPP markets, making domestic agricultural reforms even costlier and riskier to undertake.

But the prospects of Australia–EU FTA negotiations raise some new and interesting questions. The first question concerns Australia's link to New Zealand and the CER. As described above, past negotiation strategies and agricultural sensitivities suggest that Europe could start negotiating with Australia's smaller neighbour first. But given the free movement of goods and services guaranteed under the CER, it would become untenable in the long run to conclude an FTA with only one of the CER countries, as goods and services move freely between Australia and New Zealand. Similar problems would arise if both FTAs were concluded, but with highly asymmetrical outcomes (e.g. where tariffs are cut in Europe for a certain good from one CER country, but not for the other), especially if rules of origin in the two FTAs are not harmonised.

Unlike Europe's customs union with Turkey, Australia and New Zealand do not apply common external tariffs. Australia and New Zealand have concluded both joint and individually negotiated FTAs. But whenever a major FTA was concluded by one of the CER countries, the other moved in swiftly to negotiate its own FTA. However, there are also some divergent interests between Brussels, Canberra and Wellington— especially on agriculture, where New Zealand is more specialised than Australia. A region-to-region agreement between the EU and CER could be constructed in various ways and built on individual schedules, as in the AANZFTA or TPP.

Relatively ambitious agreements on regulatory cooperation already exist between Australia and the EU. The pre-existing levels of regulatory cooperation are on a par with some relatively recent EU FTAs. Should the Australia–EU FTA include a chapter and annexes on regulatory issues, its provisions are likely to be on the same level of ambition as the goals on recognition of equivalence currently negotiated under the TTIP or TPP; otherwise, it would have little value added compared to the pre-existing MRAs.

Regulatory harmonisation and cooperation bring about another dimension of complexity, in areas where the CER and TTMRA go beyond the internal liberalisation in the EU, notably on services and professional qualifications (Kenyon & Hussey 2011). Assuming that the EU cannot adopt and implement similar high-level standards internally, the scope of the Australia–EU FTA is constrained by the functional limits of the single market. Finally, there are certain discrepancies with the relationships that would need to be addressed: for example, Australia has concluded a wine agreement with the EU, and New Zealand has a received an adequacy ruling on data privacy rules, allowing for open cross-border data flows.

Both questions could either be resolved through a 'race to the top', where all parties agree to the highest standard prevailing in the three-party relationship, or 'cherry picking', where each party maintains the flexibility to define their own agreement with the other two according to the problems in that relationship. The determinants that will shape the form of the final EU–Australia agreement will be the need for such flexibility that will be balanced against the risks of asymmetrical, or even incomplete, liberalisation between the EU and Oceania.

References

Bauer, Matthias, Fredrick Erixon, Martina Ferracane & Hosuk Lee-Makiyama (2014), 'Trans-Pacific Partnership: A challenge to Europe', *ECIPE Policy Brief*, no. 9/2014.

Copenhagen Economics (2011), *Ex-Post Assessment of Six EU Free Trade Agreements*, report prepared for European Commission (Copenhagen Economics: Copenhagen). Available at trade.ec.europa.eu/doclib/docs/2011/may/tradoc_147905.pdf.

European Commission (2013a), '"Health Check" of the Common Agricultural Policy'. Available at ec.europa.eu/agriculture/healthcheck/index_en.htm.

European Commission (2013b), 'Overview of CAP Reform 2014–2020', *Agricultural Policy Perspectives Brief*, no. 5, December.

Eurostat (2013), Eurostat online database. Available at ec.europa.eu/eurostat/web/international-trade-in-goods/data/database.

FAOSTAT (Food and Agriculture Organization of the United Nations Statistics) (2012), FAOSTAT: Food and Agriculture data. Available at www.fao.org/faostat/en/.

Kawasaki, Kenichi (2011), 'Determining priority among EPAs: Which trading partner has the greatest economic impact?', FY2011 Column, Research Institute of Economic, Trade and Industry (RIETI), 31 May. Available at www.rieti.go.jp/en/columns/a01_0318.html.

Kenyon, Don & Karen Hussey (2011), 'Regulatory divergences: A barrier to trade and a potential source of trade disputes', *Australian Journal of International Affairs*, 65(4): 381–93. doi.org/10.1080/10357718.201 1.586668.

Lee-Makiyama, Hosuk (2015), 'New Zealand: The EU's Asia-Pacific partnership and the case for a next generation FTA', *ECIPE Policy Brief*, no. 7/2015.

Messerlin, Patrick (2012), 'The TPP and the EU policy in East Asia', *ECIPE Policy Brief*, no. 11/2012.

OECD STAN (Organisation for Economic Co-operation and Development STructural ANalysis Database) (2013), STAN STructural ANalysis Database. Available at www.oecd.org/industry/ind/stanstructuralanalysisdatabase.htm.

OECD STRI (2014), 'Services Trade Restrictiveness Index'. Available at stats.oecd.org/Index.aspx?DataSetCode=STRI.

OECD/FAO (Organisation for Economic Co-operation and Development/ Food and Agriculture Organization of the United Nations) (2014), *OECD-FAO Agricultural Outlook 2014* (OECD Publishing: Paris).

UN Comtrade (United Nations) (2013), UN Comtrade database. Available at comtrade.un.org/.

Vitalis, Vangelis (2015), *Regional Economic Integration and Multilateralism: The Case of the ASEAN-Australia-New Zealand FTA and the Malaysia-New Zealand FTA*, ADBI Working Paper No. 523 (Asian Development Bank Institute: Tokyo).

World Bank (2013), 'World Development Indicators'. Available at data.worldbank.org/indicator.

World Bank (2014a), 'Doing Business: Measuring Business Regulation'. Available at www.doingbusiness.org/.

World Bank (2014b), 'World Development Indicators'. Available at data. worldbank.org/indicator.

WTO (World Trade Organization) (2013), World Tariff Profiles database. Available at tariffdata.wto.org/.

12

An FTA with the EU: What Could Be Gained?[1]

Bruce Gosper

Too big to ignore

When considering international economic policy, the European Union (EU) is simply too big to ignore. In 2014, the 28 members of the EU had a combined US dollar gross domestic product (GDP) of US$18.4 trillion, making it the world's largest economy. On a purchasing power parity (PPP) basis, which adjusts for differences in spending power, the EU was again the world's largest economy in 2014, with a GDP of almost PPP$18.5 trillion.[2]

Despite ongoing economic strains within the Eurozone, the EU is also an international trade and investment superpower. In 2013, for example, it was the world's largest exporter of merchandise goods, with extra-EU exports worth US$2,307 billion, or around 15 per cent of the global total, and the world's second-largest importer of merchandise goods, with US$2,235 billion of imports, also around 15 per cent of the world total.[3]

---

1   The case addressed here is based on the economic and commercial benefits of an agreement rather than other issues.

2   GDP data are from the International Monetary Fund (IMF) (2015b).

3   Data for merchandise and commercial services trade are from the World Trade Organization (WTO) (2014). Note that the reported numbers are for world trade *excluding* intra-EU trade. This is appropriate if we are treating the EU as a single economic area, just as we do not count (say) trade between Australian states in the international figures.

The EU is also the world's largest exporter and importer of commercial services. Its extra-EU exports totalled US$891 billion, which was almost one-quarter of the global total in 2013, while its imports were US$668 billion, or almost one-fifth of the world's overall import bill.

In 2013, the EU was the source of US$250 billion of foreign direct investment (FDI) outflows, behind only the United States of America (USA). In the same year, the EU received US$246 billion of FDI inflows, making it the world's largest recipient (UNCTAD 2014).

The sheer economic heft of the EU makes it appear rather odd to many observers that the EU is the one major trading partner with which Australia does not have a free trade agreement (FTA) or even one currently under negotiation. In fact, as Mike Adams, Nicolas Brown and Ron Wickes point out in *Trading Nation* (2013), 'Australia and the European Union have purposely looked past each other in the rush for FTAs'.

This situation prevails despite the fact that, over time, there have been several calls on the Australian side for a deal with the EU. The 2008 Mortimer Review, for example, noted that the EU was 'the only major trading partner with which Australia is not negotiating or considering negotiating an FTA' and went on to propose (in recommendation 6.7) that the then government should consider the merits of negotiating a bilateral FTA with the EU, including the possibility of an agreement focused only on services and related investment, which it thought could deliver 'considerable benefits' (Mortimer & Edwards 2008). A more comprehensive FTA would of course deliver even greater benefits for both sides and beyond.

Why don't we already have an FTA with the EU?

So, why don't we have a deal already? Adams, Brown and Wickes (2013) suggest several reasons as to why an agreement has so far failed to materialise. From an Australian perspective, these include Australia's perfectly sensible focus on the large-scale opportunities offered by the Asia-Pacific region; the absence of any compelling problems in the bilateral trade and investment relationship that require substantial policy intervention (aside from agriculture, of course); the fact that market access is already relatively easy due to generally low tariffs in both economies (an observation subject to the same qualification); and the presence of existing agreements already aimed at protecting investment and intellectual property. For example, the EU–Australia Partnership Framework, which was signed in 2008, included the objective of cooperation on mutual recognition approaches to facilitating trade in industrial goods (Rollo 2011).

The same authors also note that big and long-standing differences between Canberra and Brussels over agricultural policy may also have 'drained away the reserves of energy needed by trade negotiators and political leaders to seriously contemplate another big FTA'. Certainly, as Philomena Murray and M. Bruna Zolin (2012) point out, there can be little doubt that 'one single focus of intense conflict and strong emotions in Australia–EU relations has eclipsed all other aspects of the relationship over many decades … the EU's agricultural policy and, especially, agri-food trade'.

Despite the past difficulties for the bilateral relationship posed by agriculture, and despite their own list of reasons as to why no FTA with the EU has yet been forthcoming, however, Adams, Brown and Wickes still conclude that there is a case for 'putting historical baggage to one side and taking a fresh look' at the issue.

That's a perspective that makes a great deal of sense, especially given that, under current circumstances, an FTA with the EU has the potential to deliver several important strategic and productive benefits to both Australia and the EU. This is most significant, perhaps, in key areas that foster the innovation both Australia and the EU need to drive future growth and respond to critical challenges, such as the impact of disruptive technologies, ageing and development of an appropriately skilled, mobile and competitive Australian labour market.

This chapter will concentrate on the arguments for, and benefits to, Australia from negotiating a comprehensive FTA with the EU. But there are also important benefits to the EU; for example, in better leveraging our deep integration with Asia and key areas of strength in financial services (e.g. superannuation and public–private partnerships in infrastructure financing) and in some areas of medical research and technology (e.g. neuroscience, cancer research and treatment), to name a few.

It's logical to look to a major trade and investment partner

A logical and indeed obvious place to look for prospective negotiating partners is the group of countries that comprise our major trade and investment partners. On this basis, the EU is a standout contender, particularly with respect to trade in services and foreign investment.

In 2014 the value of Australia's total trade in goods and services with the EU was about A$84 billion, around 12.6 per cent of our total trade in goods and services that year. That made the EU our second-largest trading partner in 2013–14, behind only China (which had a 24 per cent share) (DFAT 2014). By market share, in 2013–14 the EU was Australia's fourth-largest export market overall, our fourth-largest export market for goods and our largest export market for services. The EU was also the most important source of all Australian imports, our second-largest source of goods imports and our largest source of services imports (DFAT 2014).

One interesting example of the bilateral trading relationship is provided by the case of Australian Scientific Instruments, a Canberra-based company that is owned by The Australian National University. In 2012, the company finalised a multimillion dollar contract for the supply of the world-leading Sensitive High Resolution Ion Micro Probe (or SHRIMP) to the Polish National Geological Institute. This equipment allows extremely accurate data to be collected from geological samples and provides insight into geological structures, with applications for the mining, oil and gas sectors. The Austrade post in Warsaw provided a supporting role to Australian Scientific Instruments in this process (Austrade 2012).

It's probably also worth noting at this point that the large trade flows described above take place against the backdrop of what is already a *relatively* liberal trade policy environment. According to the World Trade Organization (WTO), in 2013 the simple average most-favoured-nation (MFN) applied tariff in the EU was 5.5 per cent, compared to 2.7 per cent in Australia. On a trade-weighted basis, the EU average tariff in 2013 was just 2.6 per cent, compared to 3.9 per cent in Australia in 2012.[4]

---

4   Sourced from WTO tariff profiles at stat.wto.org/TariffProfile/WSDBTariffPFHome.aspx?Language=E.

There is, however, an important sectoral element to this story: the EU has an average MFN applied tariff of 13.2 per cent applying to the agricultural sector compared to a rate of just 4.2 per cent applying to the non-agricultural sector, as Table 1 shows. For Australia, the corresponding levels of protection in 2013 were 1.2 per cent and 3 per cent. On a trade-weighted basis, the average tariff applied to agriculture by the EU in 2013 was 8.4 per cent and 2.2 per cent for non-agriculture. In the case of Australia the corresponding figures were 2.6 per cent and 4 per cent.

Table 1. MFN applied tariffs in the European Union and Australia, 2013

	European Union	Australia
Average applied tariffs		
Overall	5.5	2.7
Agricultural sector	13.2	1.2
Non-agricultural sector	4.2	3.0
Trade-weighted applied tariffs		
Overall	2.6	3.9
Agricultural sector	8.4	2.6
Non-agricultural sector	2.2	4.0

Source: WTO 2015.

Then, of course, there is the fact that not only is the EU a major trading partner for Australia, but it is similarly an extremely important source of, and destination for, foreign investment.

The EU is Australia's largest foreign investor. The total stock of EU investment in Australia as of 31 December 2014 was A$959 billion, 34 per cent of total foreign investment. Of that, A$170 billion was FDI, 25 per cent of Australia's total inward FDI.[5]

Recent inward investment stories include the following: in 2014, the Acciona-led Transcity Consortium received the Project of the Year Award from Infrastructure Partnerships Australia for Legacy Way, a A$1.5 billion project to design, construct, maintain and operate a twin tunnel roadway in Brisbane; Nestle Australia expanded its operations in Australia by investing in a state-of-the-art medical nutrition facility for the company's health sciences business; and German technology company SAP recently established a data centre in Sydney (Austrade 2013).

---

5   Data from ABS (2015).

The EU is also the second-largest destination for Australian investment overseas in general and for FDI in particular. In 2014, the stock of Australian investment in the EU was A$529.2 billion, or about 28 per cent of the total stock of our outward investment. Of that total, about A$83.5 billion was FDI, which was about 15 per cent of total outward FDI.

In summary, then, the scale of the bilateral relationship suggests that the potential pay-offs from an FTA would likely be significant. Moreover, given the relative importance of services trade and foreign investment, there are good grounds for believing that the kind of behind-the-border measures that modern FTAs address would be of particular benefit in encouraging additional economic flows between the two economies.

An EU deal is the obvious missing element in Australia's list of FTAs

The case for looking to the EU as a negotiating partner that is implied by the current depth of the bilateral economic relationship is further reinforced by taking a look at our current line-up of FTAs in order to identify any obvious gaps.

One way to approach this is to start with Australia's top 10 trading partners for goods and services. In 2013–14, these were (in descending order): China, EU, Japan, USA, Korea, Singapore, New Zealand, Malaysia, Thailand and Indonesia. Together, these 10 economies accounted for 77 per cent of total Australian trade (DFAT n.d.).[6] Of this group of 10, Australia already has FTAs covering all of them except the EU.[7] Adams, Brown and Wickes (2013) describe the EU as the 'biggest single missing jigsaw piece' in our current network of FTAs.

Table 2. Australia's bilateral trade in goods and services by top 10 partners, 2013–14

Rank	Country	Value (mln A$)	% share of total
1	China	159,643	23.9
2	European Union	83,379	12.5
3	Japan	72,173	10.8
4	United States of America	58,196	8.7

---

6   If ASEAN is included as a group, the EU rank drops to three.
7   Indonesia is the only country in the top 10 without a direct FTA, but is covered in the ASEAN–Australia–New Zealand Free Trade Agreement (AANZFTA).

Rank	Country	Value (mln A$)	% share of total
5	Republic of Korea	34,589	5.2
6	Singapore	29,510	4.4
7	New Zealand	22,689	3.4
8	Malaysia	19,887	3
9	Thailand	18,837	2.8
10	Indonesia	15,970	2.4
Total		514,873	77.1

Source: DFAT 2014.

We get a similar message if we look at our leading investment relationships. So, for example, if we examine the stock of FDI as of end 2012, the top 10 *source* economies for inward FDI were (in descending order): EU, USA, Japan, China, Singapore, Canada, Switzerland, United Arab Emirates, Hong Kong and Malaysia. The corresponding top 10 *destinations* for Australian FDI were (again in order): USA, EU, New Zealand, Singapore, China, Malaysia, Indonesia, Hong Kong, Bermuda and India.

The EU stands out as a major bilateral investment partner with which Australia does not have an FTA either in place or under negotiation.

Table 3. Foreign direct investment flows into Australia by top 10 sources, 2014

Rank	Country	Value (bln A$)	% share of total
1	European Union	169.6	24.6
2	United States of America	163.4	23.7
3	Japan	66.1	9.6
4	China	30.0	4.4
5	Singapore	28.0	4.1
6	Canada	23.6	3.4
7	Switzerland	19.0	2.8
8	United Arab Emirates	14.6	2.1
9	Hong Kong	11.5	1.7
10	Malaysia	9.6	1.4
Total		535.4	77.8

Source: ABS 2015.

Table 4. Foreign direct investment flows from Australia by top 10 destinations, 2014

Rank	Country	Value (mln A$)	% share of total
1	United States of America	136.2	25.2
2	European Union	83.5	15.4
3	New Zealand	61.6	11.4
4	Singapore	13.1	2.4
5	China	12.1	2.2
6	Malaysia	6.0	1.1
7	Indonesia	5.3	1.0
8	Hong Kong	5.1	0.9
9	Bermuda	3.6	0.7
10	India	1.6	0.3
Total		328.1	60.7

Source: ABS 2015.

Agriculture is no longer the deal breaker that it used to be—the relationship is more diverse and sensitivities have modified

To the compelling logic provided by the opportunity to plug in a critical missing piece in Australia's existing network of FTAs can be added the fact that agriculture need no longer serve as an automatic deal breaker in negotiations with the EU. As Don Kenyon and Pierre van de Eng (2014b) pointed out, in large part this is because a series of internal EU reforms have, over time, removed some of the serious market distortions that have been generated in the past by the EU's program of export subsidies.[8]

Granted, this does not mean that there are no significant issues remaining with regard to agricultural trade. The relatively high level of EU tariffs on agricultural products was noted above and the EU continues to retain significant levels of protection overall against agricultural imports that serve as a serious impediment to Australian exporters. But there are signs that the EU might be prepared to negotiate increased market access to its

---

8   Beginning with the initial common agricultural policy (CAP) reform package of 1992, the old regime of high support prices to EU farmers has gradually been replaced with direct income support (Kenyon & van der Eng 2014b).

valuable internal market for Australian farmers through the mechanism of expanded tariff quotas (TQs), with potentially significant gains in beef, grains, sugar, dairy and lamb. I say this from the perspective of being closely involved with the Commission in Doha Round discussions on market access during the last push for an agreement on the full agriculture agenda, in 2008.

At that time Australia was able to see the shape of what it might secure, albeit not easily, through implementation by the EU of Doha's proposed approach to agricultural market access. It was a discussion centred on what commercially meaningful concessions Australia might extract in return for some margin of manoeuvre for the Commission on the most sensitive areas of EU agriculture. In recent years, there has been strong cooperation between Australia and the EU on matters such as the Anti-Counterfeiting Trade Agreement and the Trade in Services Agreement (TiSA). Indeed, in the area of services trade liberalisation in the WTO, the EU and Australia have been the most like-minded collaborators not only on matters like domestic regulation but also on the need to address equity caps and bind current practice and market opening.

Australian agriculture has substantial interests in better access to the EU market, and this would need to be a part of any negotiations Australia entered into. But after decades of unsuccessfully pushing at the door, many in the sector are reluctant to talk about what they might gain until they see a real negotiation engaged. And, of course, it shouldn't be assumed that we can predict which agricultural products might do well in a more open environment.

There is ample scope for a substantive negotiating agenda

What sort of issues can we expect to arise in a negotiation between the EU and Australia? One guide can be found in our respective submissions to WTO Trade Policy Reviews. In their 2015 review of Australia's trade policy, the EU commended the openness and transparency of Australia's trade regime, its commitment to multilateralism, and its strengthening of intellectual property laws. The EU noted the cooperation with Australia on the Anti-Counterfeiting Trade Agreement. On a less positive note, the EU urged continuing regulatory reform and for Australia to join the Agreement on Government Procurement (GPA), encouraged Australia to remove the luxury car tax, and highlighted the need for aligning of Australia's sanitary and phytosanitary measures with international standards.

For its part, in its comments to the 2013 trade policy review of the EU, Australia commended the EU's strong commitment to the multilateral system and in work with Australia on the TiSA. Australia noted recent reforms to the common agricultural policy (CAP), but said some coupled payments were increasing, and urged the EU to cease use of export subsidies and increase market access. Australia asked that the EU clarify third-country access to the government procurement market, commended efforts to harmonise the internal market but asked for more consistent application, and raised concerns about technical regulations restricting the processing of products imported from outside the EU.

This might give some sense of what an agenda might look like. Both Australia and the EU have made strong liberalising commitments in tariff elimination in respect of manufactured goods. Agriculture would be a substantial element, where Australia would push new access for items such as lamb, dairy, beef, wine and seafood. Perhaps a priority would be an update of the 1995 'Andriessen Assurance', with the EU undertaking not to supply subsidised beef in specified markets in Asia and the Pacific. And perhaps the EU would ask Australia to remove our single remaining agricultural TQ on its high-value cheeses. A negative list services agreement would be a priority for both.

Similarly, a substantial investment agreement would be fundamental given the nature of our economic relationship. Both Australia and the EU are committed to strong standards of intellectual property protection, and no doubt the EU would look for some recognition of its geographical indications interests, as would Australia of its interests in the continuing use of generic names. Australia has begun to articulate its own agenda on the protection of common names in world trade, and would value the opportunity to engage with the EU on this issue. Government procurement is seen by both as a key issue. Both Australia and the EU would bring sanitary and phytosanitary and technical barriers to trade issues to the table in a negotiation. *Prima facie*, this is a substantial agenda and with plenty of potential to enhance the overall relationship.

The alternative, multilateral route continues to look underwhelming …

If we could rely on the multilateral trading system to deliver a new, broad-based international trade agreement, then targeting a separate FTA with the EU might be a questionable use of limited negotiating resources. Unfortunately, for the moment the multilateral option continues to look incapable of delivering the kind of deep economic integration that a successful FTA might be able to provide with a sharp focus on lowering non-tariff barriers (NTBs).

The most compelling piece of evidence for this proposition is the low prospects for the original ambitions for the Doha Round; ambitions that anyway fell far short of the kind of 'deep integration' agenda now pursued in modern FTAs. The replacement of those original Doha goals with an even more modest agenda, based around the worthy but limited objective of trade facilitation, has subsequently confirmed the difficulties at the multilateral level. More generally, the repeated failure of the WTO ever since the debacle surrounding the so-called Singapore Issues (at least, ex-trade facilitation) of 1996 to meet the current appetite of the developed world for the kind of behind-the-border measures involving agreements on standards and regulation, investment, intellectual property, government procurement, competition policy and so on that are of increasing salience in today's global economy suggests that the appetite for deal-making outside the WTO will only persist.

Australia remains firmly committed to the multilateral system and to the benefits of a multilateral round. The decision to eliminate export subsidies on agriculture taken at the 10th WTO ministerial meeting in Nairobi in late December 2015 demonstrates how essential the multilateral system is in achieving such important systemic changes. Of course, multilateral negotiations are needed to address domestic agricultural subsidies. It should be clear that this is a subject that cannot be dealt with, certainly in any substantial way, in an FTA. Australia is also mindful of its commitments in FTAs as a way to continue to progress liberalisation, including through inbuilt agendas, to ensure our efforts are not counter to, but support, our efforts to advance a strong multilateral rules-based system.

The global environment remains challenging …

The limited outlook for the prospects for additional multilateral trade liberalisation is accompanied by a moderate outlook for global growth. According to the International Monetary Fund's (IMF) World Economic Outlook, for example, in real terms world economic growth is slowing. Projected rates are significantly below the average growth rates before the global financial crisis hit in 2008, and private investment is yet to recover (IMF 2015a).

Subdued global growth has contributed to subdued international trade. In the same forecast, for example, the IMF estimates that the volume of world trade in goods and services will expand in 2015 by 3.7 per cent and 2016 by 4.7 per cent, at rates just above those of world GDP. That compares to annual trend growth in trade volumes that was running at more than 7 per cent before the crisis.

Moreover, while international trade has certainly not suffered from the kind of mass relapse into protectionism that some pessimists feared might be triggered by the global financial crisis and the high unemployment that followed, nevertheless there are some troubling signs of advances in so-called murky protectionism. According to the 16th *Global Trade Alert* report of the London-based Centre for Economic Policy Research, for example, between the first quarter of 2012 and the third quarter of 2014, the number of new protectionist measures implemented not only increased again, but in 2013 more new protectionist measures were imposed than in the crisis year of 2009 (Evenett 2014). More recently, the WTO's latest assessment judged that 'G-20 economies between mid-October 2014 and mid-May 2015 implemented fewer trade-restrictive measures per month than at any time since 2013'. However, the same report went on to caution that the:

> longer term trend remains one of concern with the overall stock of trade-restrictive measures introduced by G-20 economies since 2008 continuing to rise. Of the 1,360 restrictions recorded by this exercise since 2008, less than a quarter have been eliminated, leaving the total number of restrictive measures still in place at 1,031. Therefore, despite the G-20 pledge to roll back any new protectionist measures, the stock of these measures has risen by over 7% since the last report. (WTO, OECD & UNCTAD 2015)[9]

---

9   Note that the WTO coverage of protectionist measures is more restrictive than the approach taken by the *Global Trade Alert* reports.

And the world (including the EU) is moving on

With the multilateral system failing to deliver the kind of deep integration that is now a priority for policy makers and businesses alike, many leading trading nations have sought alternative approaches, including FTAs, regional agreements and most recently the so-called mega-regional deals embodied in the Trans-Pacific Partnership (TPP) and Transatlantic Trade and Investment Partnership (TTIP). In recent years, the prevailing weak global economic environment has almost certainly helped to further reinforce this trend, offering as it does the prospect of a new impetus for growth and moreover one that may be particularly attractive to fiscally constrained governments.

In the case of the EU, the initial shift in emphasis in trade policy can be traced back to at least 2006, when the then EU Trade Commissioner was given a mandate to launch a new strategy for a 'Global Europe'. This mandate was then extended and deepened in 2010 as part of the Europe 2020 strategy. The result has been an official approach that has focused on signing deep and comprehensive FTAs with attractive trading partners, with the aim of not only securing improved commercial opportunities for European businesses, but also of using the EU's weight to shape the global trade and investment policy environment (Deutsch 2012).

The EU successfully concluded its first agreement under this new approach in 2010 in the form of an agreement with Korea and has also concluded an agreement with Singapore and Vietnam. Elsewhere in the region, the EU has negotiations underway with India (since 2007), Malaysia (since 2010, but paused since 2012) and Thailand (launched in May 2015). It also commenced negotiations with Japan in April 2013. And then there is the giant of all bilateral trade negotiations the TTIP. From an Australian perspective, the fact that the EU is now negotiating with many of our key regional trading partners as well as with the USA adds to the logic of pursuing our own FTA negotiations with Brussels.

Finally in this context, another recently concluded EU agreement, the Comprehensive Economic and Trade Agreement (CETA) with Canada offers yet more support to the case for an FTA. Interestingly, Canada would not have met the original criteria set out by the EU for potential FTA partners, focused as they were on emerging economies with significant growth potential and major barriers to EU trade. The inclusion of Canada (and subsequently Japan and the USA) therefore signals an important shift in the EU's willingness to conduct bilateral agreements with developed economies.

Now CETA could provide us with a useful roadmap

Indeed, as Don Kenyon and Pierre van der Eng (2014a) point out, CETA could serve as a template or road map for a possible Australia–EU deal. For a start, there are clearly some close parallels between the Australian and Canadian economies. This suggests that much of the logic that made Canada an attractive negotiating partner for the EU should likewise apply to Australia. In addition, Australia's geographic proximity and deep integration with Asian economies is an added advantage.

More particularly, however, there is the nature of CETA itself, with its focus on removing NTBs to services and investment, and its coverage of issues such as regulatory standards, rules and people movement. So, for example, work by the EU and Canada found that trade in services between the two economies was subject to significant barriers that were estimated to increase the cost of service provision by between 20 and 50 per cent. An official joint study drew on this kind of evidence to conclude that bilateral trade could be increased by between 20 and 25 per cent in both directions if a comprehensive deal were reached, with roughly half of the effect coming from liberalisation of trade in services, and roughly one-quarter each attributable to reductions in tariffs and in technical barriers.[10]

The relative importance of services trade and investment in the Canada–EU bilateral relationship worked to encourage a focus on the importance of behind-the-border issues (Schwanen 2011). Given the similar importance of services trade and investment in the Australia–EU relationship as set out above—remember, the EU is our most important services trade partner, our largest foreign investor and our second-most important investment destination—progress in these same areas would offer the potential for significant economic gains. For example, as Kenyon and van der Eng (2014b) have emphasised in their work, large benefits

---

10 These figures also assumed that the Doha Round would be completed. If Doha was not completed, the estimated gains would likely be significantly greater (Deutsch 2012).

for business could be realised by the mutual recognition of technically divergent but functionally broadly equivalent licensing, labelling, standards, certification regulations and professional qualifications.

From an Australian perspective, the striking thing about CETA is that it is the most ambitious services trade agreement that the EU has negotiated to date, with commitments that are better than those offered in the EU's FTA with Korea and that are also superior to current EU offers in the ongoing TiSA negotiations. Notably, CETA marks the first time that the EU has adopted a 'negative list' approach in an FTA, which combines commitments that bind current market access with future liberalisation except where reservations are listed. Since this is also the approach to services liberalisation favoured by Australia, CETA represents a positive signal that a relatively liberal and dynamic outcome is possible.

Another important feature of CETA is the inclusion of an MFN obligation to extend any future preferential treatment (except in relation to the EU's own internal market or the European Economic Area), which helps 'future-proof' the deal. Canada was also successful in using CETA to persuade Brussels to reduce the number of policy space reservations across a range of sectors, including professional services, environmental services, transport services and other business services—all of which would be of great interest to Australia. The CETA provisions relating to financial services would similarly look attractive to any future Australian negotiators.

CETA also suggests that a deal with the EU would offer the opportunity to boost innovation. CETA, for example, not only includes commitments on research and development services, technical testing and analysis and other scientific and technical consulting services, but also establishes a bilateral dialogue on enhanced cooperation on science, technology, research and innovation issues.

Engaging with the new trade policy landscape

Both the specific example of CETA and the more general trend towards deep integration as exemplified by the ambitious aims of the new mega-regional deals reflect the shifting nature of international trade in today's global economy. That trade is increasingly characterised by international production networks and global value chains, which in turn are heavily reliant on close connections between services, standards, intellectual property, the role of foreign affiliates, and cross-border flows of capital and labour. As is now well known, many of these variables are most influenced not by traditional, at-the-border policy measures such as tariffs or quotas, but rather by behind-the-border measures including standards and other regulations.

Some optimists now see the FTA route in general and the mega-regional route in particular as potentially contributing to the emergence of a 'multilateral deal through the back alley', producing the kind of agreement that will end up being 'far more liberalising and comprehensive than could ever be attained in Geneva' (Suominen 2012). The argument here tends to be based around the idea of critical mass. That is, a successful TTIP would encompass an economic region that contributes about half of world trade. As a result, if these economies were to agree on a common set of standards or regulations, there will be strong incentives for exporters in the rest of the world to conform to those same standards. Since any trading partner choosing to do so would then see its overall trading costs with both the USA and the EU decline, this would tend to reduce costs (and boost competition) for international players across the board (Cernat 2013). The end-game in this optimistic version of the world would then be the emergence of a set of global rules by a process of gradual accretion.

While the optimism about an effective global agreement may well turn out to be overdone, the potential importance of this kind of effect, as well as some of the risks it entails for the rest of the world, can be seen in some of the modelling around the likely impact of a TTIP on the rest of the world. For example, the main study commissioned by the European Commission on TTIP found that liberalising trade between the EU and the USA would have a positive impact on overall world trade and income. However, it turns out that the impact on the rest of the world is critically dependent on assumptions made about the potential for international convergence on EU–USA standards, which would then become *de facto* global standards in the way described above. This would produce lower NTBs worldwide and so deliver increased market access for third countries that would help offset any trade diversion.[11] It is these assumptions about reductions in NTBs that ensure economies in the rest of the world see an increase in welfare via a reduction in global trade costs as a result of the TTIP.[12]

The impact of these assumptions is highlighted by the findings of another study of the TTIP—this time by Germany's Bertelsmann Foundation—which in marked contrast identifies the potential for a significant degree of trade diversion (Felbermayr, Heid & Lehwald 2013). This report looks at two scenarios for the TTIP, one based on the elimination of tariffs alone, and one based on the kind of deep integration produced by eliminating NTBs. The tariff-only scenario sees the main losers from TTIP-induced trade diversion concentrated in those developing and emerging economies reliant on EU and US export markets—with the biggest losses in North and West Africa. According to this model, Australia is a small loser from trade diversion, suffering a 0.6 per cent fall in real income per capita in the long run. However, the same report's 'deep integration' scenario models a much bigger hit to welfare, with Australia seeing a 7.4 per cent drop in its long-run real per capita income, alongside other big losers including Canada (–9.5 per cent), Mexico (–7.2 per cent) and Japan (–5.9 per cent).

This negative impact is in large part because this study explicitly does *not* take into account the likelihood that these countries would adopt the same standards and regulations as prevail under a completed TTIP. The study's authors highlight the fact that these results provide a strong argument for countries such as Canada that already have an agreement with one partner in TTIP to conclude another (which the Canadians have just done with CETA). Obviously, the same argument applies to Australia: if the EU and the USA are going to be in effect writing the global rule book, we will likely end up having to adopt it one way or another, or suffer increased

---

11   The study actually makes two important assumptions here. First, it assumes *direct* spillovers whereby the bilateral EU–USA streamlining of regulations and standards also provides benefits to third parties, since it will become less costly to meet these new, simplified standards. Second, it also assumes *indirect* spillovers whereby third markets choose to adopt some of the common standards agreed by the EU and the USA (Francois et al. 2013).

12   A recent study by CEPII also finds 'little trade diversion induced by a TTIP', with additional bilateral trade mostly replacing domestic production. The USA sees some trade diversion from the rest of the world, mostly concentrated in manufacturing, while in the EU there is no trade diversion overall as the trade diversion in agriculture (whereby imports from the USA displace those from third markets) is more than offset by trade creation with third countries, mainly through global value chain effects (Fontagné, Gourdon & Jean 2013).

relative trade costs. With that prospect in mind, it makes sense to seek to be an active participant in shaping the rules as far as possible, a proposition that further reinforces the case for an Australia–EU FTA.

As mentioned earlier, Australia remains committed to the multilateral system and the benefits of a comprehensive multilateral round. Australia is mindful of its commitments in FTAs as a way to continue to progress liberalisation, including through inbuilt agendas, to ensure our efforts are not counter to, but support, our efforts globally, to keep the door open for a multilateral round.

Conclusion: The case for an Australia–EU agreement

In conclusion, then, there are several good reasons for considering the case for an Australia–EU FTA. Some of these are fairly obvious. In particular, the substantial nature of the existing bilateral economic flows, particularly with regard to services trade and investment, are indicative of the scale of potential pay-off from a successful agreement. Likewise, the fact that the EU currently stands out as the 'biggest single missing jigsaw piece' in our existing and prospective network of FTAs supports the logic of a push to negotiate a deal.

Then there is the argument that there are grounds for believing that agriculture may no longer be the deal-breaker that it has been in the past, and indeed that there might now be scope to deliver improved access to the EU's high-value internal market for Australian farmers. There may also be important opportunities for Australian businesses to cooperate with European agri-supply chain operations to leverage Australia's role as a 'gateway to Asia'. On top of this, the limited opportunities currently on offer via the multilateral route, along with a sluggish global growth environment and some signs of increased protectionist pressures across the world economy, argue for valuing the general growth and liberalisation benefits on offer from pursuing a bilateral agreement with the EU.

All of these arguments are given further force by the fact that the EU is already negotiating deals with many of our key regional trading partners, as well as a prospective 'mega-regional' deal with the USA in the form of a TTIP. Since the latter in particular has the potential to set the rules of the global game across a range of issues, it would be advantageous for

Australia to maximise our input into the process and minimise the risks associated with trade diversion. Further, the EU is seemingly willing to embark on a negotiating approach compatible with Australia's significant interests.

It seems probable that an FTA with the EU would also offer Australia additional pay-offs. For example, as Jim Rollo pointed out in 2011, there would be potentially important pay-offs for Australia's exports of elaborately transformed manufactures through the reduced trade costs that could come from the mutual recognition of regulatory regimes (Rollo 2011). Similarly, there could be gains from improved deals on the movement of people, and from enhanced access to government procurement markets across the EU. There could also be significant pay-offs for domestic policies *within* Australia. For example, Adams, Brown and Wickes (2013) have suggested that the sort of major FTA that a deal with the EU would entail could also serve as a useful spur for domestic reform efforts.

Finally, joint work together in recent years—including on Doha—has underlined that Australia and the EU do share interests in global economic governance and in encouraging transparency, openness and liberalisation. Surely as Australia engages in mega-deals across regions and with other major economies, it should be working together with the EU to enhance not only bilateral linkages, but also common global interests.

In summary, then, there is, *at minimum,* a strong case from an Australian perspective to consider carefully the merits of pursuing an FTA with the EU.

References

Adams, Mike, Nicolas Brown & Ron Wickes (2013), *Trading Nation: Advancing Australia's Interests in World Markets* (UNSW Press: Sydney).

ABS (Australian Bureau of Statistics) (2015), 'International Investment Position, Australia: Supplementary Statistics, 2014. Cat No. 5352.0', Australian Bureau of Statistics, May.

Austrade (2012), *Australia-Europe Brief,* Edition 7 (September).

Austrade (2013a), *Australia-Europe Brief,* Edition 9 (March).

Austrade (2013b), *Australia-Europe Brief*, Edition 10 (June).

Cernat, Lucian (2013), 'TPP, TTIP and multilateralism: Stepping stones or oceans apart?', VoxEU.org, 8 November.

Deutsch, Klaus Gunter (2012), *Looking for Partners: The EU's Free Trade Agreements in Perspective*, EU Monitor (Deutsche Bank Research: Frankfurt am Main), 27 July.

DFAT (Department of Foreign Affairs and Trade) (2014), *Composition of Trade Australia 2013–14* (Trade and Advocacy Section, DFAT: Canberra), December.

DFAT (n.d), 'Australia's trade in goods and services 2013–14'. Available at dfat.gov.au/about-us/publications/trade-investment/australias-trade-in-goods-and-services/Pages/australias-trade-in-goods-and-services-2013-14.aspx.

Evenett, Simon J. (2014), *The Global Trade Disorder: The 16th GTA Report* (Centre for Economic Policy Research: London).

Felbermayr, Gabriel, Benedikt Heid & Sybille Lehwald (2013), *Transatlantic Trade and Investment Partnership (TTIP): Who Benefits from a Free Trade Deal?* (Bertelsmann Stiftung: Gütersloh).

Fontagné, Lionel, Julien Gourdon & Sébastien Jean (2013), *Transatlantic Trade: Whither partnership, which economic consequences?* CEPII Policy Brief No. 1 (Centre d'Etudes Prospectives et d'Informations Internationales: Paris), September.

Francois, Joseph, Miriam Manchin, Hanna Norberg, Olga Pindyuk & Patrick Tomberger (2013), *Reducing Transatlantic Barriers to Trade and Investment: An Economic Assessment*, Final Project Report (Centre for Economic and Policy Research: London), March.

IMF (International Monetary Fund) (2015a), *Uneven Growth: Short and Long Term Factors, World Economic Outlook April 2015* (International Monetary Fund: Washington, DC).

IMF (2015b), *World Economic Outlook Database. April 2015* (International Monetary Fund: Washington, DC).

Kenyon, Don & Pierre van der Eng (2014a), 'Defining the relationship between Australia and the European Union: Is the framework treaty enough?', *Australian Journal of International Affairs* 68(2): 225–42.

Kenyon, Don & Pierre van der Eng (2014b), 'Why isn't Australia negotiating an FTA with the EU?' in The Transatlantic Trade and Investment Partnership: Implications for Australia and the Asia-Pacific, *ANU Centre for European Studies Briefing Paper*, 5 (Canberra: ANU Centre for European Studies), 23–28.

Mortimer, David with John Edwards (2008), *Winning in World Markets: Meeting the Competitive Challenge of the New Global Economy: Review of the Export Market Development Grants Scheme* (Review of Export Policies and Programs: Canberra), 1 September.

Murray, Philomena & M. Bruna Zolin (2012), 'Australia and the European Union: Conflict, competition or engagement in agricultural and agri-food trade?', *Australian Journal of International Affairs* 66(2): 186–205. doi.org/10.1080/10357718.2011.646481.

OECD (Organisation for Economic Co-operation and Development) (2013), *FDI in Figures October 2013* (OECD: Paris).

Rollo, Jim (2011), 'The potential for deep integration between Australia and the European Union: What do the trade statistics tell us?', *Australian Journal of International Affairs* 65(4): 394–409. doi.org/10.1080/10357718.2011.586321.

Schwanen, Daniel (2011), 'Go big or go home: Priorities for the Canada–EU economic and trade agreement', *C.D. Howe Institute Backgrounder*, No. 143, October.

Suominen, Kati (2012), 'The surprise endgame in global trade', VoxEU.org, 20 December.

UNCTAD (United Nations Conference on Trade and Development) (2014), *World Investment Report 2014: Investing in the SDGs: An Action Plan* (United Nations: Geneva).

WTO (World Trade Organization) (2014), *International Trade Statistics 2014* (WTO: Geneva).

WTO (2015), *World Tariff Profiles 2015* (WTO: Geneva). Available at www.wto.org/english/res_e/publications_e/world_tariff_profiles15_e.htm.

WTO, OECD & UNCTAD (2015), Reports on G20 Trade and Investment Measures (mid-October 2014 to mid-May 2015), 15 June. Available at www.oecd.org/daf/inv/investment-policy/13th-G20-Report.pdf.

Conclusions

13

Australia and the EU: Partners in the New Trade Agenda

Don Kenyon and Pierre van der Eng

The chapters in this book provide detailed analyses of several aspects of the new trade agenda, and the role of Australia and the European Union (EU) in promoting it. The different context of the two entities in part determines their roles: the EU with its important influence in the Northern Hemisphere; and Australia with its focus on trade liberalisation in the Asia-Pacific region—the fastest growing region of the global economy.

Essentially, as the introduction and several chapters demonstrate, the new trade agenda is about the increasing integration of national and regional economies around the world. It is characterised by the shift away from tariffs and quotas as a major obstacle to global trade flows towards behind-the-border non-tariff barriers (NTBs). The exception here is in sectors such as agriculture, where the maintenance of domestic support in the form of governmental subsidies of one kind or another mandate the continuation of high levels of border protection.

Both Australia and the EU, therefore, are now set on a trade policy course with two objectives:

1. To conclude bilateral free trade agreements (FTAs) with key trading partners that focus increasingly on liberalising NTBs that currently go beyond the rules of the World Trade Organization (WTO), while continuing to work actively in Geneva for a successful outcome to the WTO's Doha multilateral trade negotiations; and

2. To ensure that these 'new generation' or 'WTO-plus' FTAs will be a 'stepping stone' and not a 'stumbling block' (European Union 2006a: 8) to better WTO rules and more effective multilateral trade liberalisation into the future.

How could a new generation FTA between Australia and the EU advance these objectives? What progress towards these objectives has been achieved in the new-generation FTAs already negotiated by both Australia and the EU? This concluding chapter offers some tentative answers to both questions.

Could an Australia–EU FTA produce meaningful liberalisation?

First, a few facts to underline the significance of bilateral business relations. The EU of 28 member states is Australia's second-most important trading partner, following China, in two-way trade in goods and services. In 2014, with 18 per cent of the total, the EU constituted Australia's second-largest source of imports, behind China (21 per cent), but ahead of the United States of America (11 per cent). With 5 per cent of the total, the EU ranks third as an export market for Australia, behind China (33 per cent) and Japan (18 per cent) (DFAT 2015a). The EU is also Australia's largest two-way trade partner in services, accounting for 19 per cent of the total (DFAT 2015a) and it is Australia's largest source of inward direct investment, accounting for around 25 per cent of the total stock of foreign direct investment (ABS 2015). The EU, accounting for some 25 per cent of the global economy and more than 40 per cent of world trade in goods and services, is clearly a world economic and trade super power. In addition, the EU already has or is negotiating FTAs with many of Australia's major markets in Asia and with virtually all Australia's major trading partners that are members of the Organisation for Economic Co-operation and Development (OECD). These trade realities, therefore, make a good case for an Australia–EU FTA.

Second, a negative that has long overshadowed Australia–EU relations since the early 1970s relates to agricultural trade. As Murray (2005: 98–131) explained, the EU's common agricultural policy (CAP) has been an issue of continued contention between both entities over the 20 years that followed the accession of the United Kingdom (UK) to the then European Economic Community in 1973. The CAP and particularly the agriculture export policy of the EU—specifically the subsidised export of the so-called beef, butter, sugar and grains mountains onto the world market, which depressed global food prices and adversely affected Australia's rural exports around the world—were a major trade flashpoint between Australia and the EU. It has long been said that agriculture would therefore be a major obstacle to Australia negotiating an FTA with the EU; that the continuing existence of the CAP would exclude agriculture being on the negotiating agenda.

This is now an outdated view. Australia's agricultural producers have found alternative export destinations, and are generally no longer dependent on the EU, as Murray and Zolin (2012) have demonstrated. More importantly, two developments have solved the fundamentals of this problem between Australia and the EU. First, the initial CAP reform package of 1992 and the agreement it led to on agriculture in the Uruguay Round of multilateral trade negotiations encompassed reductions on the use of export subsidies into the future; and second, the subsequent CAP reform packages from 1993 to 2003 continued the process of replacing high support prices to farmers in the EU with direct income supports. As the chapter by Daugbjerg and Swinbank in this book explains, these successive CAP reform packages reduced agricultural production in the EU, reduced further the need for export subsidies in the EU and led ultimately to the offer of the EU in the Doha negotiations to eliminate export subsidies altogether (WTO 2008). Export subsidy elimination has now been implemented through decisions taken at the 10th WTO ministerial meeting in December 2015.

Access to the EU market for the temperate agricultural products that Australia continues to export to the world, however, remains a problem. This is largely as a result of the high levels of 'tariff equivalents' against agricultural imports that the EU was permitted to maintain at the end of the Uruguay Round negotiations in 1994.[1] These tariff equivalents still operate as effective barriers against increased market access in the EU. The Doha negotiating process has, however, opened up opportunities to reduce the importance of this problem. Under the negotiating framework established by WTO in 2008, increased market access through expanded

---

1   During the Uruguay Round of multilateral trade negotiations, agreement was reached to convert all NTBs, including variable import levies in the EU, to tariff equivalents. As the high level of these tariff equivalents remained a significant barrier to imports, negotiated access to highly protected agricultural markets such as the EU was provided through tariff quotas at low or zero rates of duty.

tariff quotas (TQs) at low import duty rates would be provided for all sensitive products on which high levels of tariff equivalents continue to apply (WTO 2008).

The Doha negotiations remain uncompleted but, as Gosper's chapter in this collection foreshadows, there appears to be no compelling reason why expanded TQs at low rates of import duty could not also provide improved access for Australia's agriculture exports to the EU market in FTA negotiations. The EU has already signalled its readiness in Geneva to negotiate on improved TQ access. No doubt, agriculture-related trade interests of the EU, such as treatment accorded to genetically modified products (GMOs), recognition of an expanded list of geographic indications (GIs), and sanitary and phytosanitary regulations would also be on the negotiating agenda. Agriculture, therefore, while both an essential and difficult subject for both sides in a new-generation FTA negotiation between Australia and the EU—as it was recently in the Comprehensive Economic and Trade Agreement (CETA) negotiations with Canada, as Elijah's chapter in this volume discusses—need not be the deal-breaker it would have been in earlier years.

Where would the major benefits of a new-generation FTA between Australia and the EU lie? Improved EU market access for Australia's beef, grains, sugar, dairy products and lamb would be a big positive for Australia. It would do much to defuse an issue that has dogged the relationship since the 1960s, as mentioned above. More broadly, a new-generation FTA could go a long way towards liberalising behind-the-border regulatory NTBs across the broad spectrum of agriculture, services and manufactures trade between the EU and Australia. Two factors in particular could be important in realising such an objective in negotiations. Both Australia and the EU have well-developed regulatory standards and enjoy high equivalence of regulatory intent. This could open the way for mutual recognition of technically different but broadly equivalent standards that impact on trade across a wide range of products and services.

The importance of bilateral services trade between the EU and Australia is discussed at greater length in Kerneis's chapter. In 2014, the EU was both Australia's largest export market for services with 16 per cent of the total and the largest source of imports of services into Australia with 23 per cent of the total (DFAT 2015a). In the recent CETA negotiations, the EU agreed to the liberalisation of services trade according to the 'negative-listing' approach (European Commission 2014). Under this approach, commitments are taken on all services in bilateral trade, apart from those inscribed on a specific exceptions list. This is the first time in any trade negotiation that the EU has conceded the negative-listing approach to services liberalisation.[2] It is, however, the approach typically taken by Australia in its FTA negotiations. Now that the EU has taken the negative-listing approach with Canada, it is difficult to envisage it taking a less liberalising approach in future FTA negotiations, at least with any of its other OECD trading partners. The application of the negative-listing approach to services trade liberalisation in an FTA negotiation between Australia and the EU would be an important mutually beneficial gain, opening up the opportunity for the further expansion of trade in what is already the fastest growing area of bilateral trade.

In important specific areas of bilateral services trade between Australia and the EU, such as business and professional services, mutual recognition of broadly equivalent but technically divergent licensing and certification regulations could play an important trade-creating role in a new generation Australia–EU FTA. Even more important benefits would come from the mutual recognition of divergent but broadly equivalent professional qualifications requirements. Again, important steps towards liberalisation on this basis have been taken in the context of the CETA negotiations, which could provide a basis for a comparable outcome between Australia and the EU.

Average tariffs on non-agricultural goods are now low, at just 3 per cent in Australia and 4.2 per cent in the EU in 2014 (WTO 2015a). So there would appear to be little danger of serious trade diversion from differential tariff rates in an Australia–EU FTA, as Rollo (2011) substantiated. On the other hand, mutual recognition and/or harmonisation of standards would be trade-creating by neutralising the trade impact of regulatory divergences impacting on an expanding range of goods traded bilaterally between Australia and the EU. Current examples include food standards, packaging and labelling standards, sustainable production and environmental standards, and differing product standards on an increasingly wide range of semi-manufactured goods or components involved in intra-industry trade between Australia and the EU (Rollo 2011). There would also be practical trade benefits to both sides from reducing the negative trade and

2   In all previous FTA negotiations, including that with Korea discussed by Kang in this volume, the EU has taken the less liberal 'positive-listing' approach to services negotiations under which commitments are taken only on those services and services sectors included on a specific list.

investment impact of divergent regulations that affect public procurement policies (especially at a sub-member state level in the EU and at sub-federal level in Australia), competition policies, and investment restriction and protection policies.

Apart from agriculture, therefore, Australia–EU FTA negotiations could be even more focused than the CETA negotiation was on breaking new ground in the liberalisation of NTBs relevant to key areas that need to be resolved under the new trade agenda identified in Chapter 1. Such negotiations could play a role in advancing the twofold trade policy objectives espoused by both Australia and the EU; that is, liberalising NTBs through a bilateral FTA while ensuring that such liberalisation acts as a stepping stone rather than a stumbling block to strengthening the WTO, and enhancing scope for more effective multilateral negotiations on NTB issues into the future.

Meeting the challenges of the new trade agenda

As noted in Chapter 1, global trade rules dealing with NTBs, notably under the General Agreement on Tariffs and Trade (GATT) and since 1995 under WTO, have developed only slowly. Limited progress was made through the Tokyo Round of GATT negotiations (1973–79) in negotiating 'codes' to discipline NTBs such as anti-dumping and countervailing measures taken by governments against imports and the plurilateral 'Understanding on Government Procurement'. But, with reference to the exceptions rule in Article XX of the GATT, there were no limitations on the restrictions that importing countries could impose on services imports in terms of, for example, licensing and professional qualifications, and on goods imports in terms of, for example, technical standards and sanitary and phytosanitary import barriers.

Significantly more progress was made in this respect during the Uruguay Round (1986–94) with the General Agreement on Trade in Services (GATS) and the 'Technical Barriers to Trade' and 'Sanitary and Phytosanitary' agreements. Nevertheless, in the light of subsequent experience, the shortcomings of these agreements—particularly regulations limiting the supply of traded services; technical standards for manufactured and processed food products; and sanitary and phytosanitary regulations on imports—have become evident.

Domestic regulations on licensing, certification and professional qualifications are part of the behind-the-border decisions (both at governmental and professional association levels) that determine international trade flows of traded services. National and/or regional divergences in such regulatory decisions produce the NTBs that limit trade flows in services. The domestic regulation article of GATS (Article VI) determines that regulatory decisions '[shall] not constitute unnecessary barriers to trade [and] … [shall] not [be] more burdensome than necessary to ensure the quality of the service' (WTO 1994). This 'necessity clause' in GATS is mirrored by a similar provision in Article 2 of the Technical Barriers to Trade Agreement that is part of the Uruguay Round Agreements of 1994; namely, 'technical regulations shall not be more trade-restrictive than necessary to fulfil a legitimate objective' (WTO 1994). Similar provisions are also to be found in the Sanitary and Phytosanitary Agreement of 1994, where Article 5 contains a comparable 'necessity test' to those in the GATS and the Technical Barriers to Trade agreements, as well as a requirement to base import restrictions on 'risk assessment' to 'human, animal or plant life and health' (WTO 1994). These agreements also all contain provisions encouraging mutual recognition as a solution to regulatory divergences, especially— it appears—in circumstances where there is a high level of equivalence of regulatory intent.

These principles are all aimed at reining in the NTB effect of regulations governing the supply of services, technical standards applying to goods, and conditions aimed at limiting import restrictions in defence of sanitary and phytosanitary standards. They are ground-breaking provisions, clearly aimed at tackling behind-the-border NTBs. In practice, however, operationalising them into meaningful multilateral trade rules that can be enforced in future trade liberalisation negotiations has proven to be a challenging and so far incomplete task. The disciplinary provisions of the Sanitary and Phytosanitary Agreement in particular have been the subject of 42 separate dispute settlement cases under the tough rules of the WTO Dispute Settlement Understanding since the conclusion of the Uruguay Round (WTO 2014a). So, apart from the use of the Dispute Settlement Understanding to put flesh on the bones of the Sanitary and Phytosanitary disciplinary provisions, operationalising the 'necessity tests' of the GATS and Technical Barriers to Trade agreements have not proceeded far in WTO. In that light, what may recent FTAs negotiated by both the EU and Australia have achieved?

(a) Plurilateral and bilateral

Before answering this question, it is useful to briefly discuss the respective experiences of the EU and Australia, and of Australia and New Zealand, in seeking to deal with their regulatory divergences and resulting NTBs. In particular, the efforts of EU member states to do so in the context of creating the EU single market, of the states of Australia in creating a more integrated national entity, and of Australia and New Zealand in the context of the Closer Economic Relations (CER) agreement across the Tasman Sea.

Compared to the latter two cases, the experience of the EU is certainly of longer duration and has, over time, become more complex as the organisation grew from six original member states at comparable levels of economic development in 1957 to today's far more economically heterogeneous collection of 28 member states. During many years, the EU sought to deal with divergent technical product standards within individual member states through a painstaking process of harmonising standards. Following the *Single European Act 1986*, the EU shifted its focus to an 'equivalence' or mutual recognition approach in the creation of the single market in the EU during the 1990s. This was largely based on the *Cassis de Dijon* judgment of the European Court of Justice (1979), which found that goods lawfully produced in one EU member state cannot be banned from sale on the territory of another EU member state, even if they are produced with different technical or quality specifications. Over time, however, the enlargement of the EU reduced the levels of equivalence and trust among member states, and therefore the option of automatic acceptance of regulatory heterogeneity. Consequently, the EU has moved back towards attempting to fix detailed technical and environmental product standards on an EU-wide basis and seeking acceptance of its harmonised regulatory standards in FTAs negotiated with third countries (Messerlin 2011).

The experience inside Australia, and also between Australia and New Zealand, has been different. Concerned by continuing regulatory divergences between the states of Australia on product standards and also influenced by the *Cassis de Dijon* judgment and the EU's single-market drive through the 1990s, the Australian government of the day implemented the mutual recognition agreement (MRA) between the Australian states and territories from 1992, and in 1997 extended this to the Trans-Tasman Mutual Recognition Arrangement (TTMRA) with

New Zealand. The TTMRA therefore became the first international trade agreement for the mutual recognition of standards. It covered not only product standards (on an unconditional but 'with exceptions' basis— that is, a negative-listing approach) but also the mutual recognition of professional qualifications standards between Australia and New Zealand (Hussey & Kenyon 2011).

In its continuing efforts to deal with regulatory divergences between member states, the EU has embarked on a more recent and hopefully more enduring experiment in mutual recognition in its efforts to complete the EU single market in the services sector. The EU's 2006 Services in the Internal Market Directive, which aimed originally to implement an unconditional form of mutual recognition for a wide range of business and professional services across the EU, had a long and difficult gestation going back to the mid-1990s.

Member state negotiations over the provisions of the directive coincided with the erosion of trust within an expanding EU—to take in a growing number of former Warsaw Pact countries—to accept as 'equivalent' divergent licensing provisions in different member states for a wide range of traded business services. The outcome was a compromise based on a concept known as mutual evaluation. The mutual evaluation concept in the directive is designed to operate as a peer-review process undertaken by member state authorities. If the divergent regulation is found to be comparable in regulatory intent, mutual recognition must be accorded (European Union 2006b). Mutual evaluation is therefore intended to operate as a managed form of mutual recognition.

How does the experience of the EU, Australia, and Australia and New Zealand in dealing with NTBs (or regulatory divergences) in technical standards for goods and in licensing provisions for services—either of the unconditional, negative-listing variety demonstrated by the TTMRA or the managed mutual evaluation variety present in the EU cross-border trade in services directive—relate to the broader application of the mutual recognition principle internationally? By granting recognition to the technically divergent regulations of another jurisdiction, the certifying state is effectively saying that those regulations meet acceptable standards, which implies a high level of equivalence of regulatory intent and a high level of trust between the jurisdictions. To a significant degree, this is likely to be the case between at least those countries that are currently members of the OECD.

Past experience has shown that there are no significant problems between the states in Australia, or between Australia and New Zealand with the unconditional, negative-listing mutual recognition approach in both the MRA and the TTMRA. There do, however, appear to be problems with the mutual recognition of product standards among the 28 member states of the EU, mainly related to issues of trust across an increasingly economically heterogeneous membership (Messerlin 2011). Hopefully, the more managed form of mutual recognition present in the 2006 Services in the Internal Market Directive of the EU will work more effectively for the EU, and even between the EU and its trading partners in new-generation FTAs, and not just on services but on product and environmental (i.e. sustainable production) standards as well.

Against this background, what can some of the FTAs negotiated after 2006 tell us about progress made on liberalising NTBs? These are three examples:

1. The EU and Canada reached agreement in CETA on the recognition of professional qualifications, which appears to provide a successful example of the international application of the unconditional mutual recognition principle in so far as it provides for government-to-government agreements, confirming consensus reached at professional levels on the conditions under which mutual recognition can be agreed. Guidelines for reaching consensus within specific professions are provided in CETA (European Commission 2014).

2. The Australia–Korea FTA provides for the establishment of a working group on professional services, charged *inter alia* with making recommendations on the mutual recognition of professional qualifications between Australia and Korea (DFAT 2014b: Chapter 7, Annex A). Similar provisions exist in the Australia–Japan FTA (DFAT 2014a). These could open the door to the eventual liberalisation of professional services trade comparable to that contained in CETA. However, as these provisions are formulated in the current agreements Australia has negotiated, they are less definitive than the provisions in CETA.

3. All three agreements above provide for cross-border trade in services commitments to be made on a negative-listing basis. This represents a significant expansion of the 'national treatment' commitments so far negotiated under GATS, as all tradeable services under these FTAs are subject to commitments to maintain the same regulatory treatment

on imports as for domestic service providers. In WTO terms, such 'bindings' are considered valuable as parties to the agreement are protected (in effect multilaterally and not just bilaterally) from discriminatory treatment. Even if there is not a great deal or any actual trade liberalisation, this commitment operates as an effective ceiling on the NTB effect of regulations impacting on tradeable services.

Outside the areas of services and the scope of the WTO's Technical Barriers to Trade and Sanitary and Phytosanitary agreements, post-2006 FTAs negotiated by the EU have broken beneficial new ground in the liberalisation of other NTBs generated by new trade agenda issues. One example is the chapter on public procurement in CETA. The existing plurilateral agreement in the WTO concerns competitive tendering of procedures for public procurement contracts. Currently, 67 WTO member states are either full members or have observer status in this WTO agreement. In practice, the tendering procedures of this WTO agreement apply primarily to the agencies of central governments that are actual signatories to this agreement. The new ground broken by CETA is to apply agreed tendering procedures to sub-federal and regional government authorities both within the EU and Canada. It therefore provides a useful expansion of agreed disciplinary provisions to a broader range of public purchasing authorities (European Commission 2014).

Similarly, on investment policy some progress is being made. CETA raises the threshold to C$1.5 billion under which foreign direct investment from the EU into Canada will no longer be subject to review under the *Investment Canada Act*. In both the FTAs negotiated by Australia with Korea and Japan, the threshold under which foreign investments will not be subject to prior screening by the Australian Foreign Investment Review Board has been raised to A$1 billion. CETA also contains specific provisions for the conduct of investor–state dispute settlement (ISDS) as well as investment protection rules (Government of Canada 2013).

On competition policy, CETA incorporates specific competition policy provisions relating especially to disciplinary provisions applying to monopolies, including monopoly state-owned enterprises. Similarly, the EU–Korea FTA contains a competition policy chapter setting out competition policy principles governing the conduct of monopolies and public enterprises, as well as the control of restrictive business agreements and subsidies, transparency, dispute settlement and the relationship between the FTA chapter and the provisions of the WTO

(European Union 2011: Chapter 11). On product standards issues, the EU–Korea FTA made progress through the identification of Korean equivalents to the motor vehicle parts standards of the United Nations' Economic Commission for Europe. In the case of electronic goods and electrical appliances, the agreement reduced the scope of third-party certification by implementing the use of 'supplier's declaration of conformity'. In the EU–Singapore FTA, the chapter by Elms in this book finds that Singapore agreed to recognise EU standards and testing regimes for cars and car parts and that there was agreement on using international standards where possible in the electronics sector. Progress on resolving differences in technical barriers to trade more generally appears to have been left primarily to future regulatory cooperation within this FTA.

Based on the preliminary assessment above, it is possible to conclude that some progress on liberalising NTBs in recent FTAs has been made. CETA is the outstanding example. It also appears that more progress is being made on services, through negative-listing commitments and mutual recognition of qualifications on professional services; investment policy; public procurement, through the deepening of commitments to open tendering and transparency to sub-national purchasing authorities; and possibly also on competition policy, than on the standards and licensing NTBs that are the subject of the WTO Technical Barriers to Trade agreement and the GATS agreement on services. On standards and licensing issues, apart from the limited progress that seems to have been made through the harmonisation of divergent product standards in the EU–Korea and EU–Singapore FTAs, substantive treatment of divergent regulatory standards impacting on goods and services trade appears limited to chapters on regulatory cooperation. These chapters provide essentially for consultations aimed at encouraging greater convergence between the parties on future regulatory decisions expected to impact on trade.

The experience of both Australia and the EU internally, and their respective experience in recent FTA negotiations with others, gives rise to expectations that 'trade friendly' mutual recognition solutions to the many issues of standards and licensing raised above will be worth exploring in forthcoming Australia–EU FTA negotiations. The range of problems is likely to include mutual recognition of qualifications on traded professional services, such as architectural and engineering services; licensing and certification requirements on other traded services, including a wide range of business services; food, packaging and labelling standards; and sustainable production and environmental (e.g. biodiversity) standards;

as well as technical standards on a growing range of semi-manufactured parts and components that are traded in global supply chains, and motor vehicle standards, which are of increasing interest to the EU. Mutual recognition solutions along the lines of CETA on professional services qualifications could be explored.

An alternative to mutual recognition could be the more involved managed mutual recognition approach envisaged by the EU in, for example, the EU's 2006 Services Directive. As a consequence of this Directive, individual member states are permitted to maintain regulations on traded services in defence of 'public policy, public security, public health and the protection of the environment' (Article 16), but only through a peer-review process through which it can be demonstrated that such measures are 'non-discriminatory' against imports and necessary and 'proportionate' to the requirements of the conditions specified (European Union 2006b). There is no reason why this managed mutual recognition approach should be restricted to tradeable services between the EU member states. Its extension to a broader range of regulatory NTBs in future FTA negotiations could yield worthwhile results in reducing the NTB effects of many standards issues on both goods and services trade.

(b) Multilateral

It is possible to conclude, at least provisionally, that some of the outcomes that are emerging from recent FTA negotiations conducted by both the EU and Australia in areas such as undertaking services commitments on a negative-listing basis, mutual recognition of professional services qualifications, public procurement, investment and competition policy could well be useful as eventual stepping stones to more effective current WTO disciplinary provisions and possibly future WTO negotiations on some NTB issues. Nevertheless, this is an issue that requires further detailed study.

In considering how NTBs related to regulatory divergences on traded goods and services could be liberalised multilaterally, it may be helpful to consider existing WTO agreements. In particular, how operationalisation of the 'necessity clauses' of both GATS (Article VI) and the Technical Barriers to Trade agreement (Article 2) could be a stepping stone to stronger WTO rules and future multilateral trade liberalisation.

Progress might be made (as indicated above) by the wider use of the mutual evaluation approach to a more managed form of mutual recognition in reducing the NTB effect of regulatory divergences on technical standards for goods and services. Progress has already been made with the mutual recognition agreement on professional services qualifications in CETA and GATS, while both the WTO Technical Barriers to Trade and WTO Sanitary and Phytosanitary agreements have their separate provisions on according equivalence or mutual recognition wherever feasible. However, as noted above, mutual recognition solutions to problems of technical barriers to trade generated by the new trade agenda rely on high levels of equivalence of regulatory aims and objectives, and even more so on a high level of trust in the regulatory governance of different trading partners. Mutual recognition solutions will therefore always be problematic where these elements are lacking. What other options might be available, therefore, for use between trade partners that are part of a broader, more heterogeneous group in the context of plurilateral or multilateral discussions?

One obvious option would be to attempt to arrive at a set of 'horizontal' disciplinary provisions that expand the provisions of GATS and possibly the WTO Technical Barriers to Trade agreement. In relation to GATS, such work would be aimed at developing criteria relating to licensing, qualifications and technical standards requirements in an effort to operationalise the necessity test of GATS. Work on this task has in fact been conducted within WTO for some years now, but without yielding useful results. The horizontal disciplinary provisions route therefore does not appear to present well as a viable option.

A more productive option could be through the Trade in Services Agreement (TiSA) negotiations that are currently taking place in Geneva. TiSA is a negotiation between 53 developed and developing members of WTO (counting the 28 members states of the EU separately) aimed at the further liberalisation of trade in services. Negotiations began in April 2013 to seek an agreement that is compatible with GATS and that will 'support and feed back into multilateral trade negotiations' (DFAT 2015b: 18). As well as arriving at additional commitments across 'all services sectors', TiSA aims at developing new disciplinary provisions (trade rules) on, *inter alia*, 'domestic regulation to ensure regulatory settings do not operate as a barrier to trade in services' (DFAT 2015b: 18). According to the Australian Department of Foreign Affairs and Trade, 'positive progress' has been made on developing new trade rules on domestic regulation at recent rounds of TiSA negotiations in 2014 and 2015 (DFAT 2015c). This could be a promising sign. By November 2016, 21 negotiating rounds had been held but agreement had not yet been reached.

A still more fruitful option, and one for which there is precedence, could be the 'sectoral' or vertical approach. The existing stand-out example here is the WTO's 1998 Reference Paper on Basic Telecoms. It sets out common guidelines for a regulatory framework aimed at supporting the transition of the telecommunications sector from state monopolies to a competitive international market. These principles encompass competitive safeguards, interconnection, universal service, allocation and use of scarce resources, and the existence of independent regulators unencumbered by government controls. Some 60 WTO members are signatories to this reference paper. While the paper is as much about competition policy as it is about setting a regulatory framework for the telecommunications sector, it does provide a model of regulatory guidelines and best practice that could be adapted to the needs of other traded services on a sectoral basis applying across the broad spectrum of WTO membership (WTO 2014b).

Another example is a separate sectoral agreement in the information technology (IT) sector: the WTO's 1996 Information Technology Agreement (ITA), which was recently renegotiated and expanded. The 53 WTO members involved in the ITA negotiations have agreed to eliminate tariffs on a most-favoured-nation (MFN) basis on IT products, which currently account for 10 per cent of global trade. The new agreement also includes a commitment to identify solutions to NTBs in the IT sector (WTO 2015b).

New disciplinary provisions being negotiated in the TiSA process also include financial services, information and communications technology services, professional services, maritime transport services, air transport services, delivery services, energy services and public procurement. New opportunities for sectoral regulatory frameworks of broader plurilateral and multilateral application may therefore also emerge from this process.

A final option that might be considered could be an attempt to develop conceptual tools on the operation of standards of goods, licensing provisions and qualifications conditions in services that may be utilised on a case-by-case basis; in particular by groupings of countries that are at different stages of economic development and that span different parts of the world. This approach could have linkages to the mutual evaluation concept in the EU's 2006 Services Directive and to the principles of non-discrimination, necessity and proportionality used in developing the EU's single market in goods and services. Peer review, efforts to encourage equivalence and build trust, as well as research into appropriate dispute settlement options could be a part of this current outlier option for seeking to deal with the NTB effect of divergences in standards and licensing arrangements that apply to traded goods and services.

Conclusion

Over the last more than 20 years the new trade agenda has become the focus of trade liberalisation. Bilateral and plurilateral agreements are increasingly aimed at liberalising behind-the-border regulatory NTBs that impact on services trade (such as licensing and certification requirements); trade in goods, particularly trade in semi-manufactures within global supply chains (divergent technical standards); foreign direct investment flows; public purchasing tender processes; and competition policy issues.

The EU and Australia are pursuing similar objectives in FTA negotiations. The outcome of the GATT Uruguay Round achieved much to defuse the long-standing conflict over agricultural trade policy. This outcome, together with accompanying domestic economic reforms, resulted in the EU and Australia emerging as partners. Both continue to pursue further multilateral trade liberalisation in relation to manufactures, services and the full range of new trade agenda issues. Australia and the EU were partners pursuing a new round of multilateral trade negotiations that opened in 2002 at the WTO Doha Round. Both have been disappointed with the failure to bring the Doha Round to a successful conclusion. A contributing factor in the failure of Doha to achieve acceptable outcomes has been the continuing weakness of GATT rules to discipline NTBs that resulted from issues that are now part of the new trade agenda.

In light of sustained delays in the completion of the Doha Round, the EU and Australia have pursued bilateral and plurilateral FTAs that aim (a) to liberalise NTBs in ways that go beyond the current rules of the WTO, and (b) to ensure that these new 'deep integration' or 'GATT-plus' FTAs will be stepping stones rather than stumbling blocks to better WTO rules and to more effective multilateral negotiations into the future.

Some progress in creating such stepping stones to a better WTO has been made in recent FTAs negotiated by both Australia and the EU. The standout example to date is CETA between the EU and Canada. But stepping stones can also be identified in the FTAs Australia has negotiated with Korea and Japan, as well as in the FTAs that the EU has concluded with Korea and Singapore. In these agreements, most progress has been made in relation to services. For example, through commitments to the use of a negative-listing approach and the mutual recognition of professional qualifications. Progress has also been made on public procurement by expanding competitive tendering to the enterprises of sub-federal and regional authorities, on investment, through the relaxation of investment restrictions, and through convergence of competition policy principles. Much less progress has been made in dealing with the trade impact of divergent product standards and licensing requirements. These remain major NTBs in goods and services trade. For the most part, signatory countries rely on regulatory cooperation to deal with these issues in order to overcome future problems.

Of the possible future solutions in this respect, mutual recognition remains the clearest and simplest instrument for dealing with diverging standards and licensing requirements in a way that accommodates already existing agreements in WTO. This is underlined by the EU's experience with the creation of the single market, and Australia's experience with the creation of the 1992 mutual recognition agreement between the Australian states, and the subsequent extension of the principle to New Zealand under the Trans-Tasman Mutual Recognition Agreement, as this chapter has argued.

The chapter also stressed that mutual recognition requires high levels of equivalence of regulatory intent, capacity and trust. These conditions are not always present between potential FTA partners and may need to be nurtured. However, as this chapter has argued, strong foundations for the underlying requirements of mutual recognition exist in the current trade and business relations between Australia and the EU. With the required will and effort, it seems likely that negotiations towards an Australia–EU FTA will make better progress on mutual recognition solutions to divergent standards and licensing NTBs than has been the case in the other FTAs that they have recently negotiated. A significant conclusion of this chapter is therefore that an Australia–EU FTA is likely to be a significant stepping stone to better WTO rules and outcomes into the future.

This chapter also canvassed mechanisms through which WTO-friendly solutions applicable to a broader range of WTO members might be found to behind-the-border NTBs. It raised options to resolving this, including horizontal solutions, the most promising of which is the TiSA negotiation on services trade liberalisation between 53 developed and developing countries currently being pursued in a WTO context. Vertical or sectoral approaches also merit attention, as the discussion of the Reference Paper on Basic Telecoms and the agreement to liberalise information technology trade indicated.

Finally, the chapter has argued that scope exists for further research into the ways in which the principles that underlie existing WTO agreements for the purpose of disciplining NTBs—such as 'non-discrimination', 'necessity' and 'proportionality'—could be defined and developed into conceptual tools that would be of more practical use in future trade negotiations aimed at liberalising behind-the-border NTBs. All these options for the development of mechanisms for liberalising NTBs merit further attention, consideration and research.

As a postscript to this chapter and to the book as a whole, the UK voted in a national referendum on 23 June 2016 to leave the EU. The UK implemented Article 50 of the Treaty on European Union (the exit clause) that started a two-year period of negotiations on the terms of its departure from the EU on 28 March 2017. Whatever the outcomes of this process will be, the opportunities remain for Australia and the EU to be partners in advancing the new trade agenda.

References

ABS (Australian Bureau of Statistics) (2015), 'International Investment Position, Australia: Supplementary Statistics, 2014. Cat No. 5352.0' (Australian Bureau of Statistics: Canberra).

DFAT (Department of Foreign Affairs and Trade) (2014a), 'Japan–Australia Economic Partnership Agreement'. Available at dfat.gov.au/trade/agreements/jaepa/official-documents/Pages/official-documents.aspx.

DFAT (2014b), 'Korea–Australia Free Trade Agreement'. Available at dfat.gov.au/trade/agreements/kafta/official-documents/Pages/default.aspx.

DFAT (2015a), *Composition of Trade: Australia, 2014* (Department of Foreign Affairs and Trade: Canberra).

DFAT (2015b), 'Productivity Commission Study into Barriers to Growth in Australian Services Exports: Submission by Department of Foreign Affairs and Trade (DFAT), Australian Trade Commission (Austrade), Export Finance and Insurance Corporation (Efic)'. Available at www.pc.gov.au/inquiries/current/service-exports/submissions.

DFAT (2015c), 'Trade in Services Agreement: News'. Available at dfat.gov.au/trade/agreements/trade-in-services-agreement/news/Pages/news.aspx.

European Commission (2014), 'Draft of Consolidated CETA Text (Comprehensive Economic and Trade Agreement between Canada and the European Union)'. Available at trade.ec.europa.eu/doclib/docs/2014/september/tradoc_152806.pdf.

European Union (2006a), 'Global Europe: Competing in the World' [COM(2006) 567] (European Commission: Brussels), last updated 20 May 2009. Available at eur-lex.europa.eu/legal-content/EN/TXT/?uri=URISERV:r11022.

European Union (2006b), 'Directive 2006/123/EC on Services in the Internal Market', *Official Journal of the European Union* 49, L 376: 36–68.

European Union (2011), 'Free Trade Agreement between the European Union and its Member States, of the one part, and the Republic of Korea, on the other part', *Official Journal of the European Union* 54, L127: 1–1426.

Government of Canada (2013), 'Technical Summary of Negotiated Outcomes: Canada-European Union Comprehensive Economic and Trade Agreement', October. Available at international.gc.ca/trade-commerce/assets/pdfs/ceta-technicalsummary.pdf.

Hussey, Karen & Don Kenyon (2011), 'Regulatory divergences: A barrier to trade and a potential source of trade disputes', *Australian Journal for International Affairs* 65(4): 381–93. doi.org/10.1080/10357718.2011.586668.

Messerlin, Patrick (2011), 'The EU Single Market in Goods: Between mutual recognition and harmonisation', *Australian Journal for International Affairs* 65(4): 410–34. doi.org/10.1080/10357718.201 1.586019.

Murray, Philomena (2005), *Australia and the European Superpower: Engaging with the European Union* (Melbourne University Press: Clayton, Vic.).

Murray, Philomena & M. Bruna Zolin (2012), 'Australia and the European Union: Conflict, competition or engagement in agricultural and agri-food trade?', *Australian Journal of International Affairs* 66(2): 186–205. doi.org/10.1080/10357718.2011.646481.

Rollo, Jim (2011), 'The potential for deep integration between Australia and the European Union in Australia's trade with Europe: Potential unfulfilled', *Australian Journal for International Affairs* 65(4): 394–409. doi.org/10.1080/10357718.2011.586321.

WTO (World Trade Organization) (1994), *Results of the Uruguay Round of Multilateral Trade Negotiations: The Legal Texts* (GATT Secretariat: Geneva). Available at www.wto.org/english/docs_e/legal_e/legal_e.htm.

WTO (2008), 'Revised Draft Modalities for Agriculture', TN/AG/W/4/ Rev.4, 6 December. Available at www.wto.org/english/tratop_e/agric_e /chair_texts08_e.htm.

WTO (2014a), 'Disputes by agreement'. Available at www.wto.org/ english/tratop_e/dispu_e/dispu_agreements_index_e.htm?id=A19#.

WTO (2014b), 'Negotiating group on basic telecommunications', 24 April 1996. Available at www.wto.org/english/tratop_e/serv_e/ telecom_e/tel23_e.htm.

WTO (2015a), 'World Tariff Profiles'. Available at www.wto.org/english/ tratop_e/tariffs_e/tariff_data_e.htm.

WTO (2015b), 'Information Technology Agreement'. Available at www. wto.org/english/tratop_e/inftec_e/inftec_e.htm.

Glossary

Andriessen Assurance – 1985 guarantee by EC Agriculture Commissioner that the EC would not use export subsidies to promote European beef exports in Australia's Asian markets

anti-dumping – under the 1994 WTO Anti-Dumping Agreement, signatory countries can take retaliatory actions in substantiated cases of an exporter selling goods below the home market price or cost of production

behind-the-border trade barriers – measures that are not tariffs but restrict or impede international trade, such as labelling requirements, environmental regulations, rules of origin, etc.

bilateral investment treaties – agreements establishing the terms and conditions for private investment by nationals and companies of signatory countries. See **foreign direct investment**

change in tariff classification – pertaining to rules of origin, a product that has undergone significant transformation and as a result changed tariff classification is said to have originated in the country where that transformation occurred

Codex Alimentarius – established by Food and Agriculture Organisation and the World Health Organisation in 1963 to develop harmonised international food standards that protect consumer health and promote fair practices in food trade

conformity assessment – testing procedures to ensure that products are manufactured in conformity with national technical standards. Countries entering into a 'Conformity Assessment' agreement mutually accept each other's testing outcomes

Directorate-General for Trade of the European Commission – EU Directorate-General responsible for relations between the EU and the rest of the world involving trade of goods, services, intellectual property and investment

Dispute Settlement Body (WTO) – WTO agency adjudicating trade disputes between WTO members

Doha development agenda – since 2001, the current round of multilateral trade negotiations to lower trade barriers under WTO auspices

Doha Round – see above

duty drawback – arrangement between countries that allows exporting firms to obtain a refund of customs duties paid on imported goods where those have been processed for export

EU Single Market – a single market of EU member countries based on arrangements that seek to guarantee the free movement of goods, capital, services and people

Eurozone – monetary union of 19 of the 28 EU member states that use the euro (€) as their common currency and sole legal tender

everything but arms – 2001 EU initiative under which all imports into the EU from UN-specified least developed countries are duty and quota-free, except for armaments

feed-in tariff – policy instrument to integrate electricity from renewable energy sources into the electricity grid through payments to producers

foreign direct investment (FDI) – investment flows by companies between countries for the purpose of establishing controlling ownership in a business enterprise in a host country

geographic indications – specifications of the geographical origin or products as indications of their quality or reputation

Global Europe strategy – 2006 EU communication signalling the intent of member countries to increase trade liberalisation beyond existing multilateral WTO commitments through new generation trade agreements

Global Trade Alert – association of independent organisations that monitor and report actions by countries that are likely to discriminate against foreign trade

Group of 8 (G8) – refers to the group of eight highly industrialised nations: France, Germany, Italy, the United Kingdom, Japan, the United States, Canada and Russia

Health Check reform – 2009 reform of the EU common agricultural policy (CAP) to modernise, simplify and streamline the CAP and remove restrictions on farmers

Informational Technology Agreement (ITA) – plurilateral 1996 agreement within the WTO framework to lower taxes and tariffs on information technology products traded between signatory countries

Investment Promotion and Protection Agreements (IPPAs) – bilateral agreements for the promotion and protection of mutual investments by contracting parties

mega-FTA – free trade agreement between more than two countries that together contribute a large share to global gross domestic product (GDP) and/or to global international trade

mega-regional – deep integration partnerships between countries in a global region that together contribute a large share to global GDP and/or to global international trade

Mortimer Review – 2008 Australian Government Review of Export Policies and Programs

most favoured nation (MFN) treatment – signatories to WTO agreements cannot discriminate between other signatories and are required to give all those trade partners equal treatment

multi-annual financial framework – imposes limits on annual EU budgets, both total and for different policy areas, when the EU enters legally binding obligations of five years or more

multilateral(ism) – multiple countries cooperating on a given issue

multiparty FTA – free trade agreement that includes more than two countries, as opposed to a bilateral FTA

mutual recognition agreement (MRA) – agreement by which two or more countries agree to accept each other's divergent technical standards on products or services mutually traded

mutual recognition of professional qualifications – agreement under which two or more countries agree to accept divergent technical requirements on mutually traded professional services

negative list – listing of service sectors that retain restrictions in free trade agreements, or a listing of economic sectors that remain prohibited or restricted for FDI in investment agreements; non-listed sectors are unrestricted

new-generation FTAs – FTAs that include commitments well beyond current obligations under WTO, particularly in areas such as the elimination of non-tariff barriers, liberalisation of services trade and investment, competition policy

new trade agenda – or 'deep trade agenda', refers to new and growing trends in international business, such as internationalisation of supply chains, growth of services trade, FDI, and liberalisation of non-tariff trade barriers

plurilateral agreement – legal or trade agreement between more than two countries

'plus' (e.g. 'WTO-plus FTAs'; 'GATT-plus FTAs') – liberalisation outcomes of new-generation trade agreements that aim to surpass current commitments under WTO

positive list – listing of service sectors that open to foreign trade in free trade agreements, or a listing of economic sectors that are open to FDI in investment agreements; non-listed sectors remain restricted

producer support estimates – indicator of the annual transfers from consumers and taxpayers to support agricultural producers, arising from policy measures

protectionism – economic policy of limiting international trade through e.g. tariffs on imported goods, restrictive quotas, and a variety of non-tariff trade barriers

regional FTA – see **multiparty FTA**

rules of origin – criteria needed to determine the country of origin of a product

sanitary and phytosanitary measures – measures to protect humans, domestic, animals and plants from diseases, pests or contaminants

specific trade concern – concerns relating to specific measures imposed or maintained by WTO members brought by one or more trade partners to the WTO Technical Barriers to Trade Committee

tariff – trade policy instrument, a tax imposed on imported goods and services

tariff rate quota – trade policy instrument, a higher tariff is imposed on imported goods beyond a quota threshold

third-party countries – those countries that are not signatories to a particular trade agreement between two or more other countries

Tokyo Round – seventh round of multilateral GATT negotiations 1973–79 resulting in reductions of multilateral tariffs

Trade in Services Agreement (TiSA) – proposed international trade treaty between 23 parties, including the EU, aiming to liberalise international trade in services between signatory countries

trade liberalisation – removal or reduction of national restrictions or barriers on the international exchange of goods and services

trade-weighted effective exchange rate index – index of the foreign exchange rate of a country's currency, corrected for changes in the price level in that country relative to the price levels in countries that are its most important trade partners

trade-creating – increase in international trade

Trade-Related Aspects of Intellectual Property Rights (TRIPS) agreement – 1994 international agreement under the WTO setting minimum standards for intellectual property regulation applying to nationals of other WTO member countries and bringing TRIPS issues into the purview of WTO dispute settlement procedures

Trans-Tasman Mutual Recognition Arrangement (TTMRA) – non-treaty agreement between Australia and the Australian states and New Zealand covering sale of goods and mutual recognition of divergent goods standards and professional qualifications

Uruguay Round – eighth round of multilateral GATT negotiations 1986–1994 comprising 123 countries and resulting in several agreements to reduce trade barriers on goods and services and establish WTO

Warsaw Pact (countries) – a collective defence treaty between the Soviet Union and seven socialist countries in Central and Eastern Europe in existence during 1955–91

WTO Round – intergovernmental negotiations through the WTO to reach multilateral agreement on liberalisation of international trade. The Doha Round since 2001 is the current round

WTO-plus – negotiated commitments in addition to those in existing multilateral agreements and rules placed on a country newly acceding to WTO, or FTAs in which parties commit themselves to trade liberalisation outcomes surpassing current commitments under WTO (see '**plus**')

www.ingramcontent.com/pod-product-compliance
Lightning Source LLC
Chambersburg PA
CBHW050807270326
41926CB00026B/4603